The Definitive Guide to Machine Learning Operations in AWS

Machine Learning Scalability and Optimization with AWS

Neel Sendas
Deepali Rajale

Apress®

The Definitive Guide to Machine Learning Operations in AWS: Machine Learning Scalability and Optimization with AWS

Neel Sendas
Marietta, GA, USA

Deepali Rajale
Atlanta, GA, USA

ISBN-13 (pbk): 979-8-8688-1075-6
https://doi.org/10.1007/979-8-8688-1076-3

ISBN-13 (electronic): 979-8-8688-1076-3

Managing Director, Apress Media LLC: Welmoed Spahr
Acquisitions Editor: Celestin Suresh John
Development Editor: Laura Berendson
Coordinating Editor: Gryffin Winkler

Cover designed by eStudioCalamar

Cover Image by WikiImages from Pixabay

Distributed to the book trade worldwide by Apress Media, LLC, 1 New York Plaza, New York, NY 10004, U.S.A. Phone 1-800-SPRINGER, fax (201) 348-4505, e-mail orders-ny@springer-sbm.com, or visit www. springeronline.com. Apress Media, LLC is a California LLC and the sole member (owner) is Springer Science + Business Media Finance Inc (SSBM Finance Inc). SSBM Finance Inc is a **Delaware** corporation.

For information on translations, please e-mail booktranslations@springernature.com; for reprint, paperback, or audio rights, please e-mail bookpermissions@springernature.com.

Apress titles may be purchased in bulk for academic, corporate, or promotional use. eBook versions and licenses are also available for most titles. For more information, reference our Print and eBook Bulk Sales web page at http://www.apress.com/bulk-sales.

Any source code or other supplementary material referenced by the author in this book is available to readers on GitHub (https://github.com/Apress). For more detailed information, please visit https://www.apress.com/gp/services/source-code.

If disposing of this product, please recycle the paper

Neel: This book is for you, Dad. You were my best friend and greatest support.

Deepali: Dedicated to my daughters, Ovi and Rewa, who continuously inspire me to grow and improve in everything I do.

Table of Contents

About the Authors

Neel Sendas is a principal technical account manager at Amazon Web Services (AWS). In this role, he serves as the AWS Cloud Operations lead for some of the largest enterprises that utilize AWS services. Drawing from his expertise in cloud operations, in this book, Neel presents solutions to common challenges related to ML cloud governance, cloud finance, and cloud operational resilience and management at scale. Neel also plays a crucial role as part of the core team of machine learning technical field community leaders at AWS, where he contributes to shaping the roadmap of AWS artificial intelligence and machine learning (AI/ML) services. When he isn't helping customers, he dabbles in golf and salsa dancing. Neel is based in Georgia, United States.

Deepali Rajale is a former AWS ML specialist technical account manager, with extensive experience supporting enterprise customers in implementing MLOps best practices across various industries. She is also the founder of Karini AI, a company dedicated to democratizing generative AI for businesses. She enjoys blogging about ML and generative AI and coaching customers to optimize their AI/ML workloads for operational efficiency and cost optimization. In her spare time, she enjoys traveling, seeking new experiences, and keeping up with the latest technology trends.

About the Technical Reviewer

Karanbir Singh is an accomplished engineering leader with almost a decade of experience leading AI/ML engineering, distributed systems, and microservices projects across diverse industries, including fintech and automotive. Currently working as a senior software engineer at Salesforce, he focuses on back-end technologies as well as AI. His career has been marked by a commitment to building high-performing teams, driving technological innovation, and delivering impactful solutions that enhance business outcomes.

At TrueML, as an engineering manager, he managed a critical team to develop and deploy machine learning models in production. He successfully expanded and led engineering teams, significantly improving feature development velocity and client engagement through strategic collaboration and mentorship. His leadership directly contributed to increased revenue, client retention, and substantial cost savings through innovative internal solutions. His role involved not only steering technical projects but also shaping the company's roadmap in partnership with data science, product management, and platform teams.

Previously, at Lucid Motors and Poynt, he developed critical components and integrations that advanced product capabilities and strengthened industry partnerships. His technical expertise spans AI/ML, cloud computing, and software architecture, and he is adept at utilizing cutting-edge technologies and methodologies to drive results.

Karanbir holds a master's degree in computer software engineering from San Jose State University and has been recognized for his innovative contributions, including winning the Silicon Valley Innovation Challenge. He is passionate about mentoring and coaching emerging talent and thrives in environments where he can leverage his skills to solve complex problems and advance technological initiatives.

Foreword

In the rapidly evolving landscape of artificial intelligence and machine learning, the ability to effectively operationalize AI/ML models has become a critical differentiator for organizations seeking to harness the full potential of their data-driven initiatives across a diverse team. As we witness a new era in AI, marked by the rise of foundation models (FMs) and generative AI (GenAI), the importance of robust MLOps practices has never been more important. It is in this context that I am honored to introduce *A Definitive Guide to MLOps on AWS* by Neel Sendas and Deepali Rajale, a comprehensive resource and guide that promises to be an invaluable asset for AI practitioners, data scientists, and MLOps engineers navigating the complexities of machine learning operations in the cloud.

As a principal data scientist at Amazon with more than a decade of experience in optimization and artificial intelligence, I have witnessed firsthand the transformative impact of well-implemented MLOps practices on the success of AI projects across various industries including financial services, healthcare and life sciences, media, oil and gas, and automotive. Throughout these experiences, one truth has remained constant: the path from innovative ML models to real-world impact *at scale* is possible only if enterprises, large or small, adopt principles and best practices of MLOps.

Neel Sendas and Deepali Rajale bring a wealth of expertise to this crucial subject. Neel, drawing from his several years of experience as a principal technical account manager at AWS and his background in IoT and machine learning, brings a deep understanding of the AWS ecosystem and its application in solving real-world ML challenges. Deepali, with her extensive background in product development, cloud computing, and artificial intelligence, offers insights as both a practitioner and an innovator in the field of generative AI. Her experience as a founder of a cutting-edge startup focused on GenAI in production provides a unique perspective on the challenges and opportunities in operationalizing ML models.

As organizations increasingly turn to cloud platforms like AWS to build, train, and deploy their traditional ML models as well as foundation models, the need for a comprehensive reference like *A Definitive Guide to MLOps on AWS* is important to upskill teams by offering readers a roadmap to navigate the complexities of scaling ML operations while addressing key concerns such as resiliency, security, monitoring, observability, and cost optimization.

The authors lay a solid foundation to MLOps principles and best practices before delving into the specifics of implementing MLOps on AWS. The coverage of operational excellence, security, reliability, and performance efficiency pillars in MLOps explains what it takes to build and maintain production-grade AI systems.

Of particular note in the book, as well as my personal interest is the emphasis on cost optimization in MLOps, a critical consideration in today's economic landscape where efficiency and ROI are paramount. Cost optimization doesn't mean cutting costs; it means squeezing out the last bit of performance for the dollars you are paying a service provider. The authors' exploration of right-sizing ML resources on AWS and implementing usage-based cost monitoring and analysis provides practical guidance for organizations looking to balance innovation with fiscal responsibility. Neel and Deepali have done this on a day-to-day basis for several large enterprises as part of their full-time jobs.

The final focus of the book is MLOps for GenAI (or "FMOps"), which is both timely and forward-thinking. The authors address the unique challenges posed by foundation models, including the nuances of model selection, adaptation, evaluation, and deployment, as well as the critical considerations of data privacy and technology needs specific to these advanced AI systems, contrasting it with traditional MLOps.

As we look to the future of AI and machine learning, this book can serve as a comprehensive roadmap for organizations looking to unlock the full potential of their machine learning initiatives on the AWS cloud platform. Neel and Deepali have crafted a resource that not only addresses the current state of MLOps but also anticipates future developments in this rapidly evolving field.

To the readers of this book, whether you are a data scientist, an ML engineer, a cloud architect, or a business leader overseeing AI initiatives, I encourage you to approach this guide with an open mind and a willingness to apply its insights to your own projects and challenges. The journey of operationalizing AI/ML is complex and ever-evolving, but with the knowledge and best practices shared in these pages, you will be well-equipped to navigate this terrain and drive meaningful impact through AI in your organizations.

Dr. Shreyas Subramanian
Principal Data Scientist, Amazon

CHAPTER 1

Introduction to MLOps

Machine learning operations (MLOps) is when DevOps principles are applied to a machine learning system. This is a relatively new term as nowadays most businesses try to incorporate AI/ML systems into their products and platforms. MLOps is an engineering discipline that aims to unify ML systems development (dev) and ML systems deployment/operations (ops) to standardize and streamline the continuous delivery of high-performing models in production. MLOps aims to provide high-quality machine learning solutions in production in an automated and repeatable manner.

MLOps has three contributing disciplines: machine learning, DevOps, and data engineering. MLOps is an extension of the DevOps practice of continuously building, deploying code, and testing applied to data engineering (data) and machine learning (models), as represented in Figure 1-1.

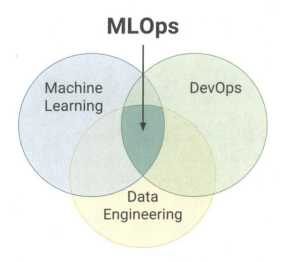

Figure 1-1. *MLOps*

© Neel Sendas and Deepali Rajale 2024
N. Sendas and D. Rajale, *The Definitive Guide to Machine Learning Operations in AWS*,
https://doi.org/10.1007/979-8-8688-1076-3_1

A machine learning model can be developed offline using training data; however. Deploying it in the production environment can be challenging. MLOps' job is not only to deploy the model but to continuously automate, monitor, manage, and update at every step of the ML systems. With a massive increase in data these days and a wide range of ML applications, automation with MLOps is the necessity within the era of AI.

MLOps Components

MLOps components can be divided into ML development and operations components, as shown in Figure 1-2.

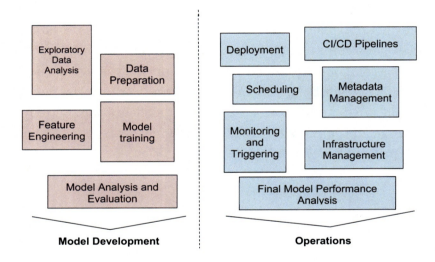

Figure 1-2. *ML development and operations components*

As displayed, all the components related to data engineering and model training fall under model development. Until model development, only half the job is done. Operations follow this process, and deployment, scheduling, monitoring, and maintenance components follow under operations.

Evolution of MLOps

In the year 2015, artificial intelligence, machine learning, and data science were at their peak with the rise in the number of data and Python libraries. With the availability of a vast number of algorithms, deep learning and neural net training ML models became easy to use and started trending. However, deploying these models in production at scale was a challenge. Very few models made it to the deployment stage with a lot of effort and time.

In 2018–2019 with the popularity of containerization, Docker and Kubernetes were used to deploy an ML model. That era was termed the *MLOps Gold Rush age* as many ML deployment platforms like DataRobot, ClearML, Amazon Sage Maker, Kubeflow, Google Cloud Platform, etc., were built with a purpose to cover the whole ML system iteration. These platforms provide automation through data analysis, model creation, deployment, maintenance, and monitoring.

Need of MLOps?

According to the Algorithma report, number 18 percent of all companies surveyed take 90 days to a year to deploy a ML model not an ML model in production. Approximately 50 percent of the companies deploy a model in 90 days or less. See Figure 1-3.

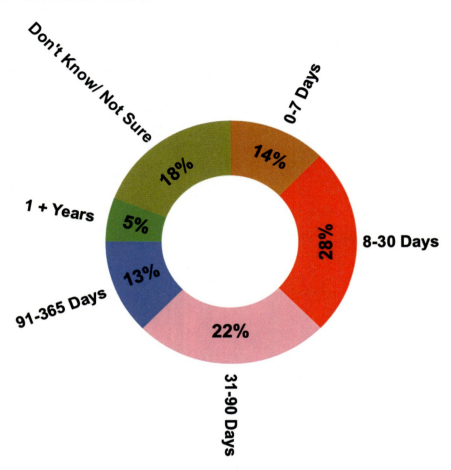

Figure 1-3. *Model deployment timeline*

According to Deeplearning.ai reports, only 22 percent of companies using machine learning have successfully deployed a model.

Now the questions arise: why is it so hard to deploy a model in production, and what is its solution?

By implementing a systematic "MLOps" process incorporating CI/CD methodology commonly used in DevOps, a business can essentially create an assembly line for each step resolving this problem. MLOps aims to streamline the data, time, modeling, and other resources required to run data science models using automation, ML, and iterative improvements on each model version.

Understanding Broad Phases of MLOps

The MLOps phasing follows an iterative-incremental process that is divided into three broad phases: designing the ML-powered application, ML experimentation and development, and ML operations. Let's take a more detailed look; see Figure 1-4.

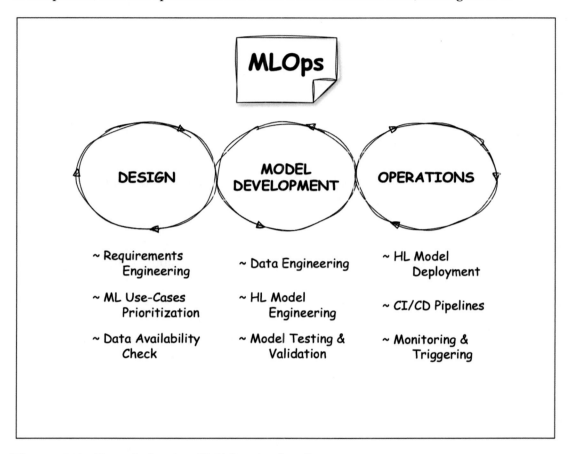

Figure 1-4. *Broad phases of MLOps in detail*

1. **Design**

   The first phase of design is devoted to business and data understanding, requirements engineering, machine learning use-case prioritization, and ML-powered application design. In this stage, the main aim is to identify the business problem by using any relevant data to design machine learning solutions for their potential user.

In the design phase, initially ML use cases are defined and prioritized. Then the data is inspected to train the model. All functional and nonfunctional requirements of the ML model are used to design the architecture of the ML application, establish the model serving strategy, and create a test suite for the future ML model.

This phase aims to set up a powerful base that increases the interactivity of machine learning applications and users' productivity.

2. **Model Development**

After the designing phase comes the "ML experimentation and development" phase. The goal in this phase is to deliver a stable quality ML model that will run in production. In this phase, the proof of concept for the ML model is implemented to verify the applicability of the ML model to our problem. Data engineering, ML model engineering, coding, hyperparameter tuning, and model testing and validation are run iteratively to identify suitable ML algorithms for business problems.

3. **Operations**

The main goal of the "ML operations" phase is to deploy the previously developed ML model in production. Deployment is completed by using established DevOps practices such as testing, versioning, and continuous integration and delivery, with regular monitoring and triggering services. For monitoring and maintenance of the ML system, continuous model evaluation is completed at this step.

All three phases are iterative, incremental, influenced, and interconnected with each other. The design decision propagates to the development phase, and the final developed model influences the deployment during the final operation phase. After a period of time after deployment, if the model decays and behaves abnormally, then we need to go back to the process of either collecting more data or re-label training data, and that triggers the re-training of the ML model.

MLOps Principles

MLOps has certain principles for successfully deploying working machine learning applications.

1. **Automation**

   Automation provides continuous integration, delivery, and deployment of trained machine learning models. It makes sure that production models always use the latest trained version and deal with dynamic data as per rapidly evolving business needs. It reduces the risk of errors, increases productivity, provides seamless updates, and increases time-to-market. Automation is executed for these processes:

   - Transformation of data

   - Feature engineering

   - Data engineering pipeline

   - ML model training pipeline

   - Hyperparameter selection

   - CI/CD pipeline for ML model deployment

   - Building application

2. **Versioning**

   Versioning is critical to ensure reproducibility and traceability. Versioning of data, code, and model is necessary. For example, there might be changes in data, the model can decay with time, or environment change might require new data or a new model, so versioning is important to maintain. Versions must be maintained for the following items:

   - Data preparation pipelines

   - Datasets

   - Features store

   - Metadata

- ML model training pipeline

- Hyperparameters

- Experiments

- Application code

- Configurations

3. **Testing**

   ML systems continuously do data, features, model, and
   infrastructure testing. Testing is required for feature pipelines,
   data pipelines, and ML model performance. Infrastructure testing
   is completed for integration and stress testing. Testing is required
   to deliver top-notch ML system output. Testing needs to be
   completed at the following steps:

   - Data validation

   - Feature creation unit testing

   - ML model training pipeline is integration-tested

   - ML model is validated before operations.

   - ML model staleness test in production

   - Model governance testing

   - Unit testing

   - Integration testing for the end-to-end pipeline

4. **Deployment**

   Model deployment should be completed based on experiment
   tracking, which includes feature stores, containerization of the
   ML stack, and the ability to run on-premise, on the cloud, or at the
   edge. A deployment service role is to ensure that the ML models,
   code, and data are stable using orchestration, logging, monitoring,
   and notification. Deployment is completed based on the following
   features:

- Feature store used in dev and production environments

- Containerization of the ML stack

- REST API

- On-premise, cloud, or edge environment

5. **Monitoring**

Continuous monitoring implies the periodic assessment of data, code, model, infrastructure resources, and model performance metrics. It helps in detecting potential errors or changes in data or environment, resulting in high product quality. Continuous monitoring is required to maintain and keep the MLOps system stable with changing data, environment, and decaying of the model. Continuous monitoring is necessary to keep checking on the following processes:

- Data distribution changes (training and serving data)

- Training and serving features

- ML model decay

- Numerical stability

- Computational performance of the ML model

- Application predictive quality in serving data

6. **Reproducibility**

Reproducibility is the ability of every phase of the ML system data processing, feature engineering, model development, and model deployment to reproduce an ML experiment and obtain the same results given the same input. A successfully deployed MLOps system must be able to reproduce the following items listed:

- Backup data

- Data versioning

- Extract metadata

- Feature engineering versioning

- Hyperparameter tuning is identical between the development and production

- Features order should be the same

- Same ensemble learning

- The model pseudocode is documented

- Versions of all dependencies in development and production are identical

- The same technical tool stack for development and production environments

- Container images or virtual machines are provided to reproduce the results

MLOps Lifecycle

Up to this point we have seen the high-level workflow for machine learning application development. Now we will explore the MLOps lifecycle in detail. which consists of six main steps, as well as several substeps (see Figure 1-5).

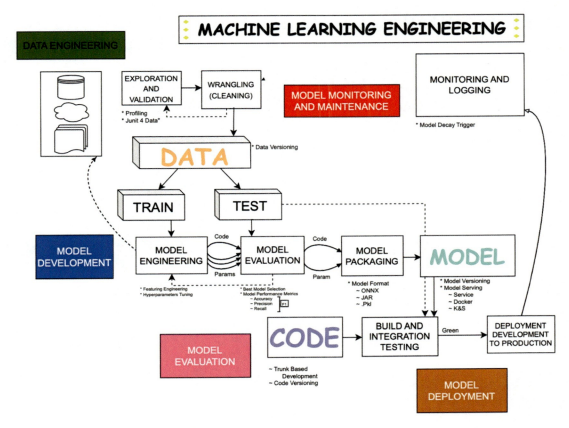

Figure 1-5. *MLOps lifecycle*

1. **Business Understanding**

   The MLOps lifecycle begins with understanding the scope of
   the machine learning application, its success criteria, and its
   data quality verification. It ensures the project's feasibility with
   a detailed understanding of the business and requirements
   before proceeding further. The following are the tasks executed in
   this phase:

   - Define business objectives

   - Define machine learning objectives

   - Collect and verify data from different sources

   - Assess the project feasibility

11

2. **Data Engineering**

   Data engineering prepares data for the model development phase. This takes care of data ingestion, data preparation, data preprocessing, data exploration and validation, data versioning, data monitoring, and data splitting. The following are tasks executed under data engineering:

   - Data selection
   - Data merging
   - Feature selection
   - Class balancing (over-sampling or under-sampling of data)
   - Data preprocessing (noise reduction, data imputation)
   - Feature engineering (data construction)
   - Data augmentation (GANs)
   - Data standardization
   - Data versioning
   - Data splitting

3. **Model Development**

   Under model development, the business objective is to translate the business objective into a machine learning model. Phases of model development are iterative so that any change in data or business goals can be incorporated easily. In this phase, the model training method's metadata is collected to become reproducible in any time of need. The following are the various tasks executed under model development:

   - Define model's quality measure
   - ML algorithm selection
   - Model specialization with domain knowledge
   - Model training

- Applying transfer learning (using pre-trained models)

- Model compression

- Ensemble learning

- Hyperparameter tuning

- Model validation

- Documenting the ML model and experiments

4. **Model Evaluation**

At the model evaluation, the performance of the ML model is evaluated on test data using model performance metrics. It is also called offline testing, which is done to check the robustness of the model. The various tasks executed under model evaluation are as follows:

- Validate model's performance

- Determine model robustness

- Decision taken (whether to deploy the model or not)

- Evaluation phase documentation

5. **Model Deployment**

This stage aims to integrate the ML model into an existing software system. It is time to successfully deploy the working ML model in the production environment. Various tasks done under model deployment are as follows:

- Model evaluation according to production environment

- Model compliance and integration

- Model deployment

- User acceptance and usability testing

- Online model testing

- Model versioning

6. **Model Monitoring and Maintenance**

After the deployment model runs on unseen real-time data, it is important to monitor and maintain the model performance in the live environment. Model performance logging, model performance monitoring, and alert and retraining services are completed under model monitoring. The following are the various tasks done for model monitoring and maintenance:

- Monitor prediction model performance

- Check if pre-specified success criteria are met or not

- Re-train model in case of model decay or requirement change

- Collect and incorporate new data

- Perform labeling of the new data points

- Repeat the tasks from the Model Engineering and Model Evaluation phases

- Continuous training, integration, and deployment of the model

MLOps Infrastructure Tool Stack

To operate the complex MLOps lifecycle. we need a well-defined project structure, process, and proper software tools. These software tools are called the MLOps infrastructure tools stack. The MLOps infrastructure stack should include tools for the following tasks:

- Data analysis

- Data, code, and model version control

- Experimentation

- Feature store

- Code repository

- ML CI/CD pipeline

- Metadata store

- Model registry

- Model serving

- Model monitoring in production

Many cloud providers are offering machine learning platforms like SageMaker by AWS, AI Platform by Google Cloud, and AzureML. In-house solutions can also be implemented for MLOps using noncloud systems like MLFlow, DVC, Sacred, etc.

Jupyter Notebooks and Python can be used for data analysis and coding. GitLab can be used for code repositories.

Look at the MLOps stack template shown in Figure 1-6 by Valohai for reference.

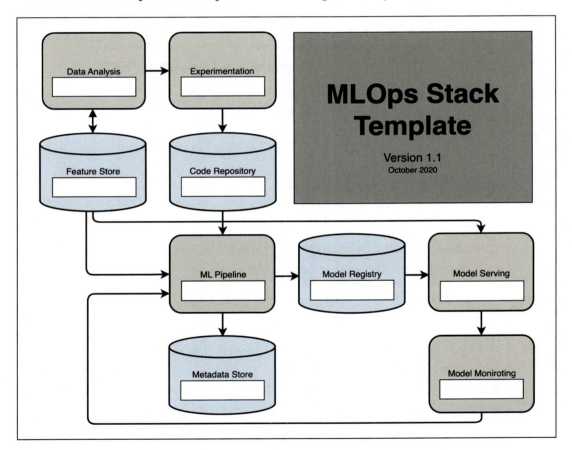

Figure 1-6. *MLOps stack template*

The MLOps stack template is attempting to simplify the workflow and architecture to a more manageable abstraction level. This guides the development teams through the MLOps building blocks and helps in identifying the necessary tools chain. There are nine components in the stack with varying requirements, and they are used depending on your specific use case.

Role of Tool Stack Components

Let's take a look at the role of the nine components of the MLOps Stack template:

1. **Data analysis**

   The first step is to collect and understand the feasibility of data so that it will be able to translate business objectives into machine learning tasks. At this step, it is important to define ML-specific and business evaluation metrics as well. For data access and analysis, various programming can be applied like R, Python, Scala, or SQL.

2. **Experimentation**

   To achieve all the tasks defined in the data analysis step, we must run experiments and implement a proof of concept. This helps in the achievable application of ML technology toward business objectives. Experimenting with different data sets and hyperparameters is necessary at this step.

3. **Feature store**

   Feature engineering is a process of transforming raw data into suitable feature vector formats for machine learning algorithms before proceeding further. The role of the feature store is the reproducibility and reuse of features across ML projects and various data science teams. This is an interface between the data engineering and model engineering phases.

4. **Code repository**

The code repository is a DevOps concept important for stable software delivery performance. This is important to maintain the code repository and its version history to track code changes and reproducibility in the future.

5. **ML pipeline**

A pipeline means implementing the construction and execution of a sequence of operations. Continuous integration (CI), continuous training (CT) of models, and continuous deployment (CD) of models make an ML pipeline.

6. **Model registry**

The model registry is an essential part of the model evaluation phase. The model registry is mandatory if you have multiple models in production and need to track them all. At the same time, the model registry ensures backward compatibility by making it easy to roll back to previously built models.

7. **Model serving**

Model serving is a process of applying a machine learning model to new input data. Model serving is implemented as a distributed service for response prediction for input requests.

8. **Model monitoring**

After the ML model deployment, it needs to be continuously monitored to ensure the model quality and correct predictions. This block of the MLOps Stack Canvas ensures the successful running of the ML system in production.

9. **Metadata store**

   The metadata store is the last block of MLOps Slack. It is a
   block used to implement the ML model governance process
   depending on the organization's regulatory requirements. The ML
   governance process relies on the ML metadata store component.

By understanding the role of different components of stacks, it will be easy for
organizations to decide their tool slack as per their requirements.

MLOps Challenges

Let's discuss some of the challenges faced by the MLOps system that opens the scope for
future enhancements.

1. **Unrealistic expectation**

   Poor analysis of business requirements and success criteria is a major
   challenge in the base layer of MLOps implementation. Machine
   learning is a trending buzzword these days, and sometimes this can
   lead to unrealistic expectations from nontechnical stakeholders
   without considering the actual background details.

2. **Data quality**

   ML system is sensitive to data quality as it is base of ML
   development and operations. If incoming data is either corrupted,
   incomplete, or not as per requirements, then it will impact ML
   models in production.

3. **Model decay**

   The performance of ML models decays over time. In real time,
   data keeps on changing, which impacts model performance in
   production, which cannot calibrate during the training phase.

4. **Locality**

   ML models are trained for certain demographics, which might be
   different for different business customers. While deploying ML
   models to new customers, demographics must remain in mind to
   meet the quality metrics.

5. **Security**

Machine learning works on sensitive data for different projects, which can be exposed to third parties. Keeping data, data pipelines, and machine learning models secure is essential for the long-term success of industries. Security patching is essential for successful ML model deployment to production as security is a challenge in any MLOps environment.

MLOps Best Practices

Implement these best practices to implement MLOps at scale.

1. **Well-organized project structure**

A well-organized project structure is particularly important in the MLOps project. It helps in navigating, maintaining, managing, and scaling our future projects. The end-to-end project structure must be maintained for the following:

- Data and code folders

- Data and code versioning

- ML model organization

- Deployment files organization

2. **Documentation**

Documentation is often ignored at various steps of the ML lifecycle. However, it is crucial to maintain documents with a consistent style for both records and reference. Documentation is required for the processes:

- Data sources records

- Labeling methods

- Experiment designs

- Model selection criteria

- Model pseudocode

- Entire deployment process

3. **Know your tool stack**

   Infrastructure tools used by an organization for MLOps
   implementation are essential. Tools depend on requirements and
   organization choices. Knowing your MLOps pipeline tool stack
   is a must.

4. **Track project expenses**

   With MLOps, we aim to minimize technical debt, but we do not
   want our expenses to rise too high and become unbearable.
   Keeping a check on financial debt along with technical debt is
   crucial.

Model Governance in MLOps

Model governance is a new challenge in MLOps that is important for model deployment
in production. Model governance should be implemented together with MLOps for
secure and stable machine learning systems across organizations.

Model governance should be implemented based on the strength of regulation and
the number of models. The following are a few of the aspects that are common in every
variant of the MLOps system where model governance needs to be implemented:

- Comprehensive model documentation and metrics reports.

- Versioning of all models

- Auditing of ML systems

- Data documentation

- Management of ML metadata

- Validation of ML models

- Continuous monitoring and logging of model metrics

Since MLOps is expanding to different verticals, building a successfully deployed
ML application is a challenging task. Keeping all MLOps principles, challenges, best
practices, and governance hand in hand, we can design, model, and deploy ML models
into production in different demographics successfully.

References

- https://cloud.google.com/devops

- https://en.wikipedia.org/wiki/MLOps

- https://github.com/adbreind/open-standard-models-2019/blob/master/01-Intro.ipynb

- https://www.deeplearning.ai/

- https://ml-ops.org/content/mlops-principles

- https://ml-ops.org/

- https://valohai.com/blog/the-mlops-stack/

CHAPTER 2

Foundations of MLOps on AWS

Machine learning (ML) has evolved from a niche field to a transformative technology that empowers businesses to make data-driven decisions, automate tasks, and enhance customer experiences. As machine learning (ML) continues to redefine the technological landscape, the transition from conceptualizing ML models to operationalizing them is at a critical juncture. MLOps, the amalgamation of practices and tools facilitating the seamless integration of ML system development and operations, emerges as the linchpin in this transformative journey.

In the realm of cloud computing, Amazon Web Services (AWS) stands as a pioneering force, providing a robust platform for deploying and managing ML workflows. This chapter serves as a guiding beacon through the fundamental principles and strategies essential for navigating the intricate landscape of MLOps in this dynamic cloud environment. Whether you're an experienced practitioner or an aspiring enthusiast, join us as we unravel the core tenets that form the bedrock of MLOps on AWS, propelling you toward operational excellence in machine learning.

The Evolution of Machine Learning in the Cloud

The evolution of machine learning (ML) in the cloud represents a significant shift from traditional, on-premises ML approaches to a more dynamic, scalable, and accessible cloud-based environment. The shift to the cloud has also meant that ML models can now be trained and deployed faster, with greater flexibility and at a lower cost than ever before. Cloud environments offer the advantage of handling large volumes of data and complex computations, which are inherent to ML workloads, without the need for substantial upfront investments in infrastructure.

© Neel Sendas and Deepali Rajale 2024
N. Sendas and D. Rajale, *The Definitive Guide to Machine Learning Operations in AWS*,
https://doi.org/10.1007/979-8-8688-1076-3_2

Amazon Web Services (AWS) has been pivotal in this transformation, offering an extensive suite of tools and services that cater specifically to the diverse needs of MLOps, facilitating seamless integration from model development to deployment and ongoing management. AWS's cloud-native architecture provides unparalleled scalability, ensuring that machine learning workflows can adapt to varying workloads and evolving requirements.

Moreover, AWS empowers practitioners to leverage advanced analytics, data storage, and computational resources, all within a secure and reliable environment. The robust ecosystem of AWS services, coupled with its commitment to innovation, makes it an ideal choice for organizations seeking to implement MLOps practices efficiently and effectively.

In essence, MLOps on AWS is not merely a partnership of convenience but a strategic alignment that unlocks the full potential of machine learning, offering unparalleled flexibility, scalability, and reliability in the operationalization of ML workflows. Whether you are a startup or an enterprise, AWS MLOps solutions cater to a diverse range of requirements.

Key Components of MLOps on AWS

The implementation of MLOps on AWS involves several key components to ensure the efficient, scalable, and reliable deployment of machine learning models and applications.

Data Management and Processing

Data is the cornerstone of any ML project. Examples of processing steps include converting data to the input format expected by the ML algorithm, rescaling and normalizing, cleaning and tokenizing text, and many more. However, data processing at scale involves considerable operational overhead: managing complex infrastructure like processing clusters, writing code to tie all the moving pieces together, and implementing security and governance. AWS provides a suite of services that cater to these needs, ensuring scalability, security, and efficiency.

Scalable Data Lakes with Amazon S3

In the realm of data analytics, companies are increasingly consolidating their dispersed data into a unified repository, commonly referred to as a *data lake*, to facilitate advanced analytics and machine learning (ML). However, the challenge arises as data volumes grow, making data movement laborious. To address this, an innovative Lake House approach on AWS has been introduced.

Unlike merely integrating a data lake and a data warehouse, the Lake House approach involves connecting the data lake, data warehouse, and purpose-built services into a cohesive architecture. This approach comprises scalable data lakes, purpose-built data services, seamless data movement, unified governance, and a focus on performance and cost-effectiveness.

Amazon Simple Storage Service (Amazon S3) is identified as the optimal choice for building a data lake due to its unparalleled durability, availability, scalability, security features, compliance, audit capabilities, performance, and diverse integration options with partners.

However, the setup and management of data lakes involve manual and time-consuming tasks. AWS addresses this challenge with AWS Lake Formation, a solution designed to simplify the process of building secure data lakes in the cloud. Lake Formation collects and catalogs data, moves it into an Amazon S3 data lake, leverages machine learning algorithms to clean and classify data, and ensures secure access to sensitive information.

Additionally, S3's flexible storage management features, such as storage classes and lifecycle policies, contribute to cost-effective data storage. Integration with other AWS analytics services enhances the ability to directly query and analyze data in the data lake, streamlining ML data processing workflows. The Lake House approach is illustrated with a diagram showcasing data movement between analytics services and data stores, both inside and outside the perimeter.

Figure 2-1. *Lake House architecture on AWS*

With a data lake in the center of the architecture, data engineering teams can apply their own tools for analytics workloads. At the same time, data science teams can also use their own separate tools to access the same data for ML workloads. Multiple separate processing clusters run by various teams can access the same data, while retaining the raw data in Amazon S3 for all teams as a source of truth. Additionally, use of a feature store for transformed data, such as Amazon SageMaker Feature Store, by data science teams helps delineate the boundary with data engineering, as well as provide benefits such as feature discovery, sharing, updating, and reuse.

Data Processing with Amazon SageMaker

SageMaker is a fully managed service that helps data scientists and developers prepare, build, train, and deploy high-quality ML models quickly by bringing together a broad set of capabilities purpose-built for ML. For data processing and data preparation, there are following capabilities.

SageMaker Data Wrangler

SageMaker Data Wrangler is a feature of SageMaker, enabled through SageMaker Studio, that makes it easy for data scientists and ML engineers to aggregate and prepare data for ML applications using a visual interface to accelerate data cleansing, exploration, and visualization. It allows you to easily connect to various data sources such as Amazon S3,

Amazon Athena, and Amazon Redshift. SageMaker Data Wrangler enables a "no-code" workflow where you can apply built-in transformations in lieu of writing code.

Additionally, you have the option to write custom transformations in PySpark, Pandas, or SQL. SageMaker Data Wrangler also includes several convenient integrations with other SageMaker features such as SageMaker Clarify for bias detection, SageMaker Feature Store (mentioned earlier), and SageMaker Pipelines (purpose-built CI/CD for ML). Finally, you can export your entire data preparation workflow into executable Python code.

SageMaker Feature Store

The machine learning (ML) development process often begins with extracting data signals also known as *features* from data to train ML models. Amazon SageMaker Feature Store makes it easy for data scientists, machine learning engineers, and general practitioners to create, share, and manage features for ML development. Feature Store accelerates this process by reducing repetitive data processing and curation work required to convert raw data into features for training an ML algorithm.

Further, the processing logic for your data is authored only once, and features generated are used for both training and inference, reducing the training-serving skew. Feature Store is a centralized store for features and associated metadata so features can be easily discovered and reused. You can create an online or an offline store. The online store is used for low latency real-time inference use cases, and the offline store is used for training and batch inference.

Figure 2-2 shows how you can use the Feature Store as part of your machine learning pipeline. First, you read in your raw data and process it. You can ingest data via streaming to the online and offline store, or in batches directly to the offline store. You first create a FeatureGroup and configure it to an online or offline store, or both. Then, you can ingest data into your FeatureGroup and store it in your store. A FeatureGroup is a group of features that is defined via a schema in the Feature Store to describe a record.

The online store is primarily designed for supporting real-time predictions that need low millisecond latency reads and high throughput writes. The offline store is primarily intended for batch predictions and model training. The offline store is an append-only store and can be used to store and access historical feature data. The offline store can help you store and serve features for exploration and model training. The online store retains only the latest feature data. Feature groups are mutable and can evolve their schema after creation.

Figure 2-2. *Amazon SageMaker Feature Store*

SageMaker Processing

SageMaker processing lets you easily run your preprocessing, post-processing, and model evaluation workloads on fully managed infrastructure. Preprocessing may include data validation, data transformation, analysis, and feature engineering. Post-processing may include steps to generate final results.

Figure 2-3 shows how Amazon SageMaker spins up a SageMaker Processing job. Amazon SageMaker takes your script, copies your data from Amazon Simple Storage Service (Amazon S3), and then pulls a processing container. The processing container image can be either an Amazon SageMaker built-in image or a custom image that you provide. The underlying infrastructure for a SageMaker Processing job is fully managed by Amazon SageMaker. Cluster resources are provisioned for the duration of your job and cleaned up when a job completes. The output of the processing job is stored in the Amazon S3 bucket you specified.

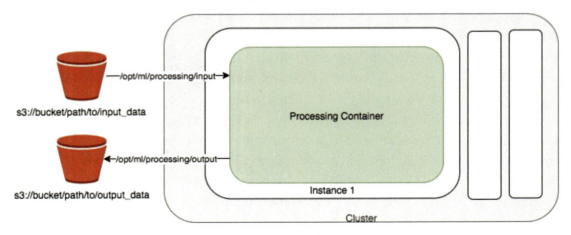

Figure 2-3. *Amazon SageMaker Processing container*

Apache Spark serves as a unified analytics engine for large-scale data processing. Amazon SageMaker offers prebuilt Docker images containing Apache Spark and necessary dependencies for distributed data processing. Using the Amazon SageMaker Python SDK, data transformations and feature extraction (feature engineering) can be seamlessly applied using the Spark framework.

You can use the sagemaker.spark.PySparkProcessor or sagemaker.spark. SparkJarProcessor class to run your Spark application inside of a processing job. Note you can set MaxRuntimeInSeconds to a maximum runtime limit of 5 days. With respect to execution time and the number of instances used, simple Spark workloads see a near-linear relationship between the number of instances versus the time to completion.

The following code example shows how to run a processing job that invokes your PySpark script *preprocess.py*:

```
from sagemaker.spark.processing import PySparkProcessor

spark_processor = PySparkProcessor(
    base_job_name="spark-preprocessor",
    framework_version="2.4",
    role=role,
    instance_count=2,
    instance_type="ml.m5.xlarge",
    max_runtime_in_seconds=1200,
)

spark_processor.run(
    submit_app="preprocess.py",
    arguments=['s3_input_bucket', bucket,
               's3_input_key_prefix', input_prefix,
               's3_output_bucket', bucket,
               's3_output_key_prefix', output_prefix]
)
```

Similarly, SageMaker Processing also supports data processing with scikit-learn using the SKLearnProcessor class from the SageMaker Python SDK. The following code example shows how the notebook uses SKLearnProcessor to run your own scikit-learn script using a Docker image provided and maintained by SageMaker, instead of your own Docker image:

```
from sagemaker.sklearn.processing import SKLearnProcessor
from sagemaker.processing import ProcessingInput, ProcessingOutput

sklearn_processor = SKLearnProcessor(framework_version='0.20.0',
                                     role=role,
                                     instance_type='ml.m5.xlarge',
                                     instance_count=1)

sklearn_processor.run(code='preprocessing.py',
                inputs=[ProcessingInput(
                    source='s3://path/to/my/input-data.csv',
                    destination='/opt/ml/processing/input')],
                outputs=[ProcessingOutput(source='/opt/ml/processing/
                output/train'),
                        ProcessingOutput(source='/opt/ml/processing/
                        output/validation'),
                        ProcessingOutput(source='/opt/ml/processing/
                        output/test')]
                )
```

You can also use `FrameworkProcessor` to run Processing jobs with a specified machine learning framework, providing you with an Amazon SageMaker–managed container for whichever machine learning framework you choose. `FrameworkProcessor` provides premade containers for the following machine learning frameworks: Hugging Face, MXNet, PyTorch, TensorFlow, and XGBoost.

Additionally, you can install libraries to run your scripts in your own processing container or, in a more advanced scenario, you can build your own processing container that satisfies the contract to run in Amazon SageMaker.

Single Universal Notebook with Built-in Integration with Amazon EMR

While SageMaker Processing lets you run your processing scripts at scale and automates your data preparation workflow, the built-in integration with Amazon EMR enables you to do interactive data preparation and machine learning at petabyte scale right within the single universal SageMaker Studio notebook. It also enables you to monitor and debug your Apache Spark jobs running on EMR from SageMaker Studio notebooks. Additionally, you can discover, connect to, create, terminate, and manage EMR clusters directly from SageMaker Studio.

You can also use AWS Service Catalog to define and roll out preconfigured templates to selected data workers to enable them to create EMR clusters right from SageMaker Studio. Data workers can visually browse through a set of templates made available to them, customize them for their specific workloads, create EMR clusters on-demand, and terminate them with just a few clicks right from SageMaker Studio. You can use these features to simplify your data preparation workflow and more optimally use EMR clusters for interactive workloads from SageMaker Studio.

Low-Code/No-Code Options for ETL Pipelines

Developing extract, transform, and load (ETL) data pipelines is one of the most time-consuming steps to keep data lakes, data warehouses, and databases up-to-date and ready to provide business insights. AWS offers several low-code (or no-code)services for ETL that are serverless and lead to faster results with minimal cost.

- **Amazon Athena:** Amazon Athena is a serverless interactive query service for transforming data using standard SQL queries, in combination with Amazon QuickSight, a serverless BI tool that offers no code, built-in visualizations. When evaluating this powerful combination, consider whether your data transformations can be accomplished with SQL. On the visualization side, an alternative to QuickSight is to use a library such as PyAthena to run SQL queries in SageMaker notebooks and visualize the results there with a declarative visualization library such as Altair (this might be considered "low code+" as it still involves minimal code).

- **AWS Glue:** Another low-code possibility involves AWS Glue, a serverless ETL service that catalogs your data and offers built-in transforms, along with the ability to write custom PySpark code. For visualizations, besides QuickSight, you can attach either SageMaker or Zeppelin notebooks to an AWS Glue development endpoint. If AWS Glue built-in transforms don't fully cover the desired set of data transforms, choosing between Athena and AWS Glue may depend upon a team's preference for implementing custom transforms using standard SQL versus PySpark code.

- **AWS Glue DataBrew:** AWS Glue DataBrew is a visual data preparation tool that enables users to clean and normalize data without writing any code. You can choose from more than 250 ready-made transformations to automate data preparation tasks, such as filtering anomalies, converting data to standard formats, and correcting invalid values. Table 2-1 compares DataBrew and SageMaker Data Wrangler.

Table 2-1. *Comparing DataBrew with SageMaker Data Wrangler*

	Glue DataBrew	SageMaker Data Wrangler
Processing resources	Serverless	Serverless
Built-in visualizations	Yes	Yes
Built-in transforms	Yes	Yes
Custom transforms	No	Yes
Bias detection integration	No	Yes (SageMaker Clarify)
Feature store integration	No	Yes (SageMaker Feature Store)
CI/CD integration	No	Yes (SageMaker Pipelines)

AWS Glue plays a pivotal role in the Extract, Transform, Load (ETL) processes crucial in preparing data for ML models. It is a fully managed ETL service that simplifies the process of preparing and transforming data for analysis. AWS Glue automatically discovers and categorizes data, making it searchable and queryable in the AWS environment.

Glue's serverless nature allows for easy scaling of ETL jobs, handling varying volumes of data without the need for manual provisioning of resources. Additionally, Glue's integration with other AWS services, like Amazon Redshift and Amazon Athena, streamlines the data preparation and loading process into various analytics and data warehousing services.

Self-Managed Stack Using Spark, Python, or R

Another option is to "roll your own" solution by deploying Spark, Python frameworks such as Dask, or R-based code in a self-managed cluster using Amazon Elastic Compute Cloud (Amazon EC2) compute resources, or the container services Amazon Elastic Container Service (Amazon ECS) or Amazon Elastic Kubernetes Service (Amazon EKS). Integration with SageMaker is most conveniently achieved using the Amazon SageMaker Python SDK. Any machine with AWS Identity and Access Management (IAM) permissions to SageMaker can use the SageMaker Python SDK to invoke SageMaker functionality for model building, training, tuning, deployment, and more.

This option provides the most flexibility to mix and match any data processing tools and frameworks. It also offers access to the widest range of EC2 instance types and storage options. As with Amazon EMR, you can use Spot Instances to optimize data processing costs for this option. Additionally, similarly to the SageMaker Savings Plans previously mentioned, you can also use Amazon EC2 Instance Savings Plans or Compute Savings Plans, which can be applied not only to EC2 resources but also to serverless compute AWS Lambda resources and serverless compute engine AWS Fargate resources.

However, keep in mind in regard to user-friendliness for data scientists and ML engineers, this option requires them to manage low-level infrastructure, a task better suited to other roles. Also, with respect to usefulness for ML-specific tasks, although there are many frameworks such as Spark and tools that can be layered on top of these services to make management easier and provide specific functionality for ML workloads, this option is still far less managed than the preceding options. It requires more personnel time to manage, tune, maintain infrastructure and dependencies, and write code to fill functionality gaps. As a result, this option also is likely to prove the most costly in the long run and cause the most workflow friction.

In conclusion, your choice of a data processing option for ML workloads typically depends on your team's preference for tools (Spark, SQL, Python, etc.) and inclination for writing code and managing infrastructure. Table 2-2 summarizes the options across several relevant dimensions. The first column emphasizes that separate services or features may be used for processing and related visualization, and the third column refers to resources used to process data rather than for visualization, which tends to be run on lighter-weight resources.

Table 2-2. *Comparing AWS Data Processing Options*

Processing/Visualization	Spark, SQL, or Custom Code	Processing Resources Available	Language
SageMaker Data Wrangler (both processing/visualization)	"No code", additional support for custom code transformations.	Serverless (with distributed support)	Python, PySpark, Pandas, SQL
SageMaker Processing/ SageMaker notebooks	Spark, SQL (Spark SQL), custom code	Managed cluster, choose number and type of (most) EC2 instances, storage.	Python, R (others possible)
SageMaker Studio Universal notebook/ built-in integration with Amazon EMR	Spark, SQL (Spark SQL), custom code, multiple options like presto, hive etc.	Most EC2 instance types in a managed EMR or EKS cluster.	Python, Scala, SQL, PySpark (others possible)
Athena/ Quicksight or SageMaker Notebooks	SQL only	Serverless	SQL
AWS Glue ETL/ SageMaker or Zeppelin notebooks	Spark, SQL (Spark SQL)	Serverless	Python, Scala
Data Brew (both processing and visualization)	"No code"	Serverless	N/A
Amazon EMR with Spark/ SageMaker Notebooks or EMR Studio	Spark, SQL (multiple options like presto, hive), custom code.	Most EC2 instance types in a managed EMR or EKS cluster. Serverless option is also available.	Python, Scala, SQL, PySpark (others possible)
Self-managed EC2/ECS/EKS Spark, Python and/or R stack	All of the above	Any EC2 instance type, in a self-managed cluster	Python, R (others possible)

Workloads evolve over time, and you don't need to be locked into one set of tools forever. You can mix and match according to your use case. When you use Amazon S3 at the center of your data lake and the fully managed SageMaker service for core ML workflow steps, it's easy to switch tools as needed or desired to accommodate the latest technologies. Whichever option you choose now, AWS provides the flexibility to evolve your tool chain to best fit the then-current data processing needs of your ML workloads.

Spark Processing with Amazon EMR

Organizations commonly utilize Spark for data processing and as a foundation for data warehouses. Amazon EMR, a managed service for Hadoop-ecosystem clusters, simplifies setup, tuning, and maintenance of Spark clusters. Data scientists and ML engineers may opt for Spark in Amazon EMR under specific circumstances:

- **Persistent clusters:** When Spark is already employed for a data warehouse or other applications with a persistent cluster, Amazon EMR allows the creation of enduring clusters, supporting analytics applications.

- **End-to-end Spark pipeline:** If there's an existing end-to-end pipeline in Spark and the team has the expertise and preference for running a persistent Spark cluster long-term, Amazon EMR is a suitable choice. Otherwise, SageMaker and AWS Glue options are generally preferred.

- **Instance types:** Amazon EMR provides a variety of instance types, including AWS Graviton2 processors and Amazon EC2 Spot Instances for cost optimization.

For visualization with Amazon EMR, options include using SageMaker Studio with its built-in SparkMagic kernel for querying, analyzing, and processing data within SageMaker. Alternatively, Amazon EMR Studio, offering fully managed Jupyter notebooks, allows logging in via AWS single sign-on. Note that EMR Studio lacks some SageMaker-specific UI integrations present in SageMaker Studio.

Model Training and Optimization

In the realm of machine learning operations (MLOps) on AWS, the focus on efficient and effective model training and optimization is paramount. This section explores the capabilities of AWS in providing scalable training environments, hyperparameter tuning with SageMaker, and strategies for cost-effective model training.

Scalable Training Environments in AWS

Scalability is a key factor in the training of machine learning models, especially when dealing with large datasets or complex algorithms. AWS provides scalable training environments that can adapt to the varying demands of ML model training. Services like Amazon EC2 (Elastic Compute Cloud) and Amazon SageMaker offer a range of instance types, including those with GPU and CPU optimizations, to cater to different training requirements.

Amazon EC2 instances, particularly those equipped with GPUs, are ideal for deep learning tasks, offering high-performance computing capabilities. AWS' auto-scaling feature allows these instances to scale up or down based on demand, ensuring efficient resource utilization. Additionally, Amazon SageMaker enables distributed training, where the training task is split across multiple instances, drastically reducing the training time for large models.

Framework Support with SageMaker

SageMaker's key features include built-in algorithms and support for popular ML frameworks, such as TensorFlow and PyTorch. SageMaker's ability to scale to handle large datasets and complex algorithms makes it an ideal choice for a wide range of ML applications. Its automatic model tuning capability, known as Hyperparameter Optimization (HPO), helps in finding the best version of a model by running multiple training jobs with different hyperparameter combinations.

SageMaker provides prebuilt Docker images for its built-in algorithms and the supported deep learning frameworks used for training and inference. Using containers, you can train machine learning algorithms and deploy models quickly and reliably at any scale. If you build or train a custom model and require a custom framework that does not have a prebuilt image, you can build a custom container.

The following decision tree illustrates the information in the previous three lists:

- Use cases for using prebuilt Docker containers with SageMaker

- Use cases for extending a prebuilt Docker container

- Use case for building your own container

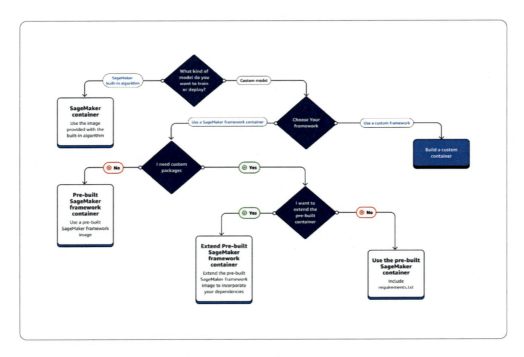

Figure 2-4. *Amazon SageMaker framework container support*

Deep Learning AMIs

AWS Deep Learning Amazon Machine Images (AMIs) provide machine images pre-installed with popular deep learning frameworks like TensorFlow, PyTorch, Apache MXNet, and others. These AMIs are optimized for high performance and scalability on AWS, reducing the setup time for deep learning environments.

These AMIs are particularly beneficial for complex models that require extensive computational power. They support various GPU and CPU configurations, ensuring efficient utilization of resources. The AMIs also come with pre-installed CUDA and cuDNN libraries, which are essential for deep learning tasks on NVIDIA GPUs. Users can also customize and save their own AMIs, creating a tailored environment that can be reused for consistent experiments.

Hyperparameter Tuning with SageMaker

Hyperparameter tuning is a critical step in optimizing machine learning models for better performance. AWS SageMaker offers an automatic model tuning feature, known as Hyperparameter Optimization (HPO). HPO uses a process called Bayesian optimization, random search, or grid search to find the best combination of hyperparameters, thereby improving model accuracy.

SageMaker's HPO service automates the process of running multiple training jobs, each with different hyperparameter settings, and then aggregates the results to find the most optimal model. This not only saves time but also ensures a more systematic and scientific approach to model tuning compared to manual experimentation.

Experiment Management

Effective management of experiments and model versions is crucial in MLOps for tracking and comparing different models. AWS SageMaker Experiments is a tool that allows users to organize, track, compare, and evaluate ML experiments and model versions.

SageMaker Experiments automatically captures input parameters, configurations, and results, enabling users to reproduce and trace back the steps in their ML workflow. This is critical for understanding model performance and making iterative improvements. The integration of SageMaker with AWS CodeCommit, CodeBuild, and CodePipeline further streamlines the version control and continuous integration/continuous deployment (CI/CD) pipelines, enhancing the MLOps lifecycle.

Cost-Effective Model Training Strategies

Cost optimization is a vital consideration in the MLOps lifecycle, particularly during the model training phase, which can be resource-intensive. AWS offers several strategies to manage and reduce costs.

One approach is to utilize Spot Instances in Amazon EC2, which allows users to take advantage of unused EC2 capacity at a lower price than On-Demand instances. This is particularly beneficial for training jobs that can tolerate interruptions.

Another strategy is to leverage the right mix of instance types. For instance, using a high-powered GPU instance for the initial intensive training phase and then switching to a less expensive CPU instance for the less intensive tasks.

AWS also provides detailed cost management tools like AWS Cost Explorer and AWS Budgets, which allow users to track and manage their spending effectively.

In summary, AWS's MLOps ecosystem offers a powerful combination of scalability, advanced tools for hyperparameter tuning, and cost-effective strategies. These capabilities are crucial for the efficient and optimized training of machine learning models, enabling organizations to harness the full potential of their ML initiatives.

Automated Model Deployment and Scaling

Deploying and managing machine learning models effectively is a critical aspect of MLOps on AWS.Key strategies for model deployment focus on real-time and batch inference, the use of SageMaker Endpoints and Elastic Inference, and managing model latency and scalability.

For managing scaling requirements, AWS Auto Scaling monitors your applications and automatically adjusts capacity to maintain steady, predictable performance at the lowest possible cost. This is crucial for ML models where demand can fluctuate.

Deployment Strategies: Real-Time vs. Batch Inference

The choice between real-time and batch inference depends on the specific requirements of an application. Real-time inference is suitable for applications that require immediate responses, such as recommendation systems or interactive user interfaces. AWS supports real-time inference through services like Amazon SageMaker, which allows the deployment of models as HTTPS endpoints. These endpoints can respond to prediction requests in real time, with low latency.

Batch inference, on the other hand, is appropriate for scenarios where the immediate response is not critical, and large volumes of data are processed in a single, non-interactive operation. AWS offers batch inference capabilities through services like Amazon SageMaker Batch Transform. This service enables efficient processing of large datasets without the need for real-time interaction, making it ideal for scenarios like daily financial risk assessments or batch processing of images.

Amazon SageMaker Endpoints provide a straightforward way to deploy machine learning models for real-time inference. These endpoints are fully managed instances that handle the heavy lifting of deploying and scaling the models. One of the key benefits of SageMaker Endpoints is their integration with AWS Elastic Inference, which allows attaching just the right amount of GPU-powered inference acceleration to a SageMaker instance. This results in cost-effective, high-performance inference.

Amazon SageMaker's deployment guardrails introduce an array of new deployment features, enabling the adoption of sophisticated deployment strategies to mitigate risks when introducing new model versions in SageMaker hosting. These strategies are tailored to suit various use cases, each employing a unique method to divert inference traffic toward one or several model versions. The selection of a particular strategy should align with the specific requirements of your machine learning (ML) application. However, any strategy should include the ability to monitor the performance of new model versions and automatically roll back to a previous version as needed to minimize potential risk of introducing a new model version with errors. Incorporating these deployment strategies into your MLOps framework is vital for establishing consistent and dependable model deployment processes. The implementation of your chosen deployment approach should be integrated into your automated deployment pipeline. Deployment guardrails work seamlessly with the existing SageMaker CreateEndpoint and UpdateEndpoint APIs, allowing you to easily modify your current deployment pipeline setups to leverage these advanced deployment functionalities.

Amazon Elastic Kubernetes Service (Amazon EKS)

For those looking to deploy ML models in containers, Amazon EKS provides a scalable and highly available Kubernetes service. Kubernetes is a powerful tool for container orchestration, and Amazon EKS simplifies its management. This service is particularly useful when you need to run ML workloads in a containerized environment. Kubernetes provides isolation, auto-scaling, load balancing, flexibility, and GPU support. These features are critical to run computationally and are data-intensive and hard to parallelize machine learning models. Declarative syntax of Kubernetes deployment descriptors make it easy for nonoperationally focused engineers to easily train machine learning models on Kubernetes.

Managing Model Latency and Scalability

Model latency and scalability are crucial factors in the deployment phase. AWS provides various tools and services to manage these aspects efficiently. Auto-scaling in SageMaker Endpoints allows automatic adjustment of instance counts based on the incoming request volume, ensuring that latency remains low even under heavy loads.

For latency-sensitive applications, AWS provides services like Amazon Elastic Kubernetes Service (EKS) and AWS Fargate, which offer fine-grained control over the deployment environment and can optimize the infrastructure for the lowest possible latency. Additionally, optimizing the model itself, such as reducing its size or complexity, can also lead to lower latency.

In summary, AWS offers a comprehensive suite of services and tools for efficient model deployment and inference in an MLOps context. Whether it's choosing between real-time or batch inference, leveraging SageMaker Endpoints with Elastic Inference for cost-effective deployment, or managing latency and scalability, AWS provides robust solutions to meet diverse deployment needs.

Continuous Integration and Continuous Deployment (CI/CD)

In the evolving landscape of MLOps, continuous integration (CI) and continuous deployment (CD) are essential practices that streamline the development and deployment of machine learning models. AWS offers robust tools to facilitate these practices, enhancing the efficiency and reliability of ML workflows.

Automating MLOps with AWS CodePipeline

AWS CodePipeline is a fully managed continuous delivery service that helps automate the release pipelines for fast and reliable updates. In the context of MLOps, CodePipeline can automate various stages of ML model development and deployment, from data preprocessing and model training to deployment and monitoring. It integrates seamlessly with other AWS services, allowing for the creation of a custom pipeline that suits the specific needs of an ML project.

Using CodePipeline, data scientists and ML engineers can define the workflow for building, testing, and deploying their ML models. For example, once a model is trained and validated, CodePipeline can automatically deploy it to a production environment, such as an Amazon SageMaker endpoint. This automation reduces manual intervention, accelerates the release process, and minimizes the scope for errors.

Building CI/CD Pipelines with AWS CodeBuild

AWS CodeBuild is a fully managed build service that compiles source code, runs tests, and produces software packages that are ready to deploy. In an MLOps pipeline, CodeBuild can be used to automate tasks such as running unit tests on ML code, building Docker containers for model deployment, or executing scripts for data validation.

Integrating CodeBuild into an MLOps CI/CD pipeline ensures that the code and model artifacts are consistently tested and built in a standardized environment. This consistency is crucial for reliable and repeatable model training and deployment. Moreover, CodeBuild can scale automatically to meet varying build volumes and can process multiple builds concurrently, thus speeding up the development process.

Version Control with AWS CodeCommit

Version control is a vital aspect of MLOps, ensuring that all changes in ML models, datasets, and code are tracked and managed effectively. AWS CodeCommit is a managed source control service that hosts secure Git-based repositories. It facilitates collaboration among ML teams, allowing them to track and share their work efficiently.

Incorporating CodeCommit into an MLOps workflow enables teams to maintain a history of changes in their ML projects, roll back to previous versions when necessary, and manage different versions of models and datasets. CodeCommit also integrates with CodePipeline and CodeBuild, providing a seamless experience for managing the lifecycle of ML models from development to deployment.

In conclusion, leveraging AWS services like CodePipeline, CodeBuild, and CodeCommit in MLOps workflows empowers teams to automate and streamline their CI/CD processes. This automation not only accelerates the pace of model development and deployment but also ensures higher quality and consistency in ML projects.

Orchestrate ML Workflows with SageMaker Pipelines

SageMaker pipelines is a purpose-built, easy-to-use continuous integration and continuous delivery (CI/CD) service for machine learning (ML). SageMaker Pipelines is directly integrated with Amazon SageMaker. SageMaker pipelines offer three components to improve the operational resilience and reproducibility of your ML workflows: pipelines, model registry, and projects. These workflow automation components enable you to easily scale your ability to build, train, test, and deploy hundreds of models in production, iterate faster, reduce errors due to manual orchestration, and build repeatable mechanisms.

SageMaker projects introduce MLOps templates that automatically provision the underlying resources needed to enable CI/CD capabilities for your ML development lifecycle. You can use a number of built-in templates or create your own custom template. While you can use SageMaker Pipelines on their own to automate workflows, combining them with SageMaker projects gives you extra CI/CD features automatically. Figure 2-5 illustrates how SageMaker Pipelines' three main parts can be used together in a typical SageMaker project.

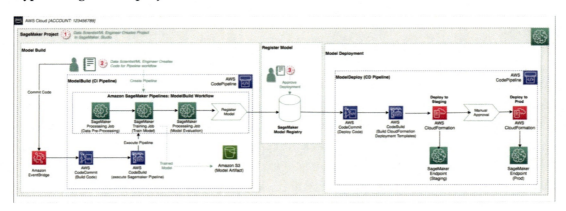

Figure 2-5. *Amazon SageMaker Pipeline*

Run ML Pipelines with AWS Step Functions

AWS offers a wide range of services to manage and run ML workflows, allowing you to select a solution based on your skills and application. If you already use AWS Step Functions to orchestrate the components of distributed applications, you can use the same service to build and automate your ML workflows.

AWS Step Functions allows you to coordinate multiple AWS services into serverless workflows. For MLOps, this means orchestrating data preprocessing, model training, and deployment with ease. By defining state machines in Step Functions, you can create robust ML pipelines that are easy to maintain and monitor.

You can use a workflow to create a machine learning pipeline. The AWS Data Science Workflows SDK provides several AWS SageMaker workflow steps that you can use to construct an ML pipeline. You can create Train and Transform steps such as these:

- **TrainingStep:** Starts a SageMaker training job and outputs the model artifacts to S3.

- **ModelStep:** Creates a model on SageMaker using the model artifacts from S3.

- **TransformStep:** Starts a SageMaker transform job.

- **EndpointConfigStep:** Defines an endpoint configuration on SageMaker.

- **EndpointStep:** Deploys the trained model to the configured endpoint.

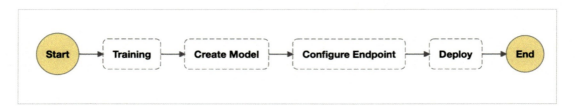

Figure 2-6. *ML pipeline workflow steps*

Finally, you can create and run the workflow using `pipeline.create()` and `pipeline.execute()`. A successful run shows each state in green.

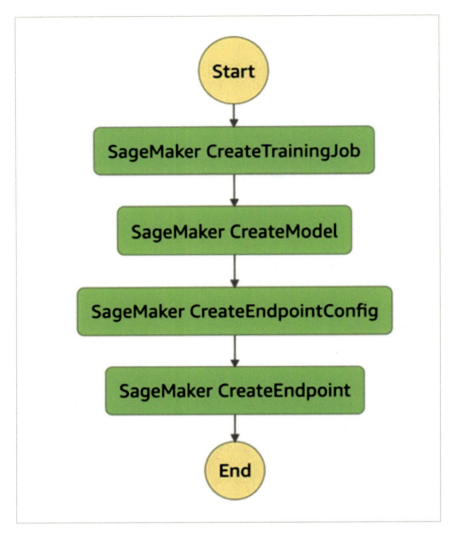

Figure 2-7. *ML pipeline successful workflow run*

Monitoring, Logging, and Model Maintenance

In the world of machine learning operations, ongoing maintenance, monitoring, and logging are essential to ensure the efficient and secure functioning of machine learning models. This chapter explores how AWS services like Amazon CloudWatch, AWS CloudTrail, and strategic approaches to model retraining and updating contribute to robust MLOps practices.

Monitoring Models with Amazon CloudWatch

Amazon CloudWatch is a monitoring and observability service designed to provide data and actionable insights to monitor applications, respond to system-wide performance changes, and optimize resource utilization. In the context of MLOps, CloudWatch plays a pivotal role in monitoring ML models. It offers the capability to track operational metrics and logs, set alarms, and react to changes in your AWS resources.

For ML models, CloudWatch can be used to monitor key metrics such as prediction latency, error rates, and the number of requests per model. These metrics are crucial for understanding the performance of a model in a production environment. Furthermore, CloudWatch allows the setting of alarms that can notify the team if the model's performance deviates from the defined threshold, enabling timely interventions to maintain model accuracy and efficiency.

Logging and Auditing with AWS CloudTrail

AWS CloudTrail is a service that provides a record of actions taken by a user, a role, or an AWS service in AWS, enabling governance, compliance, operational auditing, and risk auditing of your AWS account. In MLOps, CloudTrail can be used to log and continuously monitor account activity related to ML workflows.

The logging of API calls made to services such as Amazon SageMaker, AWS Lambda, and Amazon S3 provides visibility into user activity and resource changes. This level of detail is critical for security and compliance purposes, allowing teams to track who made what changes, when, and from where. Furthermore, CloudTrail logs can be integrated with Amazon CloudWatch Logs for real-time analysis and correlated with other data sources for comprehensive auditing.

Model Retraining and Updating Strategies

Maintaining the accuracy and relevance of ML models over time is a challenge. As data evolves, models may become less effective, necessitating retraining and updating. Effective strategies for model retraining and updating involve regular evaluation of model performance against new data, implementing automated retraining pipelines, and carefully managing the deployment of updated models.

Automated retraining pipelines can be established using AWS services, where new data is continuously evaluated, and models are retrained when a significant drift in data or model performance is detected. Additionally, techniques such as A/B testing or canary releases can be used to cautiously roll out updated models, ensuring they perform as expected in the real world without disrupting existing services.

Model Lineage Tracking

Amazon SageMaker Model Monitor is an essential tool in the machine learning (ML) ecosystem, addressing critical issues such as data drift and model drift, which can significantly impact the performance of ML models over time. Data drift occurs when the statistical properties of model input data change, leading to a mismatch between the training data and new data the model encounters in production. Similarly, model drift happens when the model's predictive performance degrades due to evolving patterns in the underlying data.

The significance of model lineage tracking cannot be overstated in this context. It involves keeping a detailed record of the data, features, parameters, and environments used in each version of a model. This tracking is crucial for diagnosing and rectifying issues like drifts, as it provides a clear history of how a model was developed, trained, and modified.

SageMaker Model Monitor effectively tackles these challenges by continuously evaluating the model's performance in production. It automatically detects and alerts any deviations in data quality or model performance, helping to identify data drift and model drift. By monitoring the incoming data to the model and the predictions made by the model, it ensures that any drift is quickly caught and addressed. Furthermore, SageMaker's integration with model lineage tracking tools provides a comprehensive view of the model's history, aiding in swift diagnosis and resolution of any issues. This holistic approach ensures that ML models deployed in production continue to perform reliably and accurately over time, adapting to changes in data patterns and maintaining their relevance and effectiveness.

In summary, robust monitoring with Amazon CloudWatch, detailed logging with AWS CloudTrail, and strategic model retraining and updating are critical components of a successful MLOps strategy on AWS. These practices enable businesses to maintain high-performing, secure, and compliant ML models in their operational environments.

Conclusion

While AWS provides a robust ecosystem for MLOps, there are challenges to overcome. These include cost management, model drift detection, and data versioning. Additionally, selecting the right instance types and storage options can significantly impact the performance and cost-effectiveness of your ML workloads.

In conclusion, MLOps on AWS offers a powerful platform to develop, deploy, and manage ML models at scale. By leveraging AWS's extensive suite of services and adhering to best practices, organizations can streamline their ML workflows, reduce time-to-market, and unlock the full potential of machine learning.

References

- https://docs.aws.amazon.com/glue/latest/dg/notebooks-chapter.html

- https://aws.amazon.com/glue/features/databrew/

- https://aws.amazon.com/blogs/machine-learning/data-processing-options-for-ai-ml/

- https://aws.amazon.com/blogs/big-data/harness-the-power-of-your-data-with-aws-analytics/

- https://aws.amazon.com/about-aws/whats-new/2021/12/amazon-sagemaker-studio-data-notebook-integration-emr/

- https://aws.amazon.com/blogs/machine-learning/building-machine-learning-workflows-with-amazon-sagemaker-processing-jobs-and-aws-step-functions/

- https://aws.amazon.com/blogs/machine-learning/take-advantage-of-advanced-deployment-strategies-using-amazon-sagemaker-deployment-guardrails/

- https://aws.amazon.com/blogs/apn/deploy-accelerated-ml-models-to-amazon-elastic-kubernetes-service-using-octoml-cli/

- https://lifesciences-resources.awscloud.com/aws-storage-blog/machine-learning-with-kubeflow-on-amazon-eks-with-amazon-efs

- https://sagemaker-examples.readthedocs.io/en/latest/step-functions-data-science-sdk/machine_learning_workflow_abalone/machine_learning_workflow_abalone.html

## CHAPTER 3

Operational Excellence in MLOps

Every business, technology, and operation strives for excellence to reach a peak level of their respective domains. An approach for continuous improvement, ameliorating efficiency with top-notch quality, and customer satisfaction at nominal expenses is called *operation excellence*. This chapter aims to achieve operational excellence in machine learning operations.

In this chapter, we will deep dive in to operational excellence in MLOps and its amalgamation in detail. We will discuss principles, phases of operational excellence, and best practices to be followed for operational excellence in MLOps. We will learn operational excellence design principles in the cloud as well as see a detailed implementation of operational excellence in AWS with code snippets.

© Neel Sendas and Deepali Rajale 2024
N. Sendas and D. Rajale, *The Definitive Guide to Machine Learning Operations in AWS*,
https://doi.org/10.1007/979-8-8688-1076-3_3

What Is Operational Excellence?

Operational excellence was first introduced by Dr. Joseph M. Juran in the early 1970s while teaching Japanese business leaders how to improve quality. Operational excellence is a business management approach that focuses on long-term sustainable growth, continuous improvement in existing processes of an organization with top-notch quality products, empowered employees, and exceeding customer satisfaction. It is often confused with continuous improvement, but operation excellence is much more than that.

Principles of Operational Excellence

The following are the principles of operation excellence:

- Quality commitment
- Innovative products
- Process superiority
- High-level safety

- Leadership engagement
- Employee involvement
- Strategic direction and focus
- Exceeds customer expectation

Phases of Operational Excellence

To continuously deliver excellence in operations, businesses need to master the five phases of operation excellence shown in Figure 3-1.

Figure 3-1. *Phases of Operational Excellence*

1. **Essentials**

    The essentials are setting standard processes for consistent and repetitive delivery of all the products and services. All the processes must be documented, and employees must be trained to execute the process successfully. Leadership must take care of allowable expense levels.

2. **Empowerment**

    It is a major phase to drive all the coming phases efficiently. Understanding leadership and the workforce and their engagement in the process is crucial to push their performances. Fairness and firmness with staff, focus on their right skills development and leadership development of higher post individuals, and their amalgamation is taken care of in this phase.

3. **Effectiveness**

    In the effectiveness phase, the focus is on delivering products and services as promised to customers within the promised timeframe and with acceptable quality. Having the right resources in the right place at the right time is the key to effectively moving to the next phase.

4. **Efficiency**

   In the efficiency phase, the focus is on improving deliverable products and services to end customers. To achieve this, at this stage continuous improvement and investment are done in technology, quality, employee efficiency, and delivery time reduction.

5. **Execution**

   Execution to the perfection possible with the right services, right people, right skills, on-time delivery, and controlled expenses. Mastering all these aspects leads to excellent execution with happy customers, happy employees, and growing businesses.

Operational Excellence and MLOps Integration

Continuous improvement is the foundation of operation excellence. When operation excellence meets with MLOps, it leads to incremental gains in terms of time, efficiency, expense control, and agility at every level. It emphasized the importance of bridging the gap between development, deployment, and operations teams to ensure faster and more reliable output.

For the proliferation of AI business, more than developing ML models is needed; their seamless deployment is crucial as then it's continuous monitoring. It is a complete cycle that needs operations to run every gear smoothly with all the manpower and automation hand in hand. In essence, operational excellence in MLOps is about ensuring that all components of an ML system, from data ingestion to models to deployment, work together in harmony. And it is the combined force of ML, DevOps, MLOps, and operation excellence that ensures this symphony.

Best Practices of Operational Excellence in MLOps

The following are some of the best practices for implementing operational excellence in MLOps.

Continuous Integration and Continuous Delivery (CI/CD) Pipelines

Continuous integration and continuous deployment (CI/CD) is the idea adapted from DevOps and implemented in MLOps to automate the process of planning, coding, development, modeling, testing, deploying, and monitoring ML models. It ensures that every change to the code or models is tested, validated, integrated, and deployed seamlessly, reducing manual errors and enabling rapid iteration.

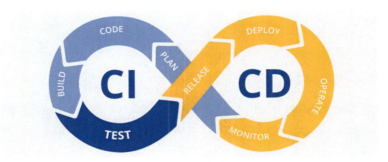

Continuous integration (CI) refers to the ML pipeline where new code is submitted at one end, and then testing and validating of data, code, models, and components is done. Every time data, code, or model is updated, the ML pipeline is rerun for versioning, testing, and validation.

Continuous delivery (CD) refers to the ML pipeline concerned with delivering a ready-for-production new release that automatically deploys another ML model into production.

MLOps goes through three levels to reach the automation of ML with CI/CD pipelines.

Level 0: Manual Process

MLOps Level 0 is a manual data science process, which is implemented at the beginning of the machine learning era. It is iterative and every step like data preparation, model training, etc., in each pipeline is executed manually. Rapid application tools like Jupyter Notebooks are used to implement manual processes. See Figure 3-2.

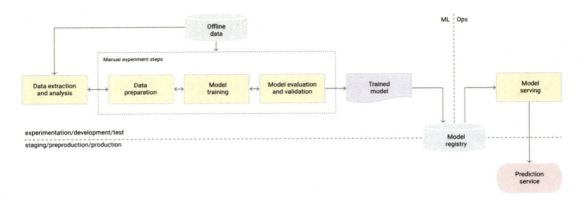

Figure 3-2. *ML manual process*

Machine Learning Steps

In any ML project, once the business requirement and its performance metrics are finalized, eight basic steps are followed for delivering the ML model to production:

1. **Data Extraction**

   The first step is to select and integrate the relevant data from different data sources for ML implementation.

2. **Data Analysis**

   Data analysis is crucial to understanding data. Exploratory data analysis (EDA) and feature engineering are two important techniques for this. This sets up the platform to decide and understand the behavior of ML models.

3. **Data Preparation**

   Data is cleaned and prepared properly for the ML task. Removing unnecessary data, imputing missing values, and splitting data for training, validation, and testing is done at this stage.

4. **Model Training**

   Various machine learning algorithms are implemented by data scientists at this stage on the prepared data to train ML models. Hyperparameter tuning is done at this step, which also contributes to identifying the best-performing model.

5. **Model Evaluation**

   The model is evaluated based on performance metrics decided at the start to assess the quality of the model.

6. **Model Validation**

   The model is validated to judge its adequacy for deployment. It is validated if its predictive performance is better than a certain baseline.

7. **Model Serving**

   On a target environment, the validated model is deployed for predictions.

8. **Model Monitoring**

   The model's predictive performance is monitored to potentially invoke a new iteration in the ML process.

The level of automation of these steps defines the maturity level of the ML process. In Level 0, all ML steps run manually; no automation exists.

Challenges with Level 0

There are many challenges with the manual process, which generates a need for ML pipeline automation.

- Burn-out in production
- Disconnect between ML and operations
- Infrequent release iterations
- No continuous integration and continuous deployment
- Lack of active monitoring systems

Level 1: ML Pipeline Automation

In MLOps level 1, an automated pipeline is implemented, which helps in continuous training (CT) of the model. This level helps provide solutions for constantly changing environments and input data. The process of model retraining is triggered whenever new data is available or at a scheduled time. With continuous training, continuous delivery of model prediction service is achieved. This level of automation also includes data and model validation steps with metadata management. See Figure 3-3.

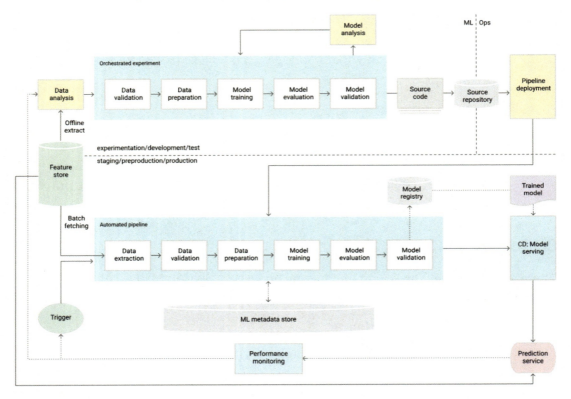

Figure 3-3. *ML pipeline automation*

Additional Components in Level 1

There are new components added in Level 1 which are as follows:

- Data validation

- Model validation

- Feature Store

- ML Metadata Store

- ML pipeline triggers

Characteristics of Level 1

Level 1 overcomes the challenges of Level 0. Its major characteristics are as follows:

- At this level, the transition between the steps is automated, which results in a quick round of experiments and appropriate results. This automation leads the whole pipeline to production in a fast and effective manner.

- At this level, the whole pipeline runs recurrently and automatically to serve the trained model to deployment unlike level 0.

- Continuous training of the model in production triggered by pipeline as new data becomes available.

- In production, the ML pipeline continuously delivers prediction services on newly trained and validated models that are trained on new data at deployment.

- Code is modularized for different components to make them reusable, composable, and potentially shared across ML pipelines.

Challenges with Level 1

There are many challenges with ML pipeline automation that generate the need for CI/CD pipeline automation.

- Less frequent deployment

- New ML ideas not considered

- Lack of continuous integration

Level 2: CI/CD Pipeline Automation

MLOps Level 2 is the final stage of MLOps where an automated CI/CD system is implemented for fast, reliable, and frequent updates of ML model deployment in production. All the steps of model building, testing, deploying, and monitoring the ML system are automated at this level. New ML ideas can be easily incorporated with continuous integration pipelines. Different technical organizations retrain and redeploy their models on their different servers daily. Intelligent systems of today's era can't survive without an end-to-end CI/CD automated MLOps cycle. See Figure 3-4.

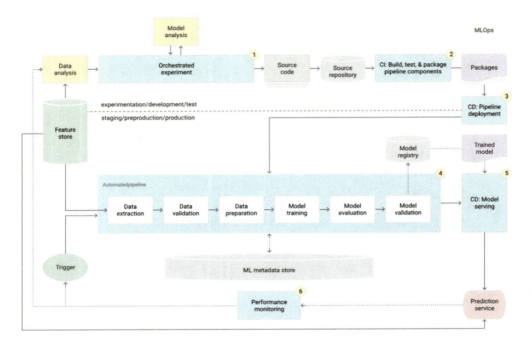

Figure 3-4. *Automated ML pipeline with CI/CD routines*

Components in Level 2

This MLOps CI/CD pipeline automation level includes the following components:

- ML pipeline orchestrator
- Source control
- Test and build services

- Pipeline deployment services

- Model registry

- Model serving

- Feature store

- ML metadata store

- Performance monitoring

Stages of the ML CI/CD Automation Pipeline

Let's see the stages of the ML CI/CD automation pipeline as shown in Figure 3-5.

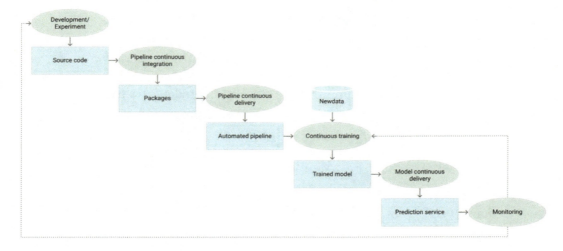

Figure 3-5. *Stages of CI/CD automated ML pipeline*

1. **Development and Experiment**

    At the stage of development and experiment, new algorithms and new models are developed, and the experiment is done with them. Its final output is the input of the next step of ML pipeline CI.

2. **Pipeline Continuous Integration**

   Various changes in requirements are integrated at this stage while building source code and testing are done. The output components like packages, executables, and artifacts are deployed to the ML pipeline CD.

3. **Pipeline Continuous Delivery**

   In the pipeline of continuous delivery artifacts and executables are deployed to the target environment.

4. **Continuous Training**

   In production, any new data triggers the model training automatically. It is a continuous training process based on schedule or response to a trigger. The output of this stage is the newly trained model, which is an input to the model registry.

5. **Model Continuous Delivery**

   At this stage, a newly trained model serves as a prediction service for the predictions. The output of this stage is a prediction model that needs to be deployed.

6. **Monitoring**

   Monitoring any system is important so that all hard work done doesn't go in vain. All the statistics and analysis of model performance are collected at this stage based on live data. The output of this stage is a trigger to execute the pipeline for a new experiment cycle.

The data analysis and model analysis steps are still manual processes for data scientists executed before a new experiment pipeline starts. With a CI/CD system new pipeline implementations can be automatically tested and deployed. These practices can be implemented gradually to help improve the automation of your ML system development and production.

Challenges with Level 2

There are a few challenges with a CI/CD pipeline automation as well.

- Human skillset challenge

- ML's huge infrastructure cost

- Operational challenges

Infrastructure as Code for Reproducible ML Environments

Huge infrastructure is required for training and testing ML models, and its manual management is adamant. MLOps needs reliable, scalable, secured, and reproducible practices to automate definition, infrastructure provisioning, deployment, and management. To streamline MLOps, infrastructure as code is implemented and managed through version control systems, which can significantly accelerate the development and deployment of ML models while also reducing errors and costs.

There are multiple tools in the market to implement IaC for ML environments, and they can be chosen to meet the organization's requirements. Some of the popular tools for implementing IaC for ML environments are `Databricks Terraform`, `AWS CloudFormation`, `Kubernetes`, and `Google Cloud Deployment Manager`.

What Is Infrastructure as Code?

Infrastructure as code (IaC) is the process of defining, managing, and infrastructure provisioning using code rather than with a manual process. With IaC, infrastructure resources, such as servers, networks, databases, and storage, are defined as code by developers. This process automates the versioning, deployment, and configuration management resulting in faster, consistent outcomes with minimized errors. Figure 3-6.

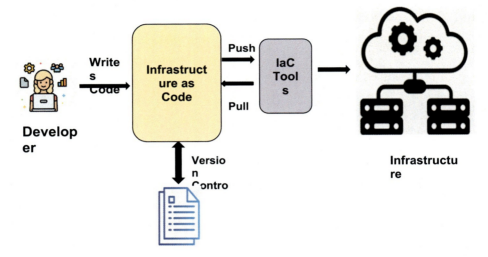

Figure 3-6. *Working of infrastructure as code*

Main Features of Infrastructure as Code for MLOps

These are the main features:

- **Automated Version Control**

    Version control refers to tracking the changes done in data, code, configurations, and models. Tracking changes in code and data makes it easier to monitor, troubleshoot, and easily recover the previous version of data, code, configurations, or model whenever necessary. Whole MLOps implementation requires a big team, and working in a big team environment version control is a necessity because its automation makes it a super-fast process.

    There are many open-source tools available to users for version control in MLOps like Git Large File System (LFS) from GitHub, MLflow from Databricks, Pachyderm from Pachyderm, and many more. Through automated version control, your MLOps team has a more efficient ability to trace bugs, roll back changes that didn't work, and collaborate with greater transparency and reliability.

- **Automated ML Pipeline Triggering**

  MLOps production is automated using automated ML pipeline triggering. The ML pipeline can be triggered manually, but automated triggering helps save a lot of time and effort. It is expensive to retrain models, so it's better to schedule the pipeline thoughtfully. ML Pipeline can be automatically triggered in any one or all of the following scenarios:

  - On a schedule basis

    Data scientists generally know the frequency of change in data accordingly, and the frequency of ML systems can be decided on a daily, weekly, or monthly basis.

  - On the availability of new training data

    A pipeline can be triggered whenever a significant amount of new training data is available.

  - On-model performance degradation

    Models can be retrained in case of degradation of model performance.

  - On significant data drift

    Data drift is crucial and necessary for retraining the model.

Benefits of Using Infrastructure as Code for ML Environments

These are the benefits:

- Reproducibility
- Scalability
- Reliability
- Security
- Accelerated deployment
- Optimized cost

Best Practices for Implementing Infrastructure as Code for MLOps

This section covers some best practices required for implementing IaC in an ML environment. These practices are necessary for the smooth and efficient functioning of ML systems.

- **Code Quality**

  Infrastructure as code is all based on code to remove the manual process. So it is crucial to ensure the IaC code is of good quality. It can be done by running tests and validating the code with high accuracy and minimal error.

- **Modularity**

  Modularity is in general good coding practice. The code will be broken into small, reusable modules that can be used in multiple configurations. It will reduce the code complexity and hence results in a high success rate.

- **Version Control System**

  It's always a good practice to maintain a version control system for IaC as we did for development code to track changes and straightforward rollback. Version control tools like Git, and DVC can be used to track changes, revert changes, and reproduce workflows when training and deploying ML models.

- **Automation Tools**

  Automation tools like Databricks Terraform, AWS CloudFormation, Kubernetes, etc., are good to be used for the accelerated automation of the ML process with streamlined infrastructure provisioning.

- **Compliance Monitoring**

  It is crucial to enforce policies and regulations for compliance monitoring of the model validation. It includes maintaining metadata and annotation policies and applying quality assurance standards to help teams monitor data, code, model, and other parameters.

Different types of organizations may have different compliance policies. They need to make sure that models are developed and deployed responsibly and ethically,

Monitoring and Observability in MLOps

Monitoring and observability are two vital components of MLOps systems. The main objective of monitoring and observability in MLOps is to ensure model performance does not degrade in the production environment. Once the model is deployed, it still needs continuous monitoring as performance can be affection any time because of the production environment or data drift. Any drift in performance at any stage should raise an alarm and alert the responsible owners.

A monitoring and alerting system is implemented in every ML system that tracks model key performance metrics, data metrics, and model degradation. Various monitoring tools are available like OpenShift, DataRobot, AWS Sage Maker, etc., that can be leveraged to establish comprehensive monitoring pipelines.

What to Monitor in MLOps?

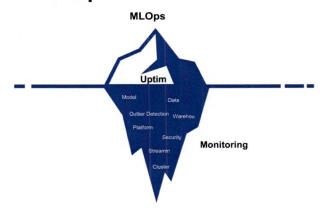

Figure 3-7. *MLOps Health*

Monitoring provides real-time health check-ups and alerts for potential issues in the ML system. Many underlying monitoring services contribute to good, successful running MLOps systems. These monitoring services are as follows:

1. **Monitoring Model Performance**

   In a live production environment, ensuring high model performance is the most important aspect of monitoring machine learning models. Performance metrics monitor model performance according to various metrics such as incoming data, their labels, model bias, correct performance metrics, and environmental factors. It is highly dependent on the label of live data in production systems. To monitor model health, monitoring dashboards for real-time visualization is implemented.

2. **Monitoring Incoming Data Metrics**

   Source of incoming data for model training varies. Moreover data undergoes multiple transformations before used for model training. With so many transitions and dynamism, it is very prone to inconsistencies and errors. With real-time data in production, model performance decreases with time. Any change in data, target variable, or transformation leads to a drift in model performance over time because of unforeseen ways. With time, model prediction becomes less accurate and needs to be monitored and alert at regular intervals.

3. **Detecting Outliers**

   Not all data is well calibrated; only training data is calibrated well, which can lead to over-fitting. Detecting outliers is a good method to flag anomalies whose model prediction cannot be trusted and cannot be used for production. As the real-world data is very noisy and not well processed, the problem of unsupervised anomaly detection will always be there, and there will always be room for monitoring and improvement.

4. **Platform Monitoring**

   Automated MLOps requires huge infrastructure and setup to monitor the whole platform regularly, and logs are maintained for this reason.

5. **Cluster Monitoring**

   Cluster monitoring is important to check if the desired number of clusters is not running. Its ignorance can lead to system failure or resource wastage.

6. **Warehouse Monitoring**

   Monitoring the warehouse is essential to understand the load profile as well as for its efficient management. Warehouse monitoring gives an exact picture of resources used and their efficiency.

7. **Streaming Monitoring**

   Streaming monitoring is essential for real-time data processing, real-time data analysis, and performing triggering actions.

8. **Security Monitoring**

   No MLOps system affords security breaches. The system needs to be secured, monitored, and watched for efficient performance. Security compliance with enhanced security monitoring is the need of time.

MLOps Observability

Observability offers a higher-level overview and end-to-end visibility into ML systems. It enables engineers to understand the system's behavior, detect problems, and improve model performance. It goes beyond monitoring and resolving the unknowns. In case your system won't run perfectly, you should able to detect and resolve before your end customers face any trouble. Observability helps in reducing both the mean-time-to-detection (MTTD) and the mean-time-to-resolution (MTTR) of incidents. The goal of MLOps observability is to keep observing the current state of all application and infrastructure components in the MLOps system.

Observability helps in understanding the internal behavior of the system, which is not possible to identify from the outside. Observability combines metrics, events, logs, and traces to help detect, investigate, and resolve unknown problems. With observation, it is easier to debug unexpected behavior and avoid future trouble. The fundamental of observability is to collect all the relevant information logged regularly and keep an eye on it for any unknown problem. Otherwise, waiting for debugging data after an incident occurs, and then finding its resolution, severely increases MTTR.

In the MLOps system, if memory utilization gets beyond a certain threshold or system real-time response time increases, many more such issues alerts are raised automatically. It uses a graphical dashboard to display logs, events, traces, and metrics, with raised alerts and alarms of the system.

Benefits of MLOps Observability

The following are the benefits of MLOps observability:

- Observability can help reduce the MTTD and MTTR of many of MLOp's internal issues.

- If the model fails, it performs root-cause analysis.

- It collects data like metrics, events, logs, and traces at all steps of the ML lifecycle.

- Give interactive and real-time visualizations.

- It becomes a lighting guide for model improvement.

MLOps Use Case

Machine learning and artificial intelligence play a crucial role in today's fast-paced growing digital world. Many industries have gravitated toward machine learning, thus resulting in the implementation of complete MLOps in production in real-world scenarios.

NatWest: MLOps Use Case

National Westminster Bank, commonly known as NatWest, is a leading retail, banking, and financial services group serving 19 million people in the United Kingdom and Ireland. NatWest is considered one of the Big Four clearing banks in the UK, and it has a large network of more than 960 branches with online banking services. NatWest handles approximately 750 million financial transactions per month. NatWest believes in championing potential and helping people, families, and businesses to thrive.

Business Goal of NatWest

The business goal in implementing MLOps is to reduce time-to-business value for NatWest Group. NatWest Group leverages analytics at scale, making it an optimized data-driven bank. But, their processes are slow and inconsistent. The fast-paced financial services industry is very competitive, and providing faster services to their 19 million customers is very challenging. NatWest explores its data and builds machine learning (ML) solutions that provide a bespoke experience based on customer demands.

To accelerate its time-to-business value with ML, NatWest turned to Amazon Web Services (AWS) and adopted Amazon SageMaker as its core ML technology. Amazon SageMaker is a service that data scientists and engineers use to build, train, and deploy ML models with fully managed infrastructure, tools, and workflows for any use case virtually. NatWest group centralized its ML processes on AWS has reduced the time that it takes to launch new products and services by several months. It also introduces a more agile culture among its data science teams. Using Amazon SageMaker, an idea on a whiteboard becomes a working ML solution in production in a few months versus one year or more before.

Challenges

The following are challenges faced by NatWest before implementing MLOps:

1. People

    There was a lack of current training and responsibilities for employees. And it is a difficult and time-consuming task.

2. Process

    Manual processes like manual handovers and governance make progress slow and sluggish, resulting in a long time to value.

3. Data

    Data, which is the first prerequisite for ML operations, was not easy to access and discover.

4. Technology

    Old technology and an out-of-date environment result in long development to deployment time.

Platform Used

NatWest Group partnered with AWS professional services to build a scalable, secure, and sustainable MLOps platform using Amazon SageMaker. The high-level architecture diagram in Figure 3-8 shows how a NatWest business application use case is deployed on AWS to build ML solutions.

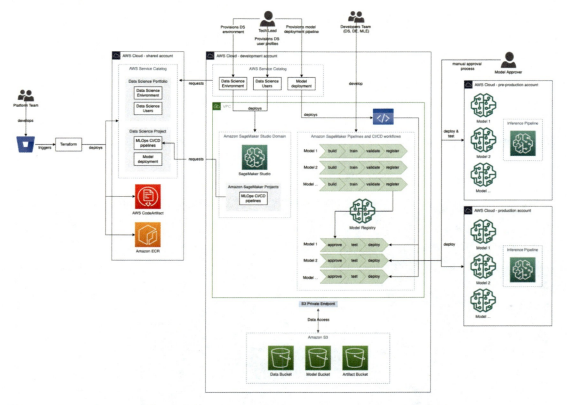

Figure 3-8. *Amazon SageMaker high-level architecture for NatWest*

Solutions

The following are various solutions implemented by NatWest:

1. NatWest uses Amazon Simple Storage Service (Amazon S3) for simple data storage and access. With simple and quick access to data and resources along with ML tools, it's easier and faster to build ML use cases.

2. NatWest Group uses AWS Service Catalog to create, organize, and govern infrastructure-as-code templates. It accelerates its employee's workflows from two to four weeks to a few hours.

3. NatWest Group has Amazon SageMaker Studio, a single web-based visual interface where all ML development steps can be performed. As it is simple to use and configure, it is user-friendly, easy to learn, and produces effective results.

4. Amazon Sage Maker integrates CI/CD pipelines workflow for production-ready use-case development. It improves quality, optimized governance, and lineage tracking.

5. With Amazon SageMaker Studio, NatWest's main goal of faster time to value has been achieved.

Key Outcomes

Figure 3-9 shows the key outcomes.

Figure 3-9. *Outcomes after MLOps implementation in NatWest Group*

These are the major key outcomes after implementing MLOps in NatWest Group:

•   Delivery of end-to-end ML solutions becomes faster as its time reduces from 12 months to less than 3 months.

•   It simplifies discovery and access to data, which usually takes five days; now it can be done in a few hours.

- The ML model has taken more than six months to be deployed in a live environment; now it can be done in less than two weeks.

- A self-service environment for end users is created that helps in issue resolution within a day.

- A time-to-business value has been reduced significantly, which puts NatWest on top of the ladder.

Final Thoughts

Automating the deployment of ML systems in production using DevOps concepts leads to MLOps. The operation excellence gives MLOps a smooth transition and execution in a real-world scenario. Although there is a gap between model creation and real-time deployment, with operational excellence advantages in MLOps, things are coming on track. Now is the time to handle data complexities, model construction, and system monitoring seamlessly. The target is to successfully deploy ML models in production with operational excellence to enjoy the full-fledged benefits of artificial intelligence technology. This can be achieved by implementing best practices of operational excellence in MLOps as elaborated on in this article along with ideas and MLOps implementation from the use case discussed.

How to Implement Operational Excellence in AWS

The operational excellence focuses on successfully deploying running systems with monitoring. Operational excellence aims to continually improve processes and procedures to deliver exceptional business values by gaining insights into workloads. To deliver business values with continuous improvement in processes, the operational excellence pillar in AWS defines its design principles, working areas, and best practices. Let's discuss them in detail.

Operational Excellence Design Principles

There are five design principles of operational excellence in the cloud:

- Perform operation procedures as code and automate response to events

- Make small incremental, frequent, and reversible changes

- Evolve operations procedures frequently

- Anticipate failures and mitigation

- Learn from all operational events and failures

Operational Excellence in the Cloud

Operational excellence in the cloud works in four areas:

- **Organization**

  To enable operational excellence in any organization, it is important to understand organization priorities, operating models, and organizational culture to support and grow in business outcomes.

- **Prepare**

  Organizations must comprehend design telemetry, workloads, and expected behaviors to optimize the entire flow and get ready for operational excellence. There is a need to build the procedures and understand operational readiness to mitigate deployment risks.

- **Operate**

  An organization reaches heights of success by understanding the health of its workload and operations. It must be able to identify organizational and business risks and able to respond to these events appropriately.

- **Evolve**

  Evolution is the continuous cycle of improvement over time.
  Learn and evaluate all operations activities and implement
  frequent small incremental changes. To evolve your operations
  over time, you must be able to learn, share, and improve.

Operational Excellence Best Practices

The operational excellence pillar aims to deliver business value by improving procedures
and supporting processes continually. Key work areas of operational excellence are
automating changes, responding to events, and managing daily operations while
meeting decided standards. This section includes nine best practices to consider while
framing the ML problem.

Establish Model Improvement Strategies

Before ML model development it is important to plan for model improvement
strategies. For optimized model performance, machine learning experimentation
is done iteratively. A variety of improvement techniques, such as data collection,
cross-validation, feature engineering, deep learning hyperparameter tuning, and
ensemble methods, are used in these experiments. Let's learn about machine learning
experimentation first.

Understanding Machine Learning Experimentation

The complete machine learning cycle is an iterative process. You need to experiment
with multiple combinations of data, feature engineering, different algorithms, and
hyperparameters while observing the impact of incremental changes on model
accuracy. This iterative experimentation led to thousands of model training runs
and model versions over time. After a few iterations, it is hard to compare the current

experiment with the past experiments to identify further changes for incremental improvements. Also, it is important to keep track of all models with their performance and input configuration, to conclude best-performing models at the end.

Developers need tools to organize, view, analyze, and compare iterative ML experimentation to gain comparative insights and track best-performing models. `Amazon SageMaker Experiments` is a managed service tool that can create, organize, view, track, analyze, and compare your machine learning experiments at scale with all the various model improvement strategies (see Figure 3-10).

Figure 3-10. *Amazon SageMaker Experiments*

Implementing Model Improvement Strategies

Let's discuss implementing various improvement strategies using Amazon SageMaker Experiments:

- **Effective Feature Selection**

  Effective feature selection is one of the most crucial parts of building a good machine learning model. Iteratively feature engineering is done with existing features, and less important features are removed to improve model accuracy and robustness. It is not only about adding new complex features but also treating the existing features effectively. Amazon SageMaker Experiments can help with data cleaning and effective feature selection.

The following sample demonstrates how to create SageMaker Scikit Estimator for feature selection by constructing a `sagemaker.sklearn.estimator.sklearn` estimator. This estimator executes the feature selection training script `sklearn_feature_selection.py`.

```python
from sagemaker.sklearn.estimator import SKLearn

script_path = "sklearn_feature_selection.py"
model_output_path = os.path.join("s3://", bucket, prefix,
"Feature_selection_model/")
sklearn_preprocessor = SKLearn(
    entry_point=script_path,
    role=role,
    output_path=model_output_path,
    instance_type="ml.c4.xlarge",
    sagemaker_session=None,
    framework_version="1.2-1",
    py_version="py3",
)

sklearn_preprocessor.fit({"train": train_input})
```

A sample "sklearn_feature_selection.py" is shown below.

```python
from sklearn.feature_selection import f_regression, mutual_info_
regression, SelectKBest, RFE

from sagemaker_containers.beta.framework import (
    content_types, encoders, env, modules, transformer, worker)

label_column = 'y'
INPUT_FEATURES_SIZE = 100

y_train = concat_data.iloc[:,number_of_columns_x-1].values
X_train = concat_data.iloc[:,:number_of_columns_x-1].values

'''Feature selection pipeline'''
feature_selection_pipe = Pipeline([
        ('svr', RFE(SVR(kernel="linear"))),# default: eliminate 50%
        ('f_reg',SelectKBest(f_regression, k=30)),
```

```
                 ('mut_info',SelectKBest(mutual_info_regression, k=10))
                     ])

feature_selection_pipe.fit(X_train,y_train)

joblib.dump(feature_selection_pipe, os.path.join(args.model_dir,
"model.joblib"))

print("saved model!")

'''Save selected feature names'''
feature_names = concat_data.columns[:-1]
feature_names = feature_names[feature_selection_pipe.named_
steps['svr'].get_support()]
feature_names = feature_names[feature_selection_pipe.named_
steps['f_reg'].get_support()]
feature_names = feature_names[feature_selection_pipe.named_
steps['mut_info'].get_support()]

joblib.dump(feature_names, os.path.join(args.model_dir, "selected_
feature_names.joblib"))
print("Selected features are: {}".format(feature_names))
```

There are two feature selection algorithms available in the
sklearn.feature_selection module.

feature_selection.RFE is a recursive feature elimination (RFE)
algorithm that chooses features by iteratively considering fewer
and smaller sets of features.

For RFE, we use Support Vector Regression (sklearn.svm.SVR)
as our learning estimator. It almost eliminates 50% of the total
features by default.

feature_selection.SelectKBest selects the best k features
that have the highest scores of a specified metric. We use f_
regression and mutual_info_regression as the score functions
that result in top 10 features.

In the previous training script, recursive feature elimination using `sklearn.feature_selection.RFE`, `sklearn.feature_selection.SelectKBest`, and `SelectKBest`, with `mutual_info_regression`, is implemented in pipeline for feature selection algorithms. These three feature selection algorithms are stacked into one `sklearn.pipeline.Pipeline` to get the top 10 selected features that are used further for training purposes.

- **Deep Learning**

    Deep learning algorithms train a large volume of training data for improved accuracy. This machine learning algorithm is based on the concept of our brain cells called *neurons*, which led to artificial neural networks (ANNs). Amazon SageMaker Experiments can train a simple classical model to a complex deep learning model to improve performance metrics related to business value.

    The following section is the sample code that demonstrates how to use TensorFlow to train deep learning models using the SageMaker Python SDK.

```python
from sagemaker.tensorflow import TensorFlow

tf_estimator = TensorFlow(
    entry_point="tf-train.py",
    role="SageMakerRole",
    instance_count=1,
    instance_type="ml.p2.xlarge",
    framework_version="2.2",
    py_version="py37",
)
tf_estimator.fit("s3://bucket/path/to/training/data")
```

    In the previous code, an instance of the `sagemaker.tensorflow.TensorFlow` estimator is created. A training script with the name `tf-train.py` is executed using the SageMsker TensorFlow estimator. It fits on the training data, which is the S3 URL path to your training data within Amazon S3.

- **Ensembling Methods**

  Ensembling combines different algorithms that can further improve accuracy. In model ensembling, combining algorithms with different model predictions and probabilities is important. Algorithms are combined considering business-specific use cases. It often offers better computational performance but with maintenance challenges. Amazon SageMaker Experiments can help organize multiple tests for different algorithms and configurations and compare them easily.

  The following section is the sample code that demonstrates the evaluation of the Linear Learner, XGBoost, and ensemble model for train, validation, and test data.

```
# Print the AUC of the combined model
print("Train AUC- Xgboost", round(roc_auc_score(train_labels,
preds_train_xgb), 5))
print("Train AUC- Linear", round(roc_auc_score(train_labels,
preds_train_lin), 5))
print("Train AUC- Ensemble", round(roc_auc_score(train_labels,
ens_train), 5))

print("=====================================")
print("Validation AUC- Xgboost", round(roc_auc_score(val_labels,
preds_val_xgb), 5))
print("Validation AUC- Linear", round(roc_auc_score(val_labels,
preds_val_lin), 5))
print("Validation AUC- Ensemble", round(roc_auc_score(val_labels,
ens_val), 5))

print("=====================================")
print("Test AUC- Xgboost", round(roc_auc_score(test_labels,
preds_test_xgb), 5))
print("Test AUC- Linear", round(roc_auc_score(test_labels,
preds_test_lin), 5))
print("Test AUC- Ensemble", round(roc_auc_score(test_labels,
ens_test), 5))
```

As the first training algorithm, the XGBoost algorithm is picked using SageMaker's managed, distributed training framework, and then the same data is trained using Linear Learner. The final modeling is done on an ensemble of XGBoost and Linear Learner on train, validation, and test data, and evaluation is done using AUC performance metrics.

- **Hyperparameters Optimization**

  The parameters of the model that control the training and fitting process of the model are called *hyperparameters*. Iteratively optimizing hyperparameters is important for a great model to obtain the best parameters for a top-performing model. The hyperparameter optimization process can be automated using Amazon SageMaker to reach the top performance via various techniques like Grid Search, Random Search, Bayesian, and Hyperband.

  The following section is the sample code that demonstrates how to manage the hyperparameter tuning using the SageMaker XGBoost and automatic model tuning using random search.

```python
from sagemaker.amazon.amazon_estimator import get_image_uri
from sagemaker.image_uris import retrieve

sess = sagemaker.Session()

container = retrieve("xgboost", region, "latest")

xgb = sagemaker.estimator.Estimator(
    container,
    role,
    base_job_name="xgboost-random-search",
    instance_count=1,
    instance_type="ml.m4.xlarge",
    output_path="s3://{}/{}/output".format(bucket, prefix),
    sagemaker_session=sess,
)
```

```python
xgb.set_hyperparameters(
    eval_metric="auc",
    objective="binary:logistic",
    num_round=10,
    rate_drop=0.3,
    tweedie_variance_power=1.4,
)
objective_metric_name = "validation:auc"

hyperparameter_ranges = {
    "alpha": ContinuousParameter(0.01, 10, scaling_
    type="Logarithmic"),
    "lambda": ContinuousParameter(0.01, 10, scaling_
    type="Logarithmic"),
}

tuner_log = HyperparameterTuner(
    xgb,
    objective_metric_name,
    hyperparameter_ranges,
    max_jobs=5,
    max_parallel_jobs=5,
    strategy="Random",
)

tuner_log.fit(
    {"train": s3_input_train, "validation": s3_input_validation},
    include_cls_metadata=False,
    job_name="xgb-randsearch-" + strftime("%Y%m%d-%H-%M-%S",
    gmtime()),
)
```

In this example, we are using SageMaker Python SDK to set up and manage the hyperparameter tuning job. Here, the XGBoost algorithm is used, and its hyperparameter tuning is done using random search. The training jobs are first configured for hyperparameter tuning, which is launched by initiating XGBoost estimator, and then static hyperparameter and objectives are defined.

- **AutoML Implementation**

  As the name suggests, AutoML automates the machine learning workflow so that you can spend more time using ML to improve business outcomes. It automates tedious, time-consuming, and iterative work like data acquisition, data cleaning, feature engineering, model training, model tuning, model deployment, and ongoing model monitoring and updating. Amazon SageMaker Autopilot is an AutoML solution for data in tabular format.

  The following sample demonstrates how to create an Amazon SageMaker Experiments using the SageMaker Python SDK.

```python
class ExperimentCallback(keras.callbacks.Callback):
    """ """

    def __init__(self, run, model, x_test, y_test):
        """Save params in constructor"""
        self.run = run
        self.model = model
        self.x_test = x_test
        self.y_test = y_test

    def on_epoch_end(self, epoch, logs=None):
        """ """
        keys = list(logs.keys())
        for key in keys:
            run.log_metric(name=key, value=logs[key], step=epoch)
            print("Epoch: {}\n{} -> {}".format(epoch, key,
            logs[key]))
```

  Next, train the Keras model in a notebook environment that carries out jobs sequentially and tracks them as experiments and displays test data accuracy at the end.

```python
from sagemaker.experiments import Run

# The run name is an optional argument to `run.init()`
with Run(experiment_name = 'my-experiment') as run:
```

```
# Define values for the parameters to log
run.log_parameter("batch_size", batch_size)
run.log_parameter("epochs", epochs)
run.log_parameter("dropout", 0.5)

# Define input artifacts
run.log_file('datasets/input_train.npy', is_output = False)
run.log_file('datasets/input_test.npy', is_output = False)
run.log_file('datasets/input_train_labels.npy', is_output
= False)
run.log_file('datasets/input_test_labels.npy', is_output
= False)

# Train locally
model.fit(
    x_train,
    y_train,
    batch_size=batch_size,
    epochs=epochs,
    validation_split=0.1,
    callbacks = [ExperimentCallback(run, model, x_test,
    y_test)]
)

score = model.evaluate(x_test, y_test, verbose=0)
print("Test loss:", score[0])
print("Test accuracy:", score[1])

# Define metrics to log
run.log_metric(name = "Final Test Loss", value = score[0])
run.log_metric(name = "Final Test Accuracy", value = score[1])
```

Establish a Lineage Tracker System

Establishing a lineage tracking system is a must to track changes in documentation, environment, model, data, code, and infrastructure in each release. A smooth tracker system allows users to roll back to any prior release. In case the user needs to reproduce any prior release results or any problem generated in that, it can be easily reproducible.

Implementing Lineage Tracker System

Let's implement a lineage tracker system with AWS SageMaker.

1. **Data and Artifacts Lineage for Tracking**

    To reproduce the model, it is essential to track all the artifacts used for the production model to meet regulatory and control requirements. Figure 3-11 illustrates the different artifacts that must be tracked and versioned to replicate the data processing, model training, configuration, and model deployment process.

Figure 3-11. *Artifacts need to be tracked*

The following artifacts need to be tracked and versioned:

- Code versioning

- Dataset versioning

- Container versioning

- Training job versioning

- Model versioning

- Endpoint metadata versioning

The following section is the sample code that demonstrates an
Amazon SageMaker artifact, which is part of a SageMaker lineage
using the SageMaker Python SDK.

```
from sagemaker.lineage import artifact

my_artifact = artifact.Artifact.create(
    artifact_name='MyArtifact',
    artifact_type='S3File',
    source_uri='s3://...')

my_artifact.properties["added"] = "property"
my_artifact.save()

for artfct in artifact.Artifact.list():
    print(artfct)

my_artifact.delete(
```

A `artifact_name`, artifact_type, and `source_uri` is given as input
to create an Amazon SageMaker artifact and save it as part of a
SageMaker lineage.

2. **Use SageMakerML Lineage Tracking**

For machine learning, systems follow an ML workflow from data
preparation to model deployment. To create and store information
about the steps of an ML workflow Amazon SageMaker ML
Lineage Tracking is used. With the SageMaker Lineage tracking, it
is easy to reproduce ML workflow steps, data set lineage, and track
model. All this tracking information helps in establishing model
governance and maintaining audit standards flawlessly.

Amazon SageMaker automatically creates an end-to-end model
training and deployment ML workflow as shown in Figure 3-12.

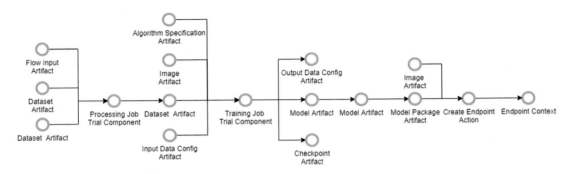

Figure 3-12. *Lineage metadata*

The following are the features of SageMaker Lineage Tracking:

- Maintain a running history of model discovery experiments.

- Establish model governance for auditing and compliance verification by tracking model lineage artifacts.

3. **Use SageMaker Studio Classic**

   Amazon SageMaker Studio Classic is a web-based interface for end-to-end ML development. It offers an integrated development environment (IDE) for machine learning to track the lineage of a SageMaker ML pipeline from uploading data to building models to deploying them. Amazon SageMaker Studio Classic offers a wide choice of purpose-built tools to perform all the ML development steps, from preparing data to building, training, debugging, deploying, and managing your machine-learning models. Figure 3-13.

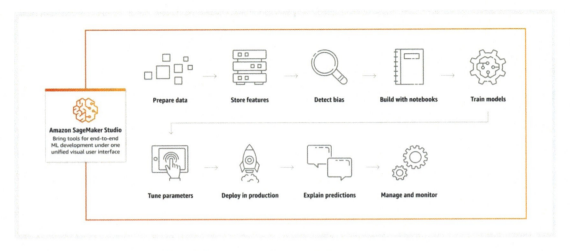

Figure 3-13. *Amazon SageMaker Studio workflow*

It is a single unified visual web-based interface where customers can perform the following tasks:

- Jupyter Notebooks to write and execute code

- Prepare data at scale for machine learning

- Build and train machine learning models with optimized performance

- Deploy the models and monitor for optimal performance and cost

- Track and debug the machine-learning experiments

- Deliver high-performance production ML models

4. **Use SageMaker Feature Store**

   Amazon SageMaker Feature Store is a purpose-built repository where you can store, share, access, and manage ML model features for training, organizing, and reusing them across ML applications and various teams. With SageMaker Feature Store processing and transforming input data into ML features can be done easily. To support MLOps practices, it builds feature pipelines to speed up the time to model deployment.

SageMaker Feature Store provides a unified store for offline feature storage during training and online storage for real-time inference and batch interference. There is no need to write additional code or create manual processes to keep features consistent.

Features from any data source, including streaming and batch, such as application logs, service logs, clickstreams, sensors, and tabular data from AWS or any other third-party data sources, can be simply ingested by the Amazon SageMaker Feature Store. Figure 3-14.

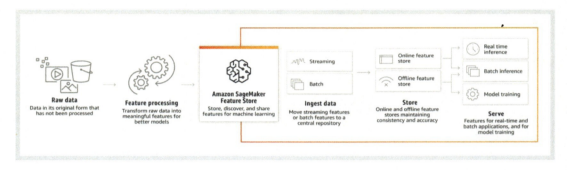

Figure 3-14. *Amazon SageMaker Feature Store*

The following are the key features of Amazon SageMaker Feature Store:

- Feature processing is done at the time of ingesting data into ML features and ingesting a high volume of data from a variety of sources with a single line of code.

- Easily store, organize, find, and utilize features with ease with Amazon SageMaker Studio's graphical user interface.

- Feature consistency by ensuring that offline and online datasets remain in sync, which is critical and can negatively impact model accuracy.

- Lineage tracking to trace features back to their data sources and view feature processing code, all in one environment to develop confidence in data scientists.

- At the time of interest retrieve the state of each feature.

- SageMaker Feature Store manages datasets and feature pipelines to speed up MLOps lifecycle tasks and eliminate duplicate feature creation.

- It implements fine-grained access controls to protect feature store data and grant access based on the role of security and compliance.

The following section sample demonstrates how to create an Amazon SageMaker Feature Store using the SageMaker Python SDK.

```
from sagemaker.feature_store.feature_store import FeatureStore

feature_store = FeatureStore(sagemaker_session=feature_store_
session)
result_df, query = feature_store.create_dataset(
    base=base_feature_group,
    output_path=f"s3://{s3_bucket_name}"
).to_dataframe()
```

By using the Feature Store Offline SDK, preprocessing data and training machine learning models, one may rapidly and simply create datasets that are ready for usage. Without having to write any SQL code, the SDK makes it simple to create datasets from SQL join, point-in-time accurate join, and event range time frames. In the previous code, the `result_df` data frame is created using the SageMaker feature store.

5. **Use SageMaker Model Registry**

   Amazon SageMaker Model Registry is used to catalog production models, manage model versions, register and deploy models, and associate metadata with a model. Model Registry enables lineage tracking.

   SageMaker Model Registry Model (Package) Groups are used to catalog production models that contain different versions of a model. A Model Group is created to track all the models trained to solve a particular problem. Every trained model is then registered as a new model version and added to the Model Group. Lastly, different categories of Model Groups are further created by organizing them into SageMaker Model Registry Collections. Figure 3-15 shows a typical workflow of SageMaker Model Registry.

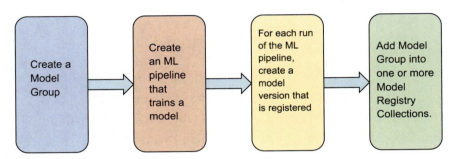

Figure 3-15. *Amazon SageMaker Model registry workflow*

The following are the key features of SageMaker Model Registry:

- Catalog models for production

- Manage model versions

- Associate metadata metrics with the model

- Manage the approval status of a model

- Deploy models to production

- Automate model deployment with CI/CD

6. **Use SageMaker Pipelines for Model Building**

   Amazon SageMaker Pipelines is a purpose-built workflow orchestration service to automate all phases of the machine learning (ML) pipeline from data preprocessing to model monitoring at scale using intuitive UI and Python SDK. With the pipeline, you can track the history of your input data, its source, and the outputs generated.

The following are the key features of Amazon SageMaker Pipelines:

- Automate all phases of ML development

- Build end-to-end LLMOP systems

- Manage huge workloads

- Compose, reuse, and schedule ML workflows

- Lift and shift your machine-learning code

- Automatic model tracking

The following section is the sample code that demonstrates how to create an Amazon SageMaker Model Building Pipelines in the Amazon SageMaker using the SageMaker Python SDK.

```python
from sagemaker.workflow.pipeline_context import PipelineSession
from sagemaker.workflow.pipeline_context import PipelineSession

pytorch_estimator = PyTorch(
    sagemaker_session=PipelineSession(),
    role=sagemaker.get_execution_role(),
    instance_type="ml.c5.xlarge",
    instance_count=1,
    framework_version="1.8.0",
    py_version="py36",
    entry_point="./entry_point.py",
)

step = TrainingStep(
    name="MyTrainingStep",
    // code just like how you trigger a training job before,
    // pipeline session will take care of delaying the start
    // of the training job during pipeline execution.
    step_args=pytorch_estimator.fit(
        inputs=TrainingInput(s3_data="s3://my-bucket/my-data/
        train"),
    ),
```

```
        displayName="MyTrainingStepDisplayName",
        description="This is MyTrainingStep",
        cache_config=CacheConfig(...),
        retry_policies=[...],
        depends_on=[...],
    )

pipeline = Pipeline(
    name="MyPipeline",
    steps=[step],
    sagemaker_session=local_pipeline_session
)

pipeline.create(
    role_arn=sagemaker.get_execution_role(),
    description="local pipeline example"
)

// pipeline will execute locally
pipeline.start()
```

The previous example shows the construction of a Pytorch
estimator and starts a TrainingJob with a SageMaker session.
Here we are using sagemaker.workflow.pipeline_context.
PipelineSession, which defines sagemaker.workflow.steps.
TrainingStep, which gets executed during pipeline execution.
This is where the pipeline session sagemaker.workflow.
pipeline_context.PipelineSession came in to execute the
entire pipeline.

Establish Feedback Loops across ML Lifecycle Phases

To share successful development trials, failures, and other operational activities
throughout phases of the ML lifecycle, it is essential to establish a feedback loop
mechanism. This facilitates continuous improvement in a future iteration of ML
workflows. ML practitioners analyze the ML implementation at every stage and revisit

monitoring and reinstruction improvement strategies with time. Various experiments are done for model training with different algorithms, hyperparameters, and data augmentation until an optimal outcome is achieved. In the iteration process, document each key learning and improvement in the process over time for future reference.

Implementing Feedback Loop Across ML Lifecycle Phases

Let's implement a feedback loop across ML lifecycle phases using Amazon SageMaker.

Establish SageMaker Model Monitoring

The first step is to establish the Amazon SageMaker Model Monitoring system. The accuracy and performance of the ML model decay with time and this phenomenon is called *model drift*. Many factors can cause model drift like model features and differences between training and inference data. Amazon SageMaker Model Monitor continually monitors machine learning models for model drift and concept drift. If there are any deviations, SageMaker Model Monitor notifies you so you can make the necessary corrections.

The different portals for model monitoring are as follows.

Use Amazon CloudWatch

Configure Amazon CloudWatch response to performance change. If model or concept drift is observed, notifications are automatically generated. Monitoring jobs can be scheduled to run at regular intervals like hourly or daily. They create actionable insights reports derived from logs as well as metrics to Amazon CloudWatch dashboards and Amazon S3.

Amazon CloudWatch collects, analyzes, and visualizes real-time logs, metrics, and event data from various applications, resources, and services run on AWS. All this data is displayed on automated CloudWatch dashboards to streamline application and infrastructure maintenance. Figure 3-16.

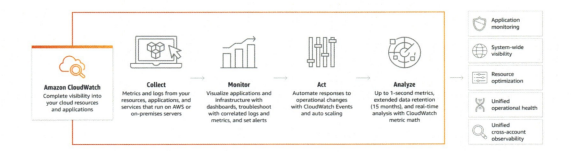

Figure 3-16. *Amazon CloudWatch*

The following sample code demonstrates how to create Amazon SageMaker CloudWatch metrics to create a CloudWatch alarm using the Amazon SageMaker Python SDK:

```
alarm_name = "MODEL_QUALITY_F2_SCORE"
alarm_desc = (
    "Trigger an CloudWatch alarm when the f2 score drifts away from the
    baseline constraints"
)
mdoel_quality_f2_drift_threshold = (
    0.625  ##Setting this threshold purposefully low to see the alarm
    quickly.
)
metric_name = "f2"
namespace = "aws/sagemaker/Endpoints/model-metrics"

cw_client.put_metric_alarm(
    AlarmName=alarm_name,
    AlarmDescription=alarm_desc,
    ActionsEnabled=True,
    MetricName=metric_name,
    Namespace=namespace,
    Statistic="Average",
    Dimensions=[
        {"Name": "Endpoint", "Value": endpoint_name},
```

```
        {"Name": "MonitoringSchedule", "Value": churn_monitor_
        schedule_name},
    ],
    Period=600,
    EvaluationPeriods=1,
    DatapointsToAlarm=1,
    Threshold=mdoel_quality_f2_drift_threshold,
    ComparisonOperator="LessThanOrEqualToThreshold",
    TreatMissingData="breaching",
)
```

In the previous code model, the metric f2 is set up, and if the metric "f2 score" drifts from the baseline threshold value of 0.625, a CloudWatch alarm is set to be triggered. By using the SageMaker CloudWatch console, you can take remedial actions such as retraining your model or updating the training dataset automatically, once the CloudWatch alarms are triggered.

Use Amazon SageMaker Model Dashboard

The Amazon SageMaker Model Dashboard extracts high-level details from each model and displays its comprehensive summary. It is a central interface to track, monitor, and review model performance and notifies you when quality issues arise. If your model is deployed for inference, the dashboard helps you track your model's performance and endpoint in real time, as shown in Figure 3-17.

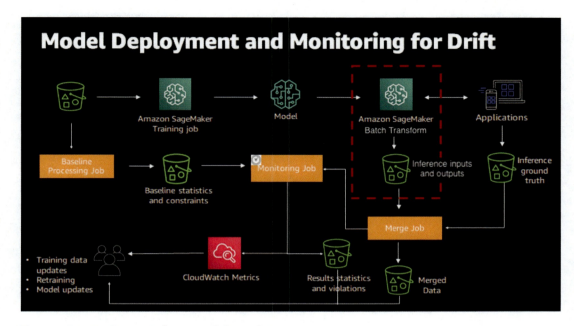

Figure 3-17. *SageMaker model working*

The Amazon SageMaker Model Dashboard displays Model Monitor status values by the following types of drift monitoring:

- Monitor **Data Drift** to maintain data quality.

- Monitor **Model Drift** for optimum model quality metrics, such as accuracy.

- Monitor **Bias Drift** in predictions for models in production.

- Monitor **Feature Attribution Drift** for models in production.

The following sample demonstrates how to create an Amazon SageMaker Model Monitor to capture real-time inference data from Amazon SageMaker endpoints.

```
from sagemaker.model_monitor import DataCaptureConfig

data_capture_config = DataCaptureConfig(
    enable_capture=True,
    sampling_percentage=100,
    destination_s3_uri='s3://path/for/data/capture'
)
```

```
predictor = model.deploy(
    initial_instance_count=1,
    instance_type='ml.m4.xlarge',
    data_capture_config=data_capture_config
)
```

For monitoring the model data quality, there is a need to capture data, which can be done using a new capture option called DataCaptureConfig. By using this setup when delivering to an endpoint, you can capture either the request payload, the response payload, or both.

These payloads are saved in the Amazon S3 location that has been specified in the DataCaptureConfig. The captured data can be viewed and downloaded using the S3Downloader utility in Amazon S3.

Automate Retraining Pipelines

Create a CloudWatch event rule that alerts on an event emitted by the SageMaker Model Monitoring system. The event rule can detect the drifts or anomalies, and start a retraining pipeline.

Use Amazon Augmented AI (A2I)

Amazon Augmented AI (Amazon A2I) allows you to conduct a human review to establish the ground truth of machine learning (ML) systems based on specific requirements. A2I guarantees precision and checks the accuracy of ML models, against which model performance can be compared. See Figure 3-18.

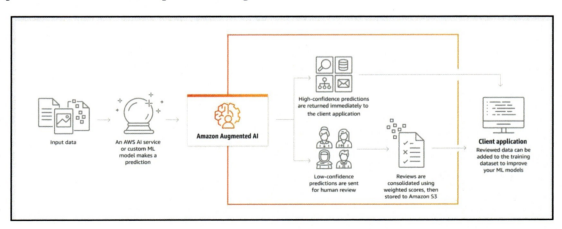

Figure 3-18. *Amazon Augmented AI (A2I)*

Review Fairness and Explainability

During each stage of the ML lifecycle fairness and explainability are expected in domains including financial services, retail, e-commerce, healthcare, education, and human resources. It is important to have less biased and more understandable machine learning models with governance compliance and external regulators. The following are the regulations that need to be in check to review for fairness and explainability:

- The objective should be explainable and fairer.

- Machine learning algorithms should be an ethical solution.

- Check for bias in labels and features.

- Data should be from versatile groups and easy to modify data to mitigate bias.

- The different number of models need to be trained to mitigate bias.

- The model needs to be evaluated using relevant fairness metrics.

- The model needs to be deployed on data for which it needs to be trained or evaluated.

- Check for unequal effects of ML solutions across users.

Implementation Plan

In the next section, let's cover some of the AWS services that one can use to implement the recommendations

Amazon SageMaker Clarify

Amazon SageMaker Clarify provides purpose-built tools to gain greater insights into your data and ML models, debug predictions, and add explainability for ML model predictions. SageMaker Clarify helps identify bias at every stage of the ML lifecycle as well as improve metrics like accuracy and robustness to improve model quality.

For tabular, computer vision, and time-series models, SageMaker Clarify provides bias and explainability reports to identify potential issues and therefore direct efforts to improve accuracy, remove bias, and increase performance.

Amazon SageMaker Clarify processing jobs at multiple stages in the lifecycle of the machine learning workflow to compute the following analysis types:

- Pre-training bias metrics

- Post-training bias metrics

- Shapely values

- Partial dependence plots (PDPs)

SageMaker Clarify processing container job interacts with an Amazon S3 bucket that contains your input datasets and with a customer model (optionally), which is deployed to a SageMaker inference endpoint, as shown in Figure 3-19.

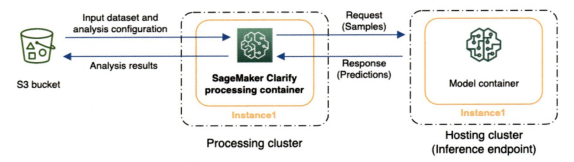

Figure 3-19. *Amazon SageMaker Clarify*

With the help of an effective implementation of Shapley Additive Explanations (SHAP), SageMaker Clarify employs a model-agnostic feature attribution technique that enables you to do the following:

- Recognize the requirements for fairness and explainability that are governance compliance.

- Helps in identifying potential issues, and measuring bias at every stage of the ML life cycle like data collection, pre-training, post-training, model tuning, and monitoring of deployed models.

- Determine whether training data is imbalanced in its features, classes, or population segments.

- When the model is in production, monitor for bias in the data strategically.

- For explainability, the simplest model works best. It's always a trade-off between model complexity and explainability.

- Generate easy-to-understand and robust model governance reports targeting risk and compliance teams and external regulators.

- Provide explanations for the predictions based on the data, models, and monitoring.

The following sample code demonstrates how to create an Amazon SageMaker Clarify used to detect bias using the Amazon SageMaker Python SDK.

```
from sagemaker import clarify
# Initialize a SageMakerClarifyProcessor to compute bias metrics and model
explanations.
clarify_processor = clarify.SageMakerClarifyProcessor(
    role=role, instance_count=1, instance_type="ml.m5.xlarge", sagemaker_
    session=sagemaker_session
)

bias_config = clarify.BiasConfig(
    label_values_or_threshold=[1], facet_name="Sex", facet_values_or_
    threshold=[0], group_name="Age"
)

clarify_processor.run_bias(
    data_config=bias_data_config,
    bias_config=bias_config,
    model_config=model_config,
    model_predicted_label_config=predictions_config,
    pre_training_methods="all",
    post_training_methods="all",
)

clarify_processor.run_explainability(
    data_config=explainability_data_config,
    model_config=model_config,
    explainability_config=shap_config,
)
```

SageMaker Clarify helps you detect possible pre-training and post-training biases using `Bias_config`, , and other parameters. BiasConfig contains configuration values for detecting `model_config` bias using a Clarify container. The parameter `pre_training_methods` is set to "all" to get all pre-training bias and parameter `post_training_methods` is set to "all" to get all post-training bias. Clarify process run `run_explainability` to run explainability predictions. All the bias reports and explainability reports can be viewed in SageMaker Studio.

Create Tracking and Version Control Mechanisms

In ML model development, there is a need to explore and iterate with different combinations of data, algorithms, and parameters. With every incremental change, there is a need to observe and keep track of model accuracy with different configuration settings. Sometimes too much experimentation leads to losing track of model development and evolution. Amazon SageMaker offers various services to track, document, automate, and version control different ML processes and improvements for future referencing and reuse.

Implementation Plan for Tracking, Version Control, and Automation

Let's track, version control, and automate the ML model development cycle using Amazon SageMaker.

Track Your ML Experiments with SageMaker Experiments

Machine learning experiments can be easily done using Amazon SageMaker Experiments. It helps in creating, managing, analyzing, and comparing different machine-learning experiments. SageMaker Experiments automatically tracks all the inputs, parameters, configurations, and different iterations as runs, as well as their results. These iterations runs can be assigned, grouped, and organized into SageMaker Experiments. It also offers a visual interface to browse your active and past experiments, compare runs on key performance metrics, and identify the best-performing models integrated with Amazon SageMaker Studio.

SageMaker Experiments aims to make the process of creating experiments, populating them with trials, adding tracking and lineage information, and running analytics across experiments and trials simple. Amazon SageMaker Experiments has the following components:

- Experiment

- Trial

- Trial component

- Tracker

The following section is the sample code that demonstrates how to run the SageMaker Experiment using the SageMaker Python SDK.

```
classsagemaker.experiments.Run(experiment_name, run_name=None,
experiment_display_name=None, run_display_name=None, tags=None, sagemaker_
session=None, artifact_bucket=None, artifact_prefix=None)
```

To run an experiment instance, `classsagemaker.experiments.Run` is initiated with various config and log parameters to invoke a training job under the context of this Run object.

Use SageMaker Processing

Amazon SageMaker Processing is used for data analysis, various data processing, and its documentation with ML model evaluation. It is also used for data validation, feature engineering, and model interpretation. Amazon SageMaker Processing offers a simplified and managed experience with data processing workloads (feature engineering, data validation, model evaluation, and model interpretation). The Amazon SageMaker Processing APIs can also be used during the experimentation phase and after the code is deployed in production to evaluate performance.

Amazon SageMaker spins up a Processing job, copies data from Amazon Simple Storage Service (Amazon S3), and then pulls a processing container. The Amazon SageMaker fully managed the underlying infrastructure for a Processing job. The output of the Processing job is stored in the Amazon S3 bucket as shown in Figure 3-20.

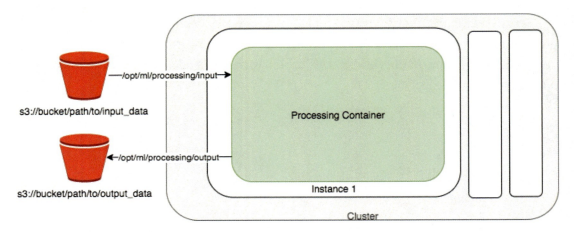

Figure 3-20. *Amazon SageMaker Processing job*

The following sample code demonstrates how to run a SageMaker Processing Job using the SageMaker Python SDK:

```python
from sagemaker.spark.processing import PySparkProcessor

# Upload the raw input dataset to a unique S3 location
timestamp_prefix = strftime("%Y-%m-%d-%H-%M-%S", gmtime())
prefix = "sagemaker/spark-preprocess-demo/{}".format(timestamp_prefix)
input_prefix_abalone = "{}/input/raw/abalone".format(prefix)
input_preprocessed_prefix_abalone = "{}/input/preprocessed/abalone".
format(prefix)

sagemaker_session.upload_data(
    path="./data/abalone.csv", bucket=bucket, key_prefix=input_
    prefix_abalone
)

# Run the processing job
spark_processor = PySparkProcessor(
    base_job_name="sm-spark",
    framework_version="3.1",
    role=role,
    instance_count=2,
```

```
    instance_type="ml.m5.xlarge",
    max_runtime_in_seconds=1200,
)

spark_processor.run(
    submit_app="./code/preprocess.py",
    arguments=[
        "--s3_input_bucket",
        bucket,
        "--s3_input_key_prefix",
        input_prefix_abalone,
        "--s3_output_bucket",
        bucket,
        "--s3_output_key_prefix",
        input_preprocessed_prefix_abalone,
    ],
    spark_event_logs_s3_uri="s3://{}/{}/spark_event_logs".format(bucket,
    prefix),
    logs=False,
)
```

The PySparkProcessor class is defined using sagemaker.spark.processing. PySparkProcessor. The PySparkProcessor class is used to define a Spark job and run it using SageMaker Processing. This is a multinode job that is specified via the instance_count and instance_type parameters. The Spark_processor runs the preprocessing script with all input and output bucket parameters.

Associate Notebook Instances with Git Repositories

SageMaker notebooks hold the data processing code and related documentation, These notebook instances can be associated with Git repositories to save the notebooks in a source control environment. After saving the SageMaker notebook instances in Git repositories, they persist after stopping or deleting the notebook instance. A notebook instance can be associated with a default repository and up to three additional repositories like AWS CodeCommit, GitHub, or any other Git server.

Associate notebook instances with Git repositories for persistence, learning, and collaboration in the source-control environment. Notebook instances can be associated with a Git repository in two ways:

- You can add a Git repository to your Amazon SageMaker account as a resource. Next, you can enter an AWS Secrets Manager secret containing credentials to gain access to the repository. In this manner, repositories that demand authentication can be accessed.

- Link a publicly accessible Git repository that isn't one of your account's resources. You won't be able to provide login credentials to access the repository if you do this.

Use SageMaker Model Registry

Amazon SageMaker Model Registry is used to catalog, manage, and deploy models. Models are cataloged by creating SageMaker Model Registry Model Groups that contain different versions of a model. A model group is created for each run of the ML pipeline, and different model versions are registered under that model group.

All models trained to solve a particular problem are registered under a Model Group as a model version. These Model Groups can be further categorized into one or more Model Registry Collections. A typical SageMaker Model Registry workflow might look like Figure 3-21.

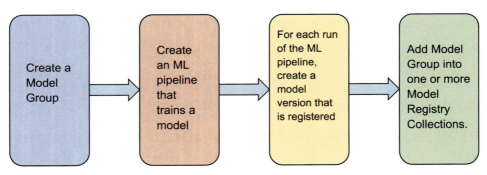

Figure 3-21. *Amazon SageMaker Model Registry workflow*

The following are key features of SageMaker Model Registry:

- Catalog models for production.

- Manage model versions.

- Associate metadata like training metrics with a model.

- Manage the approval status of a model.

- Deploy models to production.

- Automate model deployment with CI/CD.

The following sample code demonstrates how to create a SageMaker Model group using the SageMaker Python SDK.

```
import time
import os
from sagemaker import get_execution_role, session
import boto3

region = boto3.Session().region_name
role = get_execution_role()
sm_client = boto3.client('sagemaker', region_name=region)

model_package_group_name = "scikit-iris-detector-" + str(round(time.
time()))
model_package_group_input_dict = {
 "ModelPackageGroupName" : model_package_group_name,
 "ModelPackageGroupDescription" : "Sample model package group"
}

create_model_package_group_response = sm_client.create_model_package_
group(**model_package_group_input_dict)
print('ModelPackageGroup Arn : {}'.format(create_model_package_group_
response['ModelPackageGroupArn']))
```

The SageMaker Boto3 client is set up to call the `create_model_package_group` API operation and specify a name and description as parameters to create a Model Group. The response from the `create_model_package_group` call is the Amazon Resource Name (ARN) of the new Model Group.

Automate Operations Through MLOps and CI/CD

To automate the ML workload operations, appropriate MLOps mechanisms and deployments with CI/CD pipelines need to be integrated. As we discussed earlier, automated ML operations use infrastructure as code (IaC) and configuration as code (CaC). This approach ensures that developers treat infrastructure and configuration as code to provide consistency across your staging and production deployment environments. This enables version control across your hosting infrastructure and model observability.

Implementation Plan to Automate Operations

You can model and provision your application in two ways.

Use AWS CloudFormation

AWS CloudFormation enables you to create, model, provision, and manage AWS deployments by treating IaC. This can be done using a template file to create and delete a collection of resources together as a single unit (a stack) predictably and repeatedly. Using AWS CloudFormation, infrastructure is easily scalable worldwide and easy to provision and manage stacks across multiple AWS accounts and AWS regions through a single operation. See Figure 3-22.

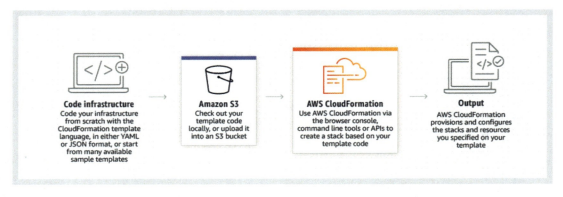

Figure 3-22. *AWS CloudFormation*

Use AWS Cloud Development Kit (AWS CDK)

An open-source software development framework called the AWS Cloud Development Kit (AWS CDK) is used to specify cloud infrastructure in code and provision it using AWS CloudFormation. In AWS CDK cloud resources can be defined and develop applications using familiar programming languages like TypeScript, JavaScript, Python, Java, C#/. Net, and Go.

The AWS CDK develops reliable, scalable, cost-effective applications in the cloud with the considerable expressive power of general programming language. There are two primary parts of AWS CDK:

- **AWS CDK Construct Library:** A collection of prewritten and reusable modules, called *constructs*, used to modify, integrate, and develop your infrastructure quickly and in a simplified manner.

- **AWS CDK Toolkit:** A command-line tool to interact with CDK apps to create, manage, and deploy AWS CDK projects. See Figure 3-23.

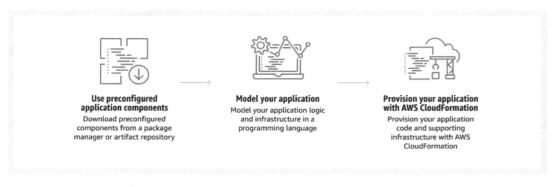

Use preconfigured application components
Download preconfigured components from a package manager or artifact repository

Model your application
Model your application logic and infrastructure in a programming language

Provision your application with AWS CloudFormation
Provision your application code and supporting infrastructure with AWS CloudFormation

Figure 3-23. *AWS Cloud Development Kit (AWS CDK)*

Various MLOps strategies to choose from based on your ML workflows.

Use SageMaker Pipelines to Orchestrate Your Workflows

Using Amazon SageMaker Pipelines, ML workflows can be created with Python SDK. The SageMaker Pipelines can be visualized using Amazon SageMaker Studio and end-to-end ML workflow can be easily managed. Amazon SageMaker Pipelines logs every step of ML workflow and scales faster by reusing workflow steps. It creates an audit trail of all the model components such as training data, platform configurations, model parameters, and learning gradients to re-create models.

The following sample demonstrates how to create SageMaker Pipelines to orchestrate your workflows using the SageMaker Python SDK.

```
base_job_prefix = "pipeline-experiment-sample"
model_package_group_name = "pipeline-experiment-model-package"

processing_instance_count = ParameterInteger(
  name="ProcessingInstanceCount", default_value=1
)

training_instance_count = ParameterInteger(
  name="TrainingInstanceCount", default_value=1
)

processing_instance_type = ParameterString(
  name="ProcessingInstanceType", default_value="ml.m5.xlarge"
)
training_instance_type = ParameterString(
  name="TrainingInstanceType", default_value="ml.m5.xlarge"
)
```

In the previous code, we have specified the pipelines that enable you to pass parameters at runtime. Here, runtime instance counts and types for processing and training, along with predefined defaults, are defined.

Use AWS Step Functions

Amazon SageMaker uses an open-source package called the AWS Step Functions Data Science SDK to automate the training of machine learning models. In AWS Step Functions, all the steps of the production-ready ML workflow are defined, and alerts are set to start the flow. It allows you to copy that workflow, experiment with new options, and then put the refined workflow into production.

To orchestrate AWS infrastructure at scale, multistep machine learning workflows are created in AWS Step Functions in the Python language. There is no need to provision and integrate the AWS services separately. A Python API offered by the AWS Step Functions Data Science SDK that can create and invoke Step Functions workflows. These workflows are easily managed and executed directly in the Python and Jupyter notebooks. See Figure 3-24.

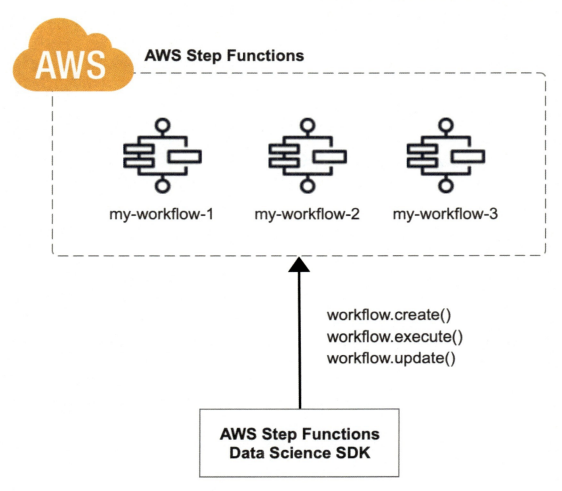

Figure 3-24. *AWS Step Functions*

The following are the key features of the AWS Step Functions Data Science SDK:

- Construct and run machine learning workflows using AWS infrastructure directly in Python easily.

- Instantiate common training pipelines.

- Using templates, create common machine learning workflows in a Jupyter Notebook.

The following section is the sample code that demonstrates how to create and execute a workflow in the AWS Step Functions Data Science SDK.

```
workflow.create()
execution = workflow.execute(inputs={
  "IsHelloWorldExample": True
})
```

The command `workflow.create` is used to create the workflow in AWS Step Functions. To execute the workflow, execute the command `workflow.execute` in AWS Step Functions.

Use Third-Party Tools

To automate model training and development, some third-party deployment orchestration tools, such as Apache Airflow, are used that integrate with AWS service APIs. This third-party tool, Amazon Managed Workflows for Apache Airflow (Amazon MWAA), uses Directed Acyclic Graphs (DAGs), which is written in Python to orchestrate your workflows. DAGs, plugins, and Python requirements reside in an Amazon Simple Storage Service (S3) bucket. DAGs can be run and monitored from the AWS Management Console, the Apache Airflow user interface (UI), a command-line interface (CLI), or a software development kit (SDK). See Figure 3-25.

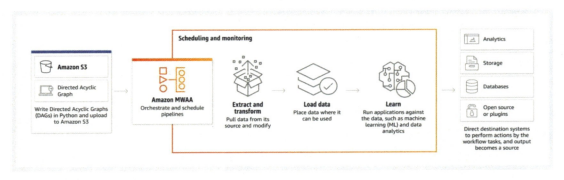

Figure 3-25. *Amazon Managed Workflows for Apache Airflow (Amazon MWAA)*

Apache Airflow deployment offers scalability, availability, and security without causing any operational burden of managing the underlying infrastructure.

Establish Deployment Environment Metrics

Measuring the performance of machine learning operations in a deployed environment is critical. Various metrics like memory and CPU/GPU usage, disk utilization, ML endpoint invocations, and latency are measured to determine the performance.

Implementation Plan to Establish Deployment Environment Metrics

Let's establish a deployment environment metrics implementation plan.

Record Performance-Related Metrics

The first step is to record performance-related metrics using AWS monitoring and observability services. These metrics include slow queries, various database transactions, I/O latency, service latency, HTTP request throughput, and other key data.

Analyze Metrics When Events or Incidents Occur

Whenever any event triggers, use monitoring dashboards and reports to understand the event and its effects in detail. It is important to understand and diagnose the impact of an occurred incident using monitoring dashboards. These dashboard views provide insight into the portions of the workload that are not performing as expected.

Establish Key Performance Indicators (KPIs)

It is important to establish and identify the key performance indicators (KPIs) that indicate whether the workload is performing as intended. KPIs are different for different kinds of industries. An e-commerce site might choose to use the number of purchases as its KPI, while an API-based workload might use overall response latency as an indication of overall performance.

Use Monitoring to Generate Alarm-Based Notifications

Use monitoring metrics for the defined KPIs to generate alarm-based notifications automatically. These alarms are generated automatically to notify when the measurements of defined KPIs are outside the expected boundaries.

Review Metrics at Regular Intervals

Reviewing metrics that were key in addressing issues and responding to different events or incidents at regular intervals needs to be part of routine maintenance. Also, it is important to identify any additional metrics that need to be added that would help to identify, address, or prevent issues.

Monitor and Alarm Proactively

Utilize KPIs in conjunction with alerting and monitoring systems to handle performance-related concerns. Alarms are used to initial automated actions to remediate issues wherever possible. If an automated response is not possible, then escalate the alarm. Use a system to predict expected KPI values, generate alerts, and automatically halt or roll back deployments if KPIs exceed the expected values.

Use Amazon CloudWatch Metrics

Observing and monitoring resources and applications on AWS, on-premises, and in other clouds is the aim of Amazon CloudWatch. Use Amazon CloudWatch metrics for SageMaker endpoints to determine the memory, CPU usage, and disk utilization. CloudWatch Dashboards are set up to visualize the environmental metrics, and CloudWatch alarms are established to initiate an alert notification via Amazon SNS to notify of the events occurring in the runtime environment. For more details, see the section "Use Amazon CloudWatch."

Two types of alarms can be created in Amazon CloudWatch.

- A metric alarm to watch a single CloudWatch metric

- A composite alarm that takes into account the alarm states of other alarms that you have created

Use Amazon EventBridge

Amazon EventBridge is a serverless event-driven application at scale across AWS that helps you receive, filter, transform, route, deliver, and respond automatically to events. These events occur in case of an increase in the compute environment capacity once it crosses a defined threshold. See Figure 3-26.

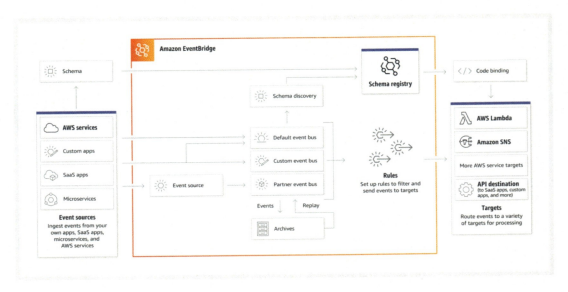

Figure 3-26. *Amazon EventBridge*

Millions of events and tasks are created, triggered, and managed from a single source with Amazon EventBridge Scheduler.

Use AWS Application Cost Profiler

Use AWS Application Cost Profiler to report granular cost insights for your multitenant applications as well as the cost per tenant (model/user). It provides you with the ability to track the consumption of shared AWS resources used by software applications and report granular cost breakdowns across the tenant base.

With the shared infrastructure approach, you may attain economies of scale while retaining a direct line of sight to comprehensive data on resource consumption across several dimensions, which lays the groundwork for a precise cost allocation model. See Figure 3-27.

Figure 3-27. *AWS Application Cost Profiler*

The following are the key features of AWS Application Cost Profiler.

- Cost efficiency

- Foundation for accurate cost allocation model

- Flexible data collection

- Margin analysis

- Customize pricing strategies for end customers

AWS Application Cost Profiler analyzes tenant metadata and generates hourly cost breakdowns for each tenant on a daily and monthly basis. Detailed data is received at your desired frequency and consumed programmatically to create your own dashboard for tracking expense patterns and margins by tenant. With Application Cost Profiler, product pricing, design, and cost data can be altered to maximize adoption and profitability.

Enable Model Observability and Tracking

Enabling model observability, monitoring mechanisms, and proactive tracking is done to identify and avoid inference issues. The performance of the ML models degrades with time due to different drifts. Thus, measuring the operational health of the underlying compute resources hosted at real-time inference endpoints is crucial. Establish lineage to trace all the steps of the ML workflow and store all the versioned inputs and model artifacts for analysis.

Implementation Plan to Enable Model Observability and Tracking

Let's enable model observability and tracking using the following resources.

Use Amazon SageMaker Model Monitor

Amazon SageMaker Model Monitor continuously keeps track of the quality of Amazon SageMaker ML models in production. It compares the results of the model in production with the results from training to evaluate the performance. For more details, see the section "Establish SageMaker Model Monitoring."

Use Amazon CloudWatch

Amazon SageMaker Model Monitor automatically sends metrics to Amazon CloudWatch so that you can gather and analyze usage statistics for your ML models. For more details see the section "Use Amazon CloudWatch."

Use SageMaker Model Dashboard

The Amazon SageMaker Model Dashboard extracts high-level details from each model and displays its comprehensive summary. It tracks the model performance hosted on real-time inference endpoints and sets up the monitor with Amazon SageMaker Model Monitor.

It finds the model that shows degradation in data quality and model quality or shows any bias drift. For more details, see the section "Use Amazon SageMaker Model Dashboard."

Use Amazon SageMaker Clarify

When feature attribution or bias drift in models occur in production, Amazon SageMaker Clarify detects and tracks several kinds of inferences. SageMaker Clarify provides tools to generate model governance reports that are used to inform the compliance teams and external regulators of risk. For more details, see the section "Amazon SageMaker Clarify."

Track Model Pipeline with SageMaker ML Lineage Tracking

Lineage tracking creates all the steps of a ML workflow, from data preparation to model deployment. It also stores information regarding all ML workflow steps. It keeps a history of model discovery experiments and tracks model lineage artifacts for auditing and compliance verification to establish model governance. For more details, see the section "Establish a Lineage Tracker System."

Use SageMaker Model Cards

Amazon SageMaker Model Cards are required to gather model information like business requirements, key decisions, and observations during model development and evaluation in a single place for streamlined governance and reporting. Catalog information includes things like a model's intended application and risk assessment, training specification and metrics, evaluation results and observations, and extra call-outs like considerations, suggestions, and customized information.

The following are the features of Amazon SageMaker Model Cards:

- Offer guidance on how a model should be used

- Support audit activities and gather all the detailed descriptions of model training and performance

- Communicate how a model is meant to achieve business goals

Using Automated Validation Capability of Amazon SageMaker

With Amazon SageMaker's automated validation capability you can compare the performance of new models against production models, by using the same real-world inference request data in real time. Amazon SageMaker routes the same inference requests to the new model as received by the production model. It then generates the performance differences across key metrics and displays them on the dashboard in real time.

Synchronize Architecture and Configuration

Synchronization of all systems and configurations is necessary across the development and deployment phases. Otherwise, differences in system architectures can result in different inference results with the same algorithm. It is important to ensure that the model gets the same range of accuracy in development, staging, and production environments. This is necessary and normal to check for skew across environments.

Implementation Plan for Synchronizing Architecture and Configuration

In the next section we cover some of the AWS services that can be use for synchronization and configuration.

Use AWS CloudFormation

AWS CloudFormation provisions a collection of related AWS and third-party resources quickly and consistently and manages them throughout their lifecycles by treating them as infrastructure as code. CloudFormation uses the template to create, update, and delete an entire stack as a single unit. AWS CloudFormation can easily manage and provision stacks, and synchronize architecture and configuration across multiple AWS environments. For more details, see the section "Use AWS CloudFormation."

Here are the key features of AWS CloudFormation:

- AWS CloudFormation standardizes the method of AWS resource creation.

- Existing CloudFormation templates can be used to re-create similar stacks to easily replicate your AWS architecture development, test, and production environments.

- CloudFormation offers various tools that define parameters, mapping, and conditions and offers customization to increase the reusability of templates.

- CloudFormation automatically rolls the resources created or updated in case any error happens during stack creation.

- CloudFormation handles failures in a fast, secure, and reliable mechanism.

- It is easy to create a CI/CD pipeline to manage your infrastructure code as a software project and automate the deployment changes using Cloud Formation.

Use Amazon SageMaker Model Monitor

SageMaker Model Monitor continuously monitors the quality of machine learning models in production using Amazon. Production model results are compared with the results from training using SageMaker Model Monitor. In case of any deviation in the model, an equality alert is raised. Timely detection of results deviation enables the engineer to take corrective actions like retraining models, auditing upstream systems, and fixing quality issues without having to monitor models manually or build additional tools. For more details, see the section "Establish SageMaker Model Monitoring."

The following types of monitoring are offered by Model Monitor:

- Monitor drifts in the data quality

- Monitor drifts model metrics

- Monitor drifts in bias for models in production

- Monitor drifts in feature attribution for models in production

References

- https://github.com/aws/amazon-sagemaker-examples/blob/main/autopilot/custom-feature-selection/Feature_selection_autopilot.ipynb

- https://sagemaker.readthedocs.io/en/stable/frameworks/tensorflow/using_tf.html#train-a-model-with-tensorflow

- https://sagemaker-examples.readthedocs.io/en/latest/introduction_to_applying_machine_learning/ensemble_modeling/EnsembleLearnerCensusIncome.html

- https://github.com/aws/amazon-sagemaker-examples-community/
  blob/215215eb25b40eadaf126d055dbb718a245d7603/training/
  sagemaker-automatic-model-tuning/hpo_xgboost_random_
  log.ipynb

- https://docs.aws.amazon.com/sagemaker/latest/dg/
  experiments-create.html

- https://sagemaker.readthedocs.io/en/stable/workflows/
  lineage/sagemaker.lineage.html

- https://docs.aws.amazon.com/sagemaker/latest/dg/feature-
  store-introduction-notebook.html

- https://sagemaker.readthedocs.io/en/stable/amazon_
  sagemaker_model_building_pipeline.html#

- https://github.com/aws/amazon-sagemaker-examples/blob/
  main/sagemaker_model_monitor/model_quality/model_quality_
  churn_sdk.ipynb

- https://sagemaker.readthedocs.io/en/stable/amazon_
  sagemaker_model_monitoring.html

- https://sagemaker.readthedocs.io/en/v2.209.0/experiments/
  sagemaker.experiments.html

- https://docs.aws.amazon.com/sagemaker/latest/dg/model-
  registry-model-group.html

- https://github.com/aws/amazon-sagemaker-examples/blob/
  main/sagemaker_processing/scikit_learn_data_processing_
  and_model_evaluation/scikit_learn_data_processing_and_
  model_evaluation.ipynb

- https://github.com/aws/amazon-sagemaker-examples/blob/main/
  sagemaker_processing/spark_distributed_data_processing/
  sagemaker-spark-processing.ipynb

- https://aws.amazon.com/blogs/machine-learning/organize-
  your-machine-learning-journey-with-amazon-sagemaker-
  experiments-and-amazon-sagemaker-pipelines/

- https://github.com/aws/aws-step-functions-data-science-sdk-python

- https://blog.cloudhm.co.th/ci-cd/

- https://cloud.google.com/architecture/mlops-continuous-delivery-and-automation-pipelines-in-machine-learning#top_of_page

- https://aws.amazon.com/blogs/machine-learning/part-2-how-natwest-group-built-a-secure-compliant-self-service-mlops-platform-using-aws-service-catalog-and-amazon-sagemaker/

- https://d1.awsstatic.com/events/Summits/reinvent2022/FSI203_NatWest-Personalizing-banking-at-scale-with-machine-learning-on-AWS.pdf

- https://aws.amazon.com/sagemaker-ai/experiments/

- https://aws.amazon.com/

- https://docs.aws.amazon.com/whitepapers/latest/build-secure-enterprise-ml-platform/data-and-artifacts-lineage-tracking.html

- https://docs.aws.amazon.com/sagemaker/latest/dg/lineage-tracking.html

- https://aws.amazon.com/sagemaker-ai/studio/

- https://docs.aws.amazon.com/sagemaker/latest/dg/feature-store.html

- https://aws.amazon.com/cloudwatch/

- https://docs.aws.amazon.com/sagemaker/latest/dg/model-monitor.html

- https://aws.amazon.com/augmented-ai/

- https://docs.aws.amazon.com/sagemaker/latest/dg/clarify-configure-processing-jobs.html

- https://docs.aws.amazon.com/sagemaker/latest/dg/
  processing-job.html

- https://aws.amazon.com/eventbridge/

- https://aws.amazon.com/aws-cost-management/aws-application-
  cost-profiler/

- https://pixabay.com/vectors/iceberg-iceburg-ice-
  glacier-frozen-2070977/

CHAPTER 4

MLOps Security in AI/ML

We have learned to deploy the machine learning model in production with operational excellence. After achieving this milestone, it's time to ensure the security and safety of the whole ML system.

MLSecOps is amalgamation of machine learning operations and security. In this chapter, we will cover the key aspects of MLSecOps, its importance at different levels of the ML lifecycle, and possible security challenges an ML system faces. We will also study best practices that need to be followed for implementing MLSecOps and its implementation in AWS with code snippets for reference.

Machine learning engineers are responsible for making ML systems secure, as systems are getting more technically advanced and intelligent with time. Security in ML systems is crucial and needs implementation at many levels to set up the foundational aspects of secured end-to-end ML systems. In this topic, we will learn about various security challenges in ML systems, the pillars of MLSecOps, and its best practices to achieve a highly secure and reliable machine learning ecosystem.

Introduction to MLOps Security

Security in MLOps (Figure 4-1) means implementing security measures to ML models, data, and the ML system infrastructure to protect them from intruders and vulnerabilities. ML models are vulnerable to attacks at different stages such as training, tuning, and deployment, which can lead to malicious exploitation, data breaches, or the manipulation of model outcomes. Addressing their unique security challenges becomes crucial with the increase in ML applications across various domains and industries.

125

© Neel Sendas and Deepali Rajale 2024
N. Sendas and D. Rajale, *The Definitive Guide to Machine Learning Operations in AWS*,
https://doi.org/10.1007/979-8-8688-1076-3_4

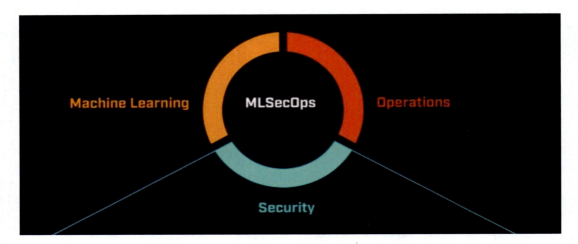

Figure 4-1. *MLSecOps*

The amalgamation of MLOps (machine learning operations) with security operations leads to MLSecOps (machine learning security operations). MLSecOps keeps security at the system's core by combining traditional methods with new practices. By incorporating security best practices and concepts into ML systems, MLSecOps seeks to reduce these risks. The following are the key aspects involved in MLSecOps:

- **Threat Modeling**

    Potential threats and vulnerabilities unique to ML systems and data are identified under threat modeling.

- **Data Security**

    Data security ensures that the data used for inference and training is secure and private, including access controls, encryption, and appropriate data handling.

- **Secure Coding**

    Coding practices need to be secured with multiple layers of security controls, input validation, and sanitization to prevent injection attacks and error handling with informative messages to ensure transparency and explainability.

- **Model Integration**

  This is the process of implementing measures to detect and prevent unauthorized attack, alteration, or tampering with ML models.

- **Secure Deployment**

  The developed model should be deployed without compromising on security and integrity by applying secure configuration and access controls.

- **Continuous Monitoring and Detection**

  Continuous monitoring of ML systems can detect anomalies in data and models. Constant monitoring and detection help identify potential attacks or any unauthorized activities in the ML system.

- **Collaboration and Incident Response**

  For secured ML systems, security teams, engineers, and data scientists must collaborate to align with security requirements and MLSecOps best practices. Together, they can create protocols for quickly responding to security events, looking into security lapses, and recovering from assaults.

Importance of MLSecOps

Every step in the ML lifecycle is vulnerable to security threats. Our machine learning systems are highly developed and advanced although they are not immune to security threats. There are threats at every level of the machine learning lifecycle such as data breaches, compromising sensitive information, model manipulation, output manipulation, and adversarial attacks. The risks associated with ML security are diverse, complex, and severe and can lead to financial losses and reputational damage. As a result, taking a proactive stance is crucial for reducing these risks and protecting the organization's assets with top-notch ML security.

MLSecOps ensures the security of different steps of the MLOps lifecycle. A machine learning engineer needs to keep check and take various actions at different levels to ensure a secure ML system.

1. **Business Understanding**

   - Specify the team member's roles and responsibilities.

   - Ensure the level of compliance that the project team of data scientists needs.

   - Identify the scope of data needed.

2. **Data Engineering**

   - Avoid data breaching.

   - Keep checking on data modifications from an untrusted source.

   - Keep checking on sensitive information.

   - Keep checking on adversarial attacks.

3. **Model Development**

   - Ensure the security of virtual machines or clusters to train the model.

   - Avoid manipulation of the machine learning model.

   - Check for security breaches in the pieces of code.

4. **Model Evaluation**

   - Keep checking on model output manipulation.

   - Keep checking on modified data inputs to achieve appropriate model output.

   - Keep checking on adversarial from malicious users to prevent the ML systems from deceiving.

5. **Model Deployment**

   - Make sure modeled packages are saved in a secure place.

   - Keep a check on the running environment before deploying the model.

- Secure every single instance of load/unload models.

6. **Monitoring and Maintenance**

- Identify potential reverse engineering attacks and keep your business value safe.

- Check and verify all the tools and technologies used in the system.

Security Challenges in ML Systems

An AI/ML system faces five major challenges.

1. **Data Poisoning**

   Data is the base of the ML systems. The efficiency and predictability of ML models are directly proportional to the quality of data they are trained on. Clean, unbiased, and comprehensive data exists only in an ideal world. However, in the real world, data is mostly incomplete, biased, noisy, and poisoned by external powers. We have methods to cope with incomplete, biased, and noisy data, but poisoned data is a serious matter for the security of ML systems. When a model receives erroneous data, it learns something not meant to be learned. Inaccurate forecasts and false alarms may arise after deployment due to the distortion of patterns that the machine learning models have acquired.

   There are four broad attack strategies in which data can be poisoned:

   a. **Label Modification**

      In supervised learning, solely labels are modified for arbitrary data points, which mislead the training model.

   b. **Data Modification**

      In this case, intruders do not have access to the learning algorithm but have access to training data so they can modify the training dataset, which leads to a corrupted training model.

c. **Data Augmentation**

In this case, intruders do not have access to training data and the learning algorithm so they can't modify the training data and algorithm but can augment new data to the training dataset. With augmentation, the training model can be corrupted easily.

d. **Logic Corruption**

When intruders have access to the learning model, they can corrupt the logic implemented.

2. **Evasion Attack**

Evasion attacks are also called adversarial attacks. The most prevalent kind of assault on a machine learning model during inference is an adversarial attack. It can easily fool humans with a slight change that is barely noticeable to the human eye. This slight change in input can completely throw off the model and data is wrongly classified by ML models. A typical example of an evasion attack is an image recognition system where some pixels of an image are changed before uploading so that the model fails to classify the result accurately. Take a look at Figure 4-2.

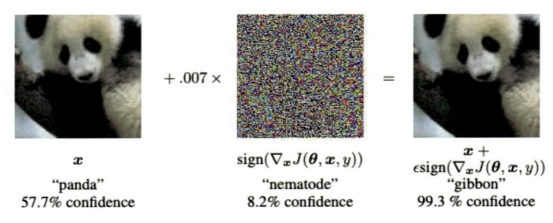

x

"panda"
57.7% confidence

$\text{sign}(\nabla_x J(\theta, x, y))$

"nematode"
8.2% confidence

$x + \epsilon \text{sign}(\nabla_x J(\theta, x, y))$

"gibbon"
99.3 % confidence

Figure 4-2. *Adversarial attack example*

In this example, a slight change in the pixel of the input image results in misclassifying the input image of "panda" as "gibbon."

With evasion attacks, the confidence level of class output prediction is highly impacted. Modified input leads to wrong model training and thus leads to the misclassification of new data.

3. **System Manipulation**

   Most of the machine learning systems are connected to the Internet during operations. This allows intruders to attach the machine learning models during training and opens a window to alter its behavior. This falls under the category of cybercrime. A cyberattack can lead to wrong input and training with altered parameters thus resulting in an altered output that is different from expected. Cybercrime is increasing with the advanced machine learning systems, and it's a real-time challenge to protect ML systems from cyber criminals.

   Although manipulating online machine learning systems is not that simple, it is so subtle and delicate that the victim won't even be aware that another person is utilizing their system.

4. **Transfer Learning Attack**

   Often pre-trained machine learning models are used to train large amounts of data, as training time is exponentially high for large datasets. Using these pre-trained models to train a new problem is called *transfer learning*. These pre-trained models can be fine-tuned according to the business requirement. As the consumer is not aware of which data was used to train these pre-trained models, it opens the scope for the intruders to penetrate and impact the model's performance by tweaking the training data. This can be exploited by the attacker who might manipulate or replace a genuine model with a malicious model.

5. **Data Confidentiality**

Ensuring the privacy and confidentiality of data is critical in today's digital world. Cyberattackers not only poison the data but also extract existing data from the training dataset. This is called *input inference*, or *model inversion*. Extraction of data just before it is going to be used for machine learning modeling can put the entire ML system at risk.

For example, in the medical field maintaining privacy about patient's personal and medical records is an important requirement and is bided by the law in a lot of nations. Breaching these medical records results in serious data confidence issues and raises a question for the organizations.

Five Pillars of MLSecOps

MLSecOps is based on five strong pillars (Figure 4-3). Various organizations implement these MLSecOps pillars to establish robust security practices and mitigate potential risks. Let's discuss them in detail.

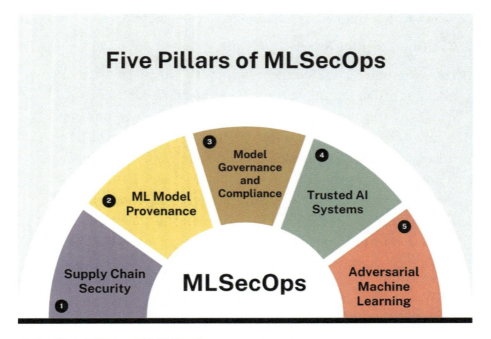

Figure 4-3. *Five Pillars of MLSecOps*

1. **Supply Chain Security**

    Supply chain vulnerability addresses the risks associated with the various components of the ML supply chain, from data collection to model deployment and their dependencies. Supply chain security key aspects include:

    a. Third-party libraries and dependencies

    b. The integrity of various data sources

    c. Model artifacts during storage, transmission, and deployment

    d. Hardware components and infrastructure

2. **ML Model Provenance**

    ML model provenance refers to the traceability, lineage, evolution, and reproducibility of ML systems throughout the ML lifecycle. It involves maintaining records of code, data, model artifacts, infrastructure, metadata, and environment to establish the authenticity and integrity of models. Key aspects of model provenance include:

    a. Tracking the version history of ML models

    b. Tracking the training data, its sources, preprocessing, and transformations

    c. Keeping track of model development steps that include feature engineering, hyperparameter tuning, and modeling

    d. Keeping track of model deployment, environment, configuration, and any subsequent updates or modifications

3. **Model Governance and Compliance**

    MLOps is interwoven with model governance to encompass a set of processes and frameworks that help in the secured deployment of ML models. The strength of the regulations depends on the business domain, the risk category of an ML model, and the business risk. The health and finance sectors follow strict regulations as they are at high risk of security breaches. If the ML model plays an important role in a company's business concept then model governance and compliance need to be more strict than the companies where ML does not play an evident role.

Model governance needs to be integrated into every step of the ML lifecycle from the start. Model governance encompasses the recording, auditing, validation, approval, and monitoring of models. Although the strength of regulation and the number of models determine how model governance should be implemented, all variants have the following aspects in common:

a. Comprehensive model documentation and reports with ML metadata

b. Validation of ML model with automated auditing of ML systems

c. Data privacy, protection, encryption, and access controls

d. Continuous monitoring and logging of model metrics

e. Regulatory compliance with the General Data Protection Regulation (GDPR), the Health Insurance Portability and Accountability Act (HIPAA), or industry-specific guidelines

f. Potential risk assessment, management, mitigation, and incident response plan development

g. By incorporating ethical rules, provide fairness, bias, accountability, and openness in your ML development process

4. **Trusted AI Systems**

MLSecOps focuses on building trusted AI systems that are transparent, reliable, accountable, and explainable. It ensures ML models make unbiased decisions while being transparent to all stakeholders. Key aspects of trusted AI include:

a. Explainable model so the user can understand the reason behind their prediction

b. Fair and unbiased outcomes throughout the process

    c. A robust and resilient AI system to withstand security challenges

    d. Continuous model monitoring and model performance evaluation to identify any degradation or anomalies

5. **Adversarial machine learning**

MLSecOps identifies and mitigates adversarial attacks that aim to manipulate or deceive ML models. By implementing techniques such as anomaly detection and adversarial training, enterprises may improve the resilience of their machine learning systems. The goal of adversarial machine learning is to protect machine learning systems from intrusions and any efforts to alter or exploit them. Key aspects of Adversarial machine learning include:

    a. Adversarial robust ML models to withstand adversarial attacks

    b. Anomaly detection and mitigation in data or model behavior

    c. Adversarial training of Ml model to improve their ability and resilience for unseen attacks

    d. Continuous learning and adaptation for new threats with online learning and dynamic model updates

Best Practices of MLSecOps

In this section, we aim to provide best practices to minimize the security risk in AI and mitigate undesired vulnerabilities. By following the practices shown in Figure 4-4, ML systems will able to unlock their full potential ensuring the ethical and conscious development of AI projects across all industrial domains. Following are the best practices that need to be followed for a secure and reliable Machine learning system.

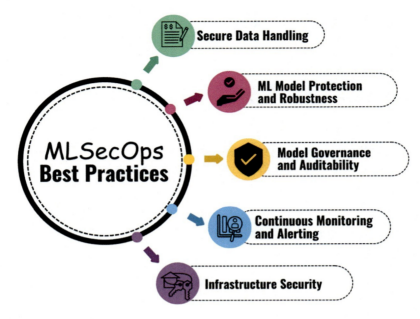

Figure 4-4. *MLSecOps best practices*

1. **Secure Data Handling**

   The first step for a secured machine learning operation is secured data handling. Data used in training and inference need to be handled properly to protect it from bias, poisoning, vulnerabilities, theft, and unauthorized access. To secure data, the following key points need to be taken care of:

   a. Data sources need to be trustworthy and with limited access controls to authorized personnel only.

   b. Sensitive data needs to be properly encrypted in storage as well as during transmission throughout the ML lifecycle.

   c. Regular data access audits should be done to detect any unauthorized activities.

2. **ML Model Protection and Robustness**

ML models are prone to attack and manipulation resulting in incorrect prediction. To make correct predictions free from bias, attack, and overfitting, ML models need to be designed, trained, and secured properly. Ensuring model robustness involves building models that are resilient to adversarial attacks, data poisoning, and other threats. Key points to protect ML models and make them robust are:

a. Limit access control of ML model parameters and configuration to ensure model integrity.

b. To track changes in ML models version control mechanisms need to be implemented.

c. Regularly run audits and assess model performance to detect any anomalies, unauthorized activities, or security breaches.

3. **Model Governance and Auditability**

Models need to be developed and maintained according to best practices and standards given by model governance and compliance. To prevent legal repercussions and preserve the confidence of stakeholders and customers, pertinent legislation must be followed. Key aspects of model governance and auditability are as follows:

a. Adopt ML security best practices to identify potential sources of bias and model performance vampires.

b. Ensure that models adhere to legal and ethical guidelines.

c. Regulatory frameworks such as GDPR or HIPAA regulations should be imposed for the protection of data and models.

4. **Continuous Monitoring and Alerting**

In MLOps, continuous monitoring and alerting are critical for the periodic assessment of model performance, data inputs, and outputs. They help in detecting any changes in model performance and potential security threats. Regular monitoring helps to identify potential threats and mitigate them by raising an alert. The following are key points for continuous monitoring and alerting:

a. Implement key monitoring tools to monitor the security and functionality of machine learning systems continuously.

b. Clearly define incident response procedures to detect and address security breaches promptly.

c. To find vulnerabilities and gauge how well security measures are working, penetration tests and security audits need to be done at regular intervals.

5. **Infrastructure Security**

Infrastructure and hardware components security is important to mitigate the risk of physical attacks. Physical attacks on infrastructure can lead to supply chain compromises. The following are key points to keep in consideration for secured infrastructure:

a. Secure execution environments must be utilized to safeguard ML model inference processes.

b. Network segmentation should be used to separate ML workloads from other systems to reduce the attack surface.

c. Keep all software and infrastructure components updated with the latest security patches.

Implementing Secure AI with MLSecOps

We now understand MLSecOps, its importance, and the pillars and best practices of MLSecOps, so it's time to implement MLSecOps effectively. Let's learn the step-by-step procedure for that (Figure 4-5).

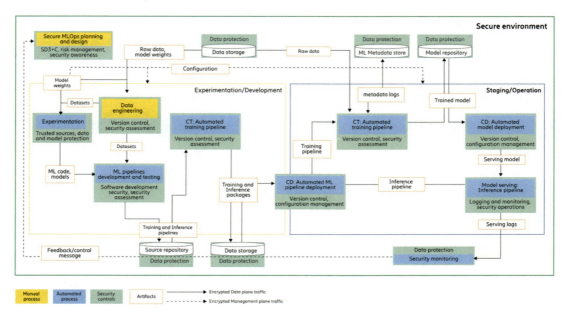

Figure 4-5. *Generalized MLSecOps architecture with security controls*

Step 1: Assess the ML System's Security Needs

The first step is to understand the ML system and its security requirements.

1. Identify all the data sources, ML models, and infrastructure used.

2. Identify potential risks and threats.

3. Conduct a risk assessment run.

4. Define clear objectives for MLSecOps implementation for security and mitigation.

Step 2: Establish a Cross-Functional Security Team

Now, establish a cross-functional security team to implement secured ML systems.

1. Establish a team of data scientists, ML engineers, IT professionals, and security experts.

2. Define clear roles and responsibilities of all team members ensuring their accountability.

Step 3: Define Policies and Procedures for MLSecOps

After defining the roles and responsibilities of members, define policies and procedures for MLSecOps.

1. Develop policies to address data handling, model development, deployment, monitoring, security, and all ML-specific tasks.

2. Develop incident response procedures in the event of a security breach.

3. Document and communicate all the MLSecOps procedures across the team for consistent implementation.

Step 4: Implement the Core Pillars of MLSecOps

Adapt, embrace, and implement the five core pillars of MLSecOps to fit your organization's data, model, ML system, and infrastructure.

Step 5: Follow the Secure Development Lifecycle

Integrate security practices during the development lifecycle, including data preprocessing, model training, validation, and deployment.

1. Educate practitioners to implement secure coding practices.

2. Implement data validation and sanitization to prevent common vulnerabilities.

3. Secure the deployment with safe configurations and limited access control.

Step 6: Implement Security Monitoring and Incident Response

After deployment, establish a security monitoring system and an incident response plan.

1. Deploy monitoring tools for ML systems to detect anomalies, adversarial attacks, and data drift in real time.

2. Define a complete incident response procedure, including roles, communication channels, and escalation paths, to ensure swift and effective response to security incidents.

Step 7: Implement Regular Audits and Assessments

Periodic security audits and assessments need to be done to assess the effectiveness of your MLSecOps implementation.

1. Conduct security audits regularly to identify vulnerabilities and improvement areas.

2. Stay updated for any future emerging threats and plan for mitigation strategies in advance.

Step 8: Conduct Employee Training and Awareness

To implement MLSecOps best practices, an organization needs to train their employees and spread awareness in the organization for the MLOps security guidelines.

1. Educate and train all the stakeholders about the security risks of MLOps, their roles and responsibilities, and how to follow MLSecOps procedures.

2. Spread awareness and encourage employees to be vigilant about potential security threats, report any suspicious activities, and adhere to MLSecOps policies.

How to Implement Security in AWS

Security is one of the key pillars of AWS's Well-Architected Framework. In fact. Security is one of the most crucial elements in every organization, and ensuring the company's security policy and standards are met is of utmost importance.

Security controls, such as, multifactor user authentication, sensitive data encryption, real-time audits, logging, and monitoring, intend to safeguard data and resource availability, confidentiality, and integrity. These administrative and technical barriers work to stop, identify, or lessen a threat actor's capacity to take advantage of a security flaw.

There are four types of security controls across the machine learning complete lifecycle: preventative, proactive, detective, and responsive. This section will discuss all security controls and focus on their AWS implementation.

Security Best Practices by ML Lifecycle Phase

The machine learning lifecycle consists of six phases (Figure 4-6). All the security best practices for AWS are divided among these phases. Let's discuss each one of them in detail.

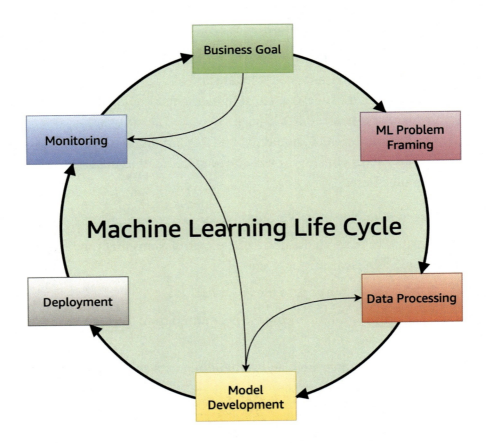

Figure 4-6. *Machine learning lifecycle*

Business Goal Identification

Business goal identification is the first and root phase of the ML lifecycle. While identifying the business goal, it is important to keep security measures in mind. It is within this time you must define and ensure the regulations needed to protect and validate data, system privacy, various permissions, software, and license terms. The best practice comes under business goal identification:

- Implementing ML Data Permissions Validation, Privacy, Software, and License Terms

  This phase establishes a process to review the privacy and license agreements for all software and ML libraries needed throughout the lifecycle. These agreements should comply with your organization's legal, privacy, and security terms and conditions and should not add any limitations to your organization's business plans. Its implementation plan is detailed here:

Ensure and Validate Data Permissions for ML

Ensure and validate all the data-related permissions that can be used for the machine learning lifecycle.

- Verify the purpose of the intended data.

- Verify if additional consent is required from the data owner or subjects.

- Have a strategy in place for handling data subjects who later decide not to give their consent.

- For compliance considerations, ensure that data permission documentation is up to date.

Bootstrap Instances with Lifecycle Management Policies

Put together a script to install the necessary packages and a reference to your package repository in a lifecycle configuration. Lifecycle management policies are created to manage the ML lifecycle instances, and automate the transition to tiered storage.

Evaluate Package Integrations

Package integration evaluation that requires external lookup services is done at this stage for security control.

- When it's essential, opt out of data gathering based on your requirements for data privacy.

- Data exposure through trusted relationships should be minimized.

- Examine the license agreements and privacy policies for any ML programs that may gather data.

Use Prebuilt Containers

Start with optimized, prepackaged, and verified containers to deploy the ML environment quickly. These pre-built containers support commonly used dependencies that automatically improve performance with optimized model training. TensorFlow, PyTorch, and Apache MXNet are some of the deep learning framework libraries and tools available in AWS deep learning containers. See Figure 4-7.

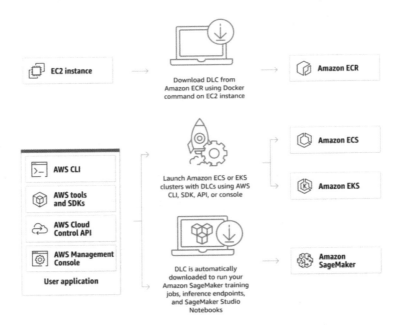

Figure 4-7. *AWS deep learning containers*

AWS deep learning containers are Docker images that are preconfigured and tested and contain the most recent iterations of well-known deep learning frameworks. With deep learning containers, you can quickly deploy custom ML environments without starting from scratch with environment creation and optimization.

ML Problem Framing

The main business challenge in this section includes best practices to formulate a machine learning problem, with the labels or target variables being what is observed and what should be forecasted. In machine learning, it is important to determine what to predict and how performance must be optimized. Following these stages will help frame ML problems per business requirements like so:

- Define the success criteria of the project.

- Define an observable and quantifiable performance metric for the project, such as accuracy, AUC, etc.

- Establish the relationship between performance metrics and the business outcome (for example, sales).

- Ensure that defined performance metrics are understood and agreed upon by business stakeholders.

- Formulate the ML question regarding inputs, desired outputs, the model's goal, and the performance metric to be optimized.

- To reach the desired business outcome, iterate the model by obtaining additional data, fine-tuning the parameters, or adding more complexity.

The best practice under ML Problem Framing is detailed here:

- Implementing Design Data Encryption and Obfuscation

  The security pillar includes the capacity to safeguard information, assets, and systems while utilizing cloud computing to enhance security. For a secure machine learning system, handling personally identifiable information, designing data encryption, and protecting credentials are important. Its implementation plan is detailed here:

Audit Data for Special Treatment Attributes

Data needs to be audited for the attributes that require special treatment related to security. There are three ways to audit data and offer security.

- *PII Data Identification and Handling*

  Special treatment is required for personally identifiable information (PII) and sensitive data by applying advanced transformations like redaction, replacement, encryption, and decryption. Because of the exponential data growth, businesses are managing vast amounts of heterogeneous data, including personally identifiable information (PII), streaming into their platform. Sensitive data identification and protection at scale has grown more difficult, costly, and time-consuming. AWS offers Glue Data Brew for identifying, processing, and handling PII data. See Figure 4-8.

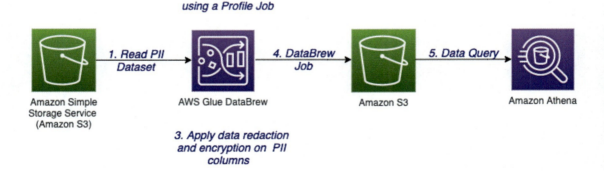

Figure 4-8. *AWS Glue Data Brew architecture*

AWS Glue Data Brew facilitates data privacy and protection with added PII data handling transformations that let you do operations on your sensitive data, such as data masking, encryption, and decryption. DataBrew has launched PII statistics, which identifies PII columns and provides their data statistics when you run a profile job on your dataset.

Design Data Encryption

Implementing design data encryption and data masking is necessary as the first line of defense to block unauthorized users from reading your data and model artifacts. Data encryption needs to be done while in transit as well as at rest. Client-side data encryption is done before uploading it to AWS, and server-side data encryption is done at its destination by the application or service that receives it. See Figure 4-9.

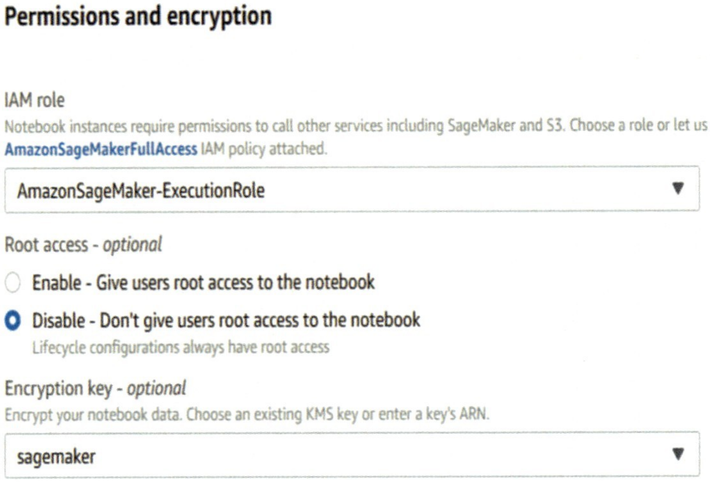

Permissions and encryption

IAM role
Notebook instances require permissions to call other services including SageMaker and S3. Choose a role or let us create a role with the **AmazonSageMakerFullAccess** IAM policy attached.

AmazonSageMaker-ExecutionRole ▼

Root access - *optional*

○ Enable - Give users root access to the notebook

◉ Disable - Don't give users root access to the notebook
Lifecycle configurations always have root access

Encryption key - *optional*
Encrypt your notebook data. Choose an existing KMS key or enter a key's ARN.

sagemaker ▼

Figure 4-9. *AWS encrypt/decrypt permissions snapshot*

Protect Credentials

Ensure the data is handled correctly, encrypted, and securely before going for inference and training. Rather than embedding credentials for accessing the database into the code, AWS recommends using AWS Secrets Manager to store your credentials, and then grant permissions to your SageMaker IAM role to access Secrets Manager from your notebook. See Figure 4-10.

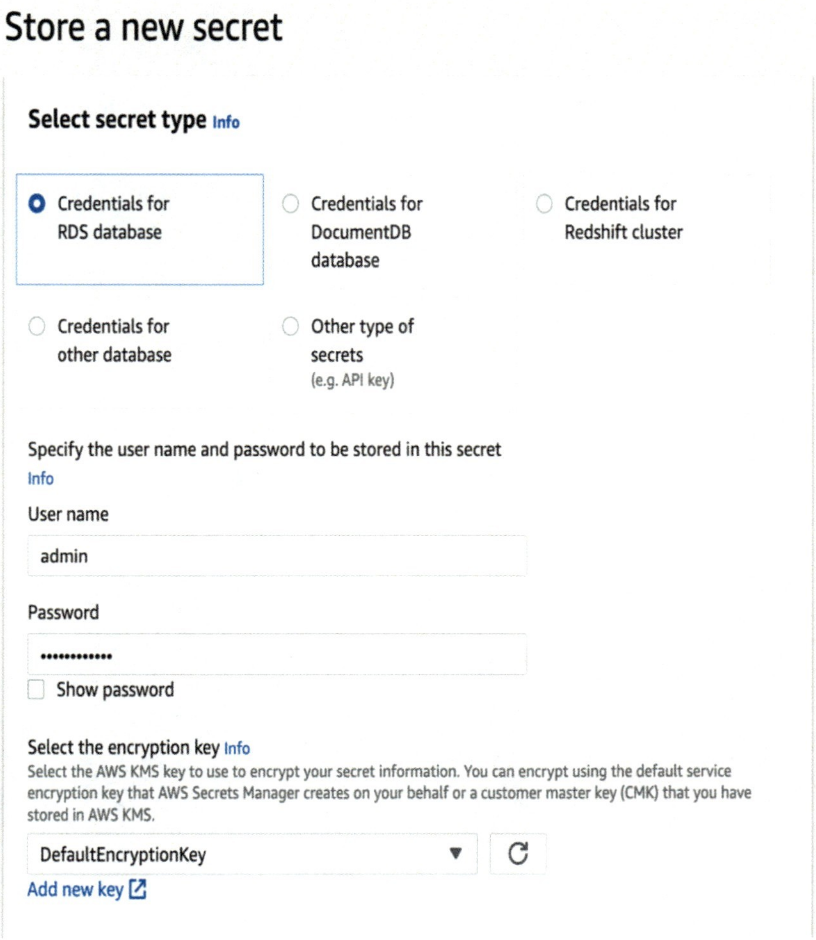

Store a new secret

Select secret type Info

○ Credentials for
  RDS database

○ Credentials for
  DocumentDB
  database

○ Credentials for
  Redshift cluster

○ Credentials for
  other database

○ Other type of
  secrets
  (e.g. API key)

Specify the user name and password to be stored in this secret
Info
User name

admin

Password

••••••••••••

☐ Show password

Select the encryption key Info
Select the AWS KMS key to use to encrypt your secret information. You can encrypt using the default service
encryption key that AWS Secrets Manager creates on your behalf or a customer master key (CMK) that you have
stored in AWS KMS.

DefaultEncryptionKey ▼   C

Add new key ☒

Figure 4-10. *Storing credentials in the AWS Secrets Manager Console*

- Using AWS Secret Manager is a secure way to protect credentials from third parties. The secret manager must rotate credentials as per the specified schedule to drastically lower the likelihood of secrets being compromised.

Data Processing

Data processing consists of data collection and data preparation (data processing and feature engineering). The first step of data processing is data collection, aggregation, ingestion, and proper labeling. Under data preprocessing, data cleaning, feature scaling (normalization or standardization), augmentation, and partition are done. The final step is feature engineering where feature selection, new feature creation, feature transformation, and extraction are done for better results. For better data understanding and exploration, Exploratory Data Analysis (EDA) and visualizations are created.

It is critical to remember that the inference requests must be processed using the same set of procedures as the training data. Data positioning, data breaching, and adversarial attacks happen at this stage. The best practices under data processing are detailed here:

Implementing Least Privileged Access

The first rule is to implement the least privileged access across all phases of the ML lifecycle to protect resources like data, code, algorithms, hyperparameters, trained models, configurations, and infrastructure. Allocate dedicated network environments with dedicated resources and services to operate any project. Its implementation plan is detailed here:

Restricted Access Based on Business Roles for Individuals

Access needs to be restricted based on the business roles in the organization.

- Identify the roles of the individuals in the project.

- Implement role-based authentication by mapping roles to the access required.

- Depending on the needs of each project, grant the least privileged access to private information, resources, and services.

Use Account Separation and AWS Organizations

Understand the workflows of the different user types, use account separation, and provide role-based access grants accordingly with a multi-account design that divides workloads across development, test, and production and applies the proper governance based on data sensitivity and compliance requirements. AWS Service Catalog is used to deploy pre-provisioned environments quickly. It lets you centrally manage your cloud resources to achieve governance and compliance requirements at the scale of your infrastructure as code (IaC) templates. It helps in establishing tagging for data and buckets that contain sensitive workloads. These tags are used to grant access to individuals at a granular level. See Figure 4-11.

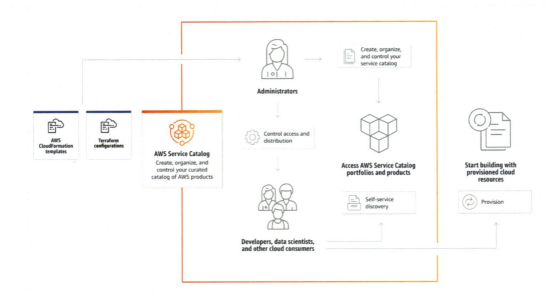

Figure 4-11. *AWS Service Catalog*

Service Catalog has the following features:

- It finds and deploys approved, self-service cloud resources quickly.

- It shows agility while improving governance and compliance over resources across multiple accounts.

- Use AWS Service Catalog's AppRegistry to obtain current, accurate application definitions and related metadata.

Break Out ML Workloads by Access Patterns and Organizational Structure

The ML workload break-up is needed based on the organizational structure and authorized access.

- Break out the ML workloads and delegate specific access to specific people like data analysts, scientists, and administrators as required.

- Enforce best practices for each access type and group using guardrails and service control policies (SCPs).

- Limit infrastructure access to administrators.

- Ensure that only specialized, isolated, and restricted environments are used to access sensitive data.

Implementing Secure Data and Modeling Environment

It's time to enable model development and safeguard the system hosting the data. End-to-end environments need to be secure like encrypt training data and store it in secure repositories. Execute data preparation in a tightly secured cloud environment. Encrypted data moves from data repositories to the tightly controlled destination compute instances. Its implementation plan is detailed here:

Build a Secure Analysis Environment

During the data preparation and feature engineering phase, Amazon AWS offers many services for data analysis in the secure environment mentioned below.

- Amazon SageMaker is a managed notebook environment.

- Amazon EMR is the market leader in the cloud big data space for petabyte-scale data processing, interactive analytics, and machine learning using open-source frameworks such as Apache Spark, Apache Hive, and Presto.

- Amazon Athena offers a simplified, flexible, serverless, interactive analytics service to analyze petabytes of data where it lives.

- AWS Glue is a serverless data integration service that discovers, prepares, moves, and integrates data efficiently with simplified ETL pipeline development for machine learning and application development. It supports various processing frameworks and workloads. See Figure 4-12.

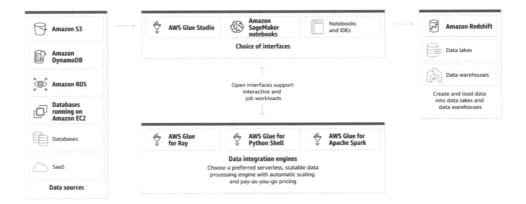

Figure 4-12. *AWS Glue*

Create dedicated AWS IAM and KMS Resources

This approach limits the scope of credentials and key impact.
A dedicated AWS Identity and Access Management and Key
Management Service resources are created. Version management
for the data and intellectual property (IP) is enabled in AWS by
implementing a centralized data lake through the use of AWS Lake
Formation on Amazon S3. Securing, accessing, and monitoring
a data lake on Amazon S3 is achieved using a combination of
granular AWS services like AWS IAM policies, S3 bucket policies,
S3 Access Logs, Amazon CloudWatch, and AWS CloudTrail. See
Figure 4-13.

Figure 4-13. *AWS Identity and Access Management*

The following are the various policies implemented via AWS Identity and Access Management to securely manage identities and access to AWS services and resources.

- Identity-based policies

- Resource-based policies

- Permissions boundaries

- Organizations SCPs

- Access control lists (ACLs)

- Session policies

The following sample demonstrates how to work with AWS Identity and Access Management (IAM) with an AWS software development kit (SDK) for Python (Boto3). AWS services can be securely controlled through the use of IAM, a web service. With IAM, permissions can be centrally managed in your AWS account. The following Python code example shows how to use CreateAccessKey using the create_key function.

```
def create_key(user_name):
    """

    :param user_name: The name of the user.
    :return: The created access key.
    """
```

```
try:
    key_pair = iam.User(user_name).create_access_key_pair()
    logger.info(
        "Created access key pair for %s. Key ID is %s.",
        key_pair.user_name,
        key_pair.id,
    )
except ClientError:
    logger.exception("Couldn't create access key pair for %s.",
    user_name)
    raise
else:
    return key_pair
```

This code creates an access key for the specified user. There is a maximum of two keys per user.

Use Secrets Manager and Parameter Store to Protect Credentials

Secrets Manager enables you to replace hard-coded secrets in your code, such as credentials, with an API call to decrypt and retrieve the secret programmatically. Application configuration variables, such as license keys or AMI IDs, can be stored in the Parameter Store, which was intended for broader use cases than secrets or passwords. With AWS Secrets Manager and Parameter Store, you can store your credentials and then grant permissions to your SageMaker IAM role to access Secrets Manager from your notebook. See Figure 4-14.

Figure 4-14. *AWS Secret Manager*

The following are AWS Secrets Manager's main features:

- Using fine-grained policies to control access to your apps, services, and IT resources and keep confidential information securely

- Satisfying your security and compliance needs, secrets are automatically rotated

- Securely encrypting database credentials and API keys

The following sample demonstrates how to use AWS SDK for Python (Boto3) to work with AWS Secrets Manager. Secrets Manager facilitates the safe encryption, archiving, and retrieval of login credentials for databases and other services. The following code example shows the implementation of the function get_secret to get a secret value:

```
class GetSecretWrapper:
    def __init__(self, secretsmanager_client):
        self.client = secretsmanager_client

def get_secret(self, secret_name):
        try:
```

```
            get_secret_value_response = self.client.get_secret_value(
                SecretId=secret_name
            )
            logging.info("Secret retrieved successfully.")
            return get_secret_value_response["SecretString"]
        except self.client.exceptions.ResourceNotFoundException:
            msg = f"The requested secret {secret_name} was not found."
            logger.info(msg)
            return msg
        except Exception as e:
            logger.error(f"An unknown error occurred: {str(e)}.")
            raise
```

In this code, the get_secret_value API is implemented to retrieve individual secrets from AWS Secrets Manager. Here, the parameter secret_name is passed and returns a secret string as output.

Automate Managing Configuration

Automate all the lifecycle configuration that manages Jupyter Notebook instances that install custom packages, preload datasets, and set up source code repositories. Changes can be done once, and updated configurations are applied across multiple notebook instances. This gives developers, data scientists, and security teams the flexibility and control over the system. AWS Service Catalog is used to simplify configuration for end users.

Create Private, Isolated, Network Environments

Amazon Virtual Private Cloud (Amazon VPC) creates and enables connectivity to isolated secured services and users as per the requirements. The Amazon SageMaker notebook instance is deployed in an Amazon VPC to enable network-level controls to limit communication to the hosted notebook. VPC Flow Logs capture network calls into and out of the notebook instance to enable additional visibility and control at the network level. VPC allows query data sources such as relational databases in Amazon RDS or Amazon Redshift data warehouses.

The following are the main features of Amazon Virtual Private Cloud (Amazon VPC):

- Implementing secure and monitored connections, screen traffic, and restricting instance access inside your virtual network.

- Saves time with setting up, managing, and validating your virtual network.

- Manages and controls the environment by customizing your virtual network by choosing your IP address range, creating subnets, and configuring route tables.

Restrict Access

Web-based access to the underlying operating system on an EC2 instance is made possible by the Jupyter Notebook server. This allows you to install additional software packages or Jupyter kernels to customize your environment. The access is granted by default to a user with root access or superuser on the operating system, giving them total control of the underlying EC2 instance. This access should be restricted to prevent the user from assuming root privileges while retaining control over their local user environment.

Secure Ml Algorithms

Models and algorithms are trained and hosted using Amazon SageMaker using container technology. Once your containers are created, host them privately to an Amazon Elastic Container Repository (Amazon ECR). See Figure 4-15.

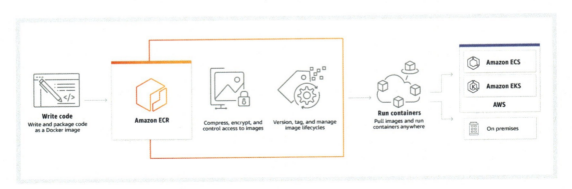

Figure 4-15. *Amazon ECR*

Amazon Elastic Container Registry (ECR) can easily store, share, and deploy your container software anywhere.

- Container images are pushed to Amazon ECR without any need for scaling or installation of the infrastructure.

- ECR aids in downloading and sharing images securely with automatic encryption and access controls over Hypertext Transfer Protocol Secure (HTTPS).

Enforce Code Best Practices

Code best practices are enforced using secured Git repositories through fully managed AWS CodeCommit for storing code. See Figure 4-16.

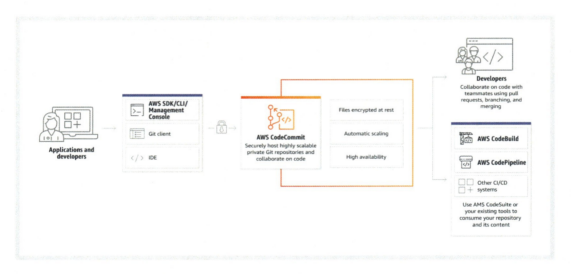

Figure 4-16. *AWS Code Commit*

The following are AWS Code Commit's main features:

- Securely hosting highly scalable private Git repositories and collaborating on code close to build, staging, and production environments on AWS

- Offering customizable user-specific access to Git repositories with automatically encrypted files in transit

- Eliminating the need to scale, backup, host, and operate your source control servers

Implement a Package Mirror for Consuming Approved Packages

Several ML Python packages are used across the ML lifecycle such as Pandas, PyTorch, Keras, TensorFlow, NumPy, and Scikit-learn. The business requirements evaluation for license terms to these Python packages is required as per the determined criteria. An automated mechanism is set up that runs the script to download the necessary package versions from approved repositories and install them with dependency checks. Once the packages are downloaded, validation is necessary to confirm the validity and safety of the packages.

SageMaker notebooks support the two following package installation tools:

- conda install

- pip install

Here is their sample code:

```
# Create a custom conda environment
source "$WORKING_DIR/miniconda/bin/activate"
KERNEL_NAME="custom_python"
PYTHON="3.6"

conda create --yes --name "$KERNEL_NAME" python="$PYTHON"
conda activate "$KERNEL_NAME"

pip install --quiet ipykernel

# These lines can be customized to install the required packages
conda install --yes numpy
pip install --quiet boto3
```

In this code, numpy is installed using conda, and boto3 is installed using pip. These lines as codes can be customized as per the package installation requirement.

Implementing Sensitive Data Privacy Protection

Sensitive data identification and classification are crucial at this stage for protection against unintended disclosure. Strategies like removing, masking, tokenizing, principal component analysis (PCA), and best governance practices are used for sensitive data protection. Its implementation plan is detailed here:

Use Automated Mechanisms for Data Classification

Amazon offers an automated mechanism for data classification named Amazon Macie. It provides automated, continuous, intelligent, cost-efficient, and organization-wide visibility into your S3 buckets for sensitive data. The following are the main features of Amazon Macie:

- Inspecting for personally identifiable information (PII), financial data, and AWS credentials.

- Building and continuously maintaining an interactive data map that shows where your sensitive data is stored in Amazon S3, along with a sensitivity score for every bucket.

- Logging specific S3 items.

- Macie also updates statistics, inventory data, and other information about your Amazon S3 data.

Use Tagging

Tags are used to distinguish between sensitive resources and models that need protection from those that don't, containing sensitive features. Storage can be categorized by using object tags. Each tag works in a key-value pair, where keys and values are case-sensitive.

The following are the key features of tags:

- Tags can be added to new objects while uploading or can be added to existing objects.

- Up to 10 tags can be associated with an object, and each tag must have unique tag keys.

- The length of a tag key and tag value can each be up to 128 and 256 Unicode characters, respectively. UTF-16 is used internally by Amazon S3 object tags.

- Fine-grained access control of permissions is made possible by object tags.

- Fine-grained object lifetime management is made possible by object tags, which allow you to define a tag-based filter in a lifecycle rule in addition to a key name prefix.

Assume that your S3 bucket is where you keep project files. You might tag these objects with a value and the key Project, as demonstrated here:

```
Project=Yellow
```

Encrypt Sensitive Data

Sensitive data can be encrypted using the following services.:

- Client-side encryption.

- **AWS Key Management**: The AWS Key Management Service lets you encrypt data with control cryptographic keys using AWS encryption SDK across your AWS workloads, digital signs, applications, and AWS services. See Figure 4-17.

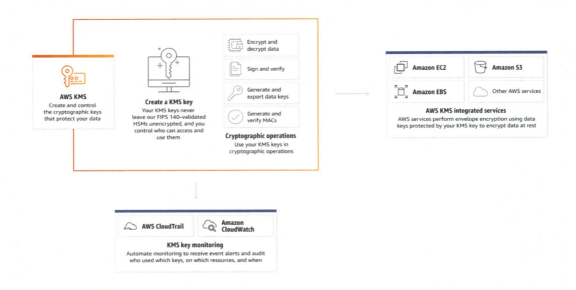

Figure 4-17. *AWS Key Management Service*

The following sample AWS SDK for Python (Boto3) code
demonstrates how to encrypt text by using the specified key with
AWS KMS:

```python
class KeyEncrypt:
    def __init__(self, kms_client):
        self.kms_client = kms_client

    def encrypt(self, key_id):
        """

        text = input("Enter some text to encrypt: ")
        try:
            cipher_text = self.kms_client.encrypt(
                KeyId=key_id, Plaintext=text.encode()
            )["CiphertextBlob"]
        except ClientError as err:
            logger.error(
                "Couldn't encrypt text. Here's why: %s",
                err.response["Error"]["Message"],
            )
```

```
        else:
            print(f"Your ciphertext is: {cipher_text}")
            return cipher_text
```

This code takes the input parameter `param key_id`, which is the ID of the key to use for encryption and returns the encrypted version of the text.

- **The AWS Encryption SDK:** To utilize the AWS Encryption SDK, keyrings or master key providers can be configured with wrapped keys or AWS KMS. For the AWS Encryption SDK to interface with the AWS KMS, it requires the AWS SDK for the programming language of your choice. To support master keys kept in AWS KMS, the AWS Encryption SDK client library collaborates with the AWS SDKs.

Reduce Data Sensitivity

Determine which data should be anonymized or de-identified to reduce data sensitivity and assess. Developing a serverless tokenization system is the best way to conceal sensitive data and lower the possibility of unwanted access. The process of turning a piece of data into a random character string known as a token is *tokenization*. Tokenization makes use of a database often referred to as a *token vault* that holds the connection between the token and the sensitive value. Next, the data within the vault is frequently protected via encryption. The token value can replace the original data in a variety of applications. Amazon Cognito is used for client authentication and receives an authorization token.

- Implementing Enforce Data Lineage

  Data lineage is necessary to audit, monitor, and track data origins and their transformation over time. Integrity checks must be applied against training data to identify any unexpected deviations brought on by loss, corruption, or manipulation to carefully regulate data access. Data lineage enables visibility and helps trace the root cause of data processing errors. Its implementation plan is detailed here:

Track Records for Any Update

Amazon SageMaker ML Lineage Tracker is used to store information about the steps of an ML workflow from data preparation to model deployment.

The following information can be extracted by lineage tracking:

- The workflow steps can be reproduced, and model and dataset lineage can be tracked.

- Follow model lineage artifacts to verify compliance and establish model governance and audit standards.

- Think of origin data as the ultimate source of truth.

- The running history of model discovery experiments is maintained.

- Ingest, process, and maintain mappings for datasets that are derived from them. Iterate from the result back to the original data element.

- Apply these concepts not just to data, as well as to the code, models, pipelines, and infrastructure. Verify that you can track and audit any activity about pipeline actions, data, or machine intelligence models.

  The following sample code demonstrates the basics of lineage entities and how to create and associate different lineage entities to track your workflows. You can further transverse the association between the different lineage entities.

```
from datetime import datetime
from sagemaker.lineage.context import Context
from sagemaker.lineage.action import Action
from sagemaker.lineage.association import Association
from sagemaker.lineage.artifact import Artifact

unique_id = str(int(datetime.now().replace(microsecond=0).
timestamp()))

print(f"Unique id is {unique_id}")
# create an example context
```

```
# the name must be unique across all other contexts
context_name = f"machine-learning-workflow-{unique_id}"

ml_workflow_context = Context.create(
    context_name=context_name,
    context_type="MLWorkflow",
    source_uri=unique_id,
    # properties services as a method to store metdata on
        lineage entities in additional to Tags
    properties={"example": "true"},
)
```

In this code, the context entity is created using sagemaker.lineage.context. A unique ID is created and a unique name is assigned to context across all other entities and its properties are defined.

Implementing Keep Only Relevant Data

machine learning systems should be designed to manage data throughout its lifecycle. The system needs to keep data that is relevant to the use case and outdated data should be automatically deleted at a given time. To lower the data exposure risk, save data across computing environments (such as development and staging) and implement mechanisms to enforce a lifecycle management process across the data. Its implementation plan is detailed here:

Establish a Data Lifecycle Plan

Every piece of data undergoes a data lifecycle, going from its raw to its processed state, and the final user uses the results to make better decisions.

Organizations use AWS Cloud services at every phase of the data lifecycle to process data quickly and affordably. We need to create a data lifecycle plan to comprehend consumption and need patterns for operational and debugging chores; this will eventually lead to data sprawl reduction and derive more value from data. See Figure 4-18.

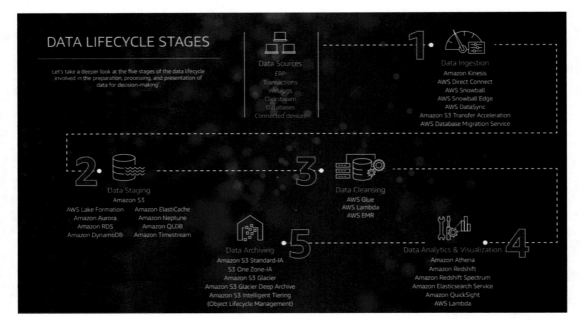

Figure 4-18. *Data lifecycle stages*

There are five data lifecycle stages.

- *Data Ingestion*

    Data ingestion takes data from various verified high-value data sources like transaction files, ERP, databases, weblogs, etc., and is imported to a location where data analytics and machine learning can be applied. These data files are kept safe and backed up on the AWS cloud. The cloud stores data in a way that is economical, safe, long-lasting, and, most crucially, available to a wide range of users. s. AWS services available during this stage include Amazon Kinesis, AWS Direct Connect, AWS Snowball/Snowball Edge/Snowmobile, AWS DataSync, Amazon S3 Transfer Acceleration, AWS Database Migration Service, and AWS Storage Gateway.

- *Data Staging*

    Data staging involves performing some housekeeping tasks before making data available to users. Businesses store data in different places, such as databases, spreadsheets, text files, and data warehouses in different ways. By avoiding different storage methods,

AWS makes it simple to stage data or build a data lake in one place like Amazon S3. AWS services available in the data staging stage include Amazon S3, Amazon Aurora, Amazon RDS, and Amazon DynamoDB.

- *Data Cleaning*

  Before data analysis, data cleansing needs to be done for defects, corrupted data, or inaccurate data. Data cleansing involves all or some of the following processes:

  - Identifying corrupt or dirty data

  - To increase the accuracy of the analytical output, adding or editing dirty data

  - Turning speech to text data

  - Translating files as per required input

  - Converting audio and image data to digital format for processing, or including metadata tags to facilitate categorization and search

  - Ultimately, the last step is to transform data so it's optimized for code (e.g., ETL).

  AWS services available for data cleaning include AWS Glue Data Catalog, AWS Glue (ETL), Amazon EMR, and Amazon SageMaker Ground Truth.

- *Data Analytics and Visualization*

  At this point, the true value of the data can be discovered. Analytics and visualization tools are used by data engineers and decision-makers to anticipate customer demands, enhance operations, fix faulty processes, and innovate to stay competitive. Executives and mission owners do not need to rely on expensive and error-prone guesswork when they have access to data. AWS services available for analytics and visualization include Amazon Athena, Amazon Redshift, Amazon QuickSight, Amazon SageMaker, Amazon Comprehend, Amazon Comprehend Medical, and AWS DeepLens

- *Data Archiving*

  By making data archiving easier, the AWS Cloud frees up IT teams' resources to devote greater attention to other phases of the data lifecycle. These storage solutions come with built-in encryption, and have many security certifications and compliance standards, allowing for compliance right away. AWS services used for data archiving include Amazon S3 Glacier, Amazon S3 Glacier Deep Archive, and AWS Storage Gateway.

Design for Privacy

Design data for privacy and remove unwanted sensitive information while maintaining data usability. Detect personally identifiable information (PII) and features for future iterations of business problems. AWS offers the use of ML capabilities of Amazon Comprehend to detect and redact PII from a variety of sources, including product reviews, social media, support issues, emails from customers, and more. See Figure 4-19.

Figure 4-19. *Amazon Comprehend Architecture*

The following are the main features of Amazon Comprehend:

- Uncovers valuable insights from text in documents, customer support tickets, emails, product reviews, and more

- Protects and controls who has access to sensitive data by detecting PII entities from documents and redacting the text from it

- Preserves privacy and abides by local rules and regulations by redacting PII entities

The following sample demonstrates code to perform real-time analysis using the Amazon Comprehend on AWS CLI.

```
aws comprehend detect-pii-entities \
--language-code en \
--text \
" Good morning, everybody. My name is Van Bokhorst Serdar, and today I feel like sharing a whole l
```

The previous code output is the JSON response object that contains the detected PII entities. The service returns the confidence score metric, type of PII, and other parameters, for each entity.

- Model Development

  The model development phase consists of model building, training, hypertuning, and evaluation. The best practices under model development are detailed here:

  - Implementing a Secure Governed ML Environment

    ML development and operations environment are protected with detective and preventive guardrails. The configuration of the development environment is managed and monitored continuously with self-service provisioning for the users. Incident management and response are also implemented for a secure governed ML environment. Its implementation plan is detailed here:

    Break Out ML Workloads

    ML workloads are broken out according to the access patterns of organizational units. This will make it possible to assign each group, like administrators, data analysts, etc., access.

    Use Guardrails and Service Control Policies (SCPs)

    Use detective and preventive guardrails with Service Control policies to enforce best practices for each type of ML environment. Administrators are provided with limited access to infrastructure for security.

171

Verify All Sensitive Data

Verification should be done for all sensitive data and check for access through restricted and isolated environments. Make sure there are dedicated resources, network isolation, and service dependencies are checked.

Secure ML Algorithm Implementation

ML algorithm must be implemented using a secured and restricted development environment. Observe the security procedures necessary for your firm to ensure the safety of model training and container hosting.

- Implementing Secure Inter-Node Cluster Communications

For the inter-node cluster communications, coefficient information is a must to share. The shared data must remain synchronized across nodes for the algorithms to function. While being transferred, data must be encrypted. Its implementation plan is detailed here:

Enable Inter-Node Encryption in Amazon SageMaker

In distributed computing environments, Inter-node encryption is enabled in Amazon through SageMaker to automatically instruct the data transmitted between nodes through transverse wide networks. To ensure that data is sent over an encrypted tunnel for your training task, encrypt inter-container communication.

Enable Encryption in Transit in Amazon EMR

There are many applications and execution engines in the Hadoop ecosystem, providing a variety of tools to match the needs of your ML and analytics workloads. Amazon EMR has distributed cluster capabilities and is also an option for running data processing, interactive analytics, and machine learning jobs on the data that is either stored locally on the cluster or in Amazon S3. See Figure 4-20.

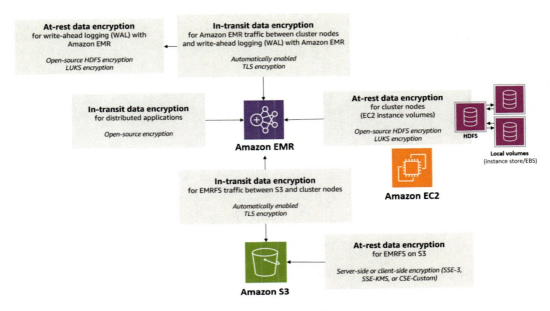

Figure 4-20. *Amazon EMR data encryption options*

The following are the main features of Amazon EMR:

- At less than half the cost of on-premises systems, Amazon EMR runs petabyte-scale data analytics and big data apps more quickly.

- Obtain up to two times faster time-to-insights with open-source, interoperable Spark, Hive, and Presto versions, which are optimized for performance.

- It offers lots of fast and easy options for data encryption.

The following sample demonstrates how to create a security configuration with the Amazon EMR console. It shows references for the various parameters that comprise encryption and configuration.

```
aws emr create-security-configuration --name "MyS3EncryptionConfig"
--security-configuration '{
  "EncryptionConfiguration": {
    "EnableInTransitEncryption": false,
    "EnableAtRestEncryption": true,
    "AtRestEncryptionConfiguration": {
```

```
    "S3EncryptionConfiguration": {
      "EncryptionMode": "SSE-S3"
    }
  }
 }
}'
```

The function of the previous code is to disable the in-transit data encryption and enable at-rest data encryption. Additionally, it disables local disc encryption and activates Amazon S3 encryption using the "SSE-S3" encryption mode.

- Implementing Protect against Data Poisoning Threats

  Data poisoning that pollutes the training dataset is the most common threat to data and protection against data injection and manipulation is necessary. Corrupt training data can be added by data injections, which can lead to inaccurate models and outputs. Data manipulations have the potential to alter labels or features in the data, which can result in imprecise and weak prediction models. Security methods and anomaly detection algorithms can identify corrupt data and inaccurate models. Ensure installed third-party packages don't contain dangerous malware or ransomware to preserve the immutability of datasets. Its implementation plan is detailed here:

  Use Only Trusted Data Sources for Data Training

  Before training, verify the training data's quality to look for significant outliers and perhaps erroneous labels. Audit controls must be done regularly to keep a review of activities and changes done by whom, when, and where.

  Look for Underlying Shifts in the Patterns of Training Data

  Determine the effect on prediction variance by keeping an eye on data drift. These skews can provide an early warning of unauthorized access aimed at the training data, as well as underlying data drift.

Identify Model Updates That Negatively Impact the Results

Check to see if the outcomes of the retrained model differ from the previous model iteration and if it's deteriorating before sending it to production. As a baseline, historical test results and model iterations should be used.

Have a Rollback Plan

Always be ready with a rollback plan in case of a failure scenario. Follow versioned training data and versioned models so it is easy to revert to a known good working model.

Use Low-Entropy Classification Cases

Look for significant, unexpected, and low-entropy classification changes. Keep an eye out for big, unexpected developments. Establish the boundaries of thresholds, spot classifications you wouldn't anticipate seeing, and sound an alert if the retrained model surpasses them.

- Model Deployment

  After all the security measures are implemented for ML problem framing, data processing and model development, evaluation, and validation, now is the time to deploy the model into production and implement security measures for it. Predictions and inferences are made against the secured model and secured deployment environment. The best practice under model deployment is detailed here:

- Implementing Protect against Adversarial and Malicious Activities

  Increase security and protection both within and outside of the code that has to be deployed to identify malicious inputs that could lead to inaccurate predictions. Detect illegal modifications automatically by closely scrutinizing the inputs and repairing them before they are added back to the pool. Its implementation plan is detailed here:

Evaluate the Robustness of the Algorithm

Analyze your use case and identify inaccurate classifications or forecasts. To determine how susceptible the algorithm is to manipulate inputs, use sensitivity analysis to assess the method's robustness against progressively altered inputs.

Build for Robustness from the Start

Choose a variety of features to strengthen the algorithm's resistance to outliers. Think about utilizing ensemble models to improve robustness around decision points and to boost diversity in decisions.

Identify Repeats

Amazon SageMaker Model Monitor runs a processing job on a periodic interval to analyze the inference data to detect repeated inputs to the model to identify possible threats to the decision boundaries. This can be done by using a technique known as *model brute forcing*, in which attackers repeatedly try a small number of variables to see what affects decision points and assess the feature's importance.

Lineage Tracking

Before retraining a replacement model, ensure that in the case of any model, skew is tracked back to the data and trimmed if retraining on untrusted or unvalidated inputs. We have discussed lineage tracking in detail under operation excellence in AWS.

Use Secure Inference API Endpoints

Host the model so that it can be securely used for inference by a model consumer. Permit users to monitor model interactions, limit access to the underlying model, and establish relationships using the API.

- Model Monitoring

  A model monitoring system ensures continuous monitoring and maintenance of the model to achieve the desired level of performance. Model monitoring helps in the early detection of security threats and allows for mitigation of them. The best practices under model monitoring are detailed here:

  - Restrict Access to Intended Legitimate Consumers

    At the deployed model endpoint, restricted access needs to be provided using least-privileged permissions. Provide access via secure API to the consumers who are external to the workload environment. Its implementation plan is detailed here:

    Use Secure Inference API Endpoints

    Provide a safe environment for a model consumer to conduct inference against the model by hosting it. Permit users to establish the relationship, limit access to the underlying model, and offer model interaction monitoring through the API.

    Secure Inference Endpoints

    Secure inference points by allowing only authorized personnel to make inferences against ML models. Ensure to go by the AWS Well-Architected Framework's instructions when it comes to providing network restrictions, such as bot control and limiting access to particular IP limits. The HTTPS requests for these API calls should be signed, so that the requester's identity can be verified, and the requested data is protected in transit.

  - Monitor Human Interactions with Data for Anomalous Activity

    Ensure you monitor the human interaction with data. Keep auditing for anomalous data access or access from abnormal locations and exceeding the threshold limit. Logs need to be maintained for the data access and authorization. Various tools can be used that support anomalous activity alerting, and combine their use with data classification to assess risk. Evaluate using services to aid in monitoring data access events. Its implementation plan is detailed here:

Enable Data Access Logging

Verify you have data access logging in place for any human CRUD (create, read, update, and delete) actions. This log should include information about who accessed what, when, from where, and what action they took.

Classify Your Data

AWS's fully managed data security solution, Amazon Macie, safeguards and categorizes training and inference data in Amazon S3. It uses machine learning and pattern matching to automatically discover, classify, and protect sensitive data in AWS. The service is capable of identifying sensitive data, including intellectual property and PII. See Figure 4-21.

Figure 4-21. *Amazon Macie*

Amazon Macie has the following features:

- Protecting and classifying sensitive data

- Discovering sensitive data automatically, continually, and cost-effectively at scale in Amazon S3

- Reducing triage time with actionable reporting of sensitive data, which is found in Amazon S3

- Increasing visibility for business-critical data

Monitor and Protect

Amazon GuardDuty combines ML and integrated threat intelligence from AWS to monitor for malicious and unauthorized activities on

your AWS accounts and workloads. This enables the protection
of AWS accounts, workloads, and data stored in Amazon S3 with
intelligent threat detection and provides thorough security findings
that can be seen and fixed. See Figure 4-22.

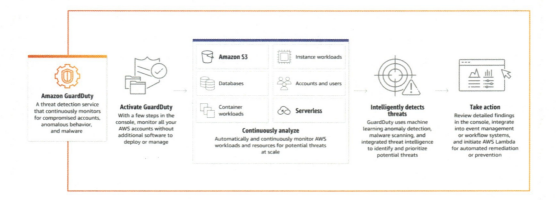

Figure 4-22. *Amazon GuardDuty*

Amazon GuardDuty has the following features:

- Keeps an eye out for possible dangers all over the Amazon
  environment

- Uses anomaly detection, behavioral modeling, machine learning
  (ML), and threat intelligence feeds from AWS and reputable third
  parties to swiftly uncover threats

- Accurately identifies hazards and take action quickly before they
  become more serious issues that could affect your business

- End-to-end visibility into AWS compute Cloud (Amazon EC2)
  workloads, serverless workloads, and container workloads

Final Thoughts

An organization is looking for a complete solution in MLOps for an end-to-end secured ML system implementation. Organizations can safeguard themselves from security threats like data poisoning, quick injection attacks, ML adversarial attacks, model inversion attacks, and others by integrating MLSecOps' five fundamental pillars and adhering to ML security best practices. As machine learning security advances, ongoing monitoring, and preventative measures become more important for secured machine learning at scale, to accelerate the organization's growth and revenue production.

References

- https://ml-ops.org/content/model-governance

- https://medium.com/@bijit211987/adopting-mlsecops-securing-machine-learning-at-scale-1a5647d01a64

- https://towardsdatascience.com/as-mlops-hits-maturity-its-time-to-consider-cybersecurity-ebd45e350532

- https://www.ericsson.com/en/reports-and-papers/white-papers/mlsecops-protecting-the-ai-ml-lifecycle-in-telecom

- https://www.harrisonclarke.com/blog/mastering-mlops-best-practices-for-secure-machine-learning-systems

- https://www.linkedin.com/pulse/mlsecopsmachine-learning-security-devops-mukund-kumar-choudhary/

- https://arxiv.org/pdf/1412.6572.pdf

- https://docs.aws.amazon.com/wellarchitected/latest/machine-learning-lens/best-practices-by-pillar.html

- https://docs.aws.amazon.com/wellarchitected/latest/machine-learning-lens/mlsec-01.html

- https://aws.amazon.com/blogs/big-data/introducing-pii-data-identification-and-handling-using-aws-glue-databrew/

- https://aws.amazon.com/blogs/security/7-ways-to-improve-security-of-your-machine-learning-workflows/

- https://github.com/aws/amazon-sagemaker-examples/blob/main/sagemaker-lineage/sagemaker-lineage.ipynb

- https://aws.amazon.com/iam/

- https://aws.amazon.com/kms/

- https://docs.aws.amazon.com/emr/latest/ManagementGuide/emr-create-security-configuration.html

- https://github.com/awsdocs/aws-doc-sdk-examples/tree/main/python/example_code/iam#code-examples

- https://aws.amazon.com/secrets-manager/

- https://github.com/aws-samples/amazon-sagemaker-notebook-instance-lifecycle-config-samples/blob/master/scripts/persistent-conda-ebs/on-create.sh

- https://docs.aws.amazon.com/code-library/latest/ug/python_3_secrets-manager_code_examples.html

- https://aws.amazon.com/codecommit/

- https://aws.amazon.com/ecr/

- https://docs.aws.amazon.com/wellarchitected/latest/machine-learning-lens/security-pillar-best-practices-3.html

- https://aws.amazon.com/comprehend/

- https://aws.amazon.com/macie/

- https://aws.amazon.com/guardduty/

- https://aws.amazon.com/vpc/?vpc-blogs.sort-by=item.additionalFields.createdDate&vpc-blogs.sort-order=desc"vpc-blogs.sort-order=desc

- https://aws.amazon.com/blogs/publicsector/building-a-data-analytics-practice-across-the-data-lifecycle/

CHAPTER 5

MLOps Reliability in AI/ML

Reliability is the third pillar of MLOps. In previous chapters, we discussed operational excellence and security in MLOps.

In this chapter, we are going to discuss reliability in MLOps, its principles, and importance of reliability in MLOps in detail. We will cover the three pillars of reliability and best practices that need to be implemented for reliable MLOps systems. We'll also show their implementations in AWS with code snippets for reference.

© Neel Sendas and Deepali Rajale 2024
N. Sendas and D. Rajale, *The Definitive Guide to Machine Learning Operations in AWS*,
https://doi.org/10.1007/979-8-8688-1076-3_5

Introduction to MLOps Reliability

Reliability in MLOps is ML architecture's best, most efficient, and most resilient pillar and helps identify improvement areas. It ensures accurate, consistent, and high-quality workload performance when expected. It encompasses the workload's capacity to bounce back from disturbances in infrastructure or services. MLOps engineers implement practices to enhance the reliability of the entire machine learning operations lifecycle, from data pipeline to model development to deployment. The machine learning system's reliability guarantees that it will function as planned under typical and unknown circumstances.

MLOps reliability is all about availability, resilience, and disaster recovery. It covers the system's functionality and workload testing during its whole lifecycle. In traditional on-premises setups, achieving reliability is difficult due to single points of failure, little automation, and low elasticity. Reliability makes it possible for the workload to be available as per requirement. It also dynamically adds processing power to the system to match demand and lessen interruptions from setup errors and temporary network problems.

MLOps Reliability Principles

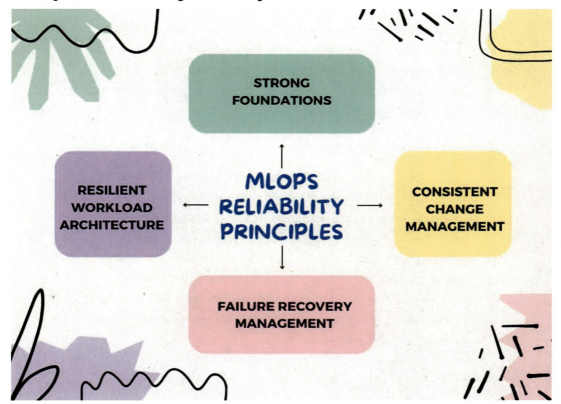

The following are the four principles on which MLOps reliability is based:

- **Strong Foundations**

  A strong foundation is necessary before architecting any reliable ML system.

  Strong fundamental foundation requirements are not limited to a single workload or project. A strong foundation can be implemented and used in various workloads and projects.

  The following are the focus points for this pillar:

- **Service Quota and Constraint Management**

  When planning your design, the service quotas and integrated services constraints should be taken into account. Quota management guards against service misuse and helps avoid inadvertently allocating more resources than required. It should be planned with adequate room to scale based on any anticipated increase in load requests.

- **Network Topology Planning**

  Workloads often exist in multiple cloud environments, so it is necessary to design your network topology. Network planning is necessary to ensure that the network is highly available, redundant, and scalable. This includes taking into account factors like intrasystem and intersystem connectivity, public and private IP address management, and domain name resolution. It should be able to address possible failures and accommodate future growth and integration with other systems and their networks.

- **Resilient Workload Architecture**

  The architecture of MLOps workloads must be resilient when creating design services across many business domains. Both software and infrastructure workload design decisions need to be robust and reliable. It should incorporate features like timeouts, throttle, retries, queue management, and emergency levers to prevent failures. To scale and innovate more quickly, use continuous improvement to break down your system into distributed services.

The following are the focus points for this section:

- **Workload Service Architecture Designing**

  A highly scalable, reliable, and resilient workload architecture is designed using a service-oriented architecture (SOA) or microservices architecture. A service-oriented architecture is the practice of making software components reusable via service interfaces. Common communication standards are used by SOA interfaces, allowing them to be quickly integrated into new workloads.

  Microservices architecture advanced by one step by making components smaller and simpler. They enable you to distinguish between the levels of availability needed for various services, allowing you to target investments more precisely at the microservices that require the highest levels of availability.

- **Interactive Distributed System Design to Prevent Failures**

  Distributed systems use communication networks to link their many components, including servers and services. In these networks, data loss or latency must not affect the dependability of your workload. The distributed system's components work together without interfering with one another or with the task. These practices increase the mean time between failures and prevent failures.

- **Consistent Change Management**

  To achieve reliable workload operations, any change in workload or its environment must be accommodated consistently throughout the MLOps lifecycle. These changes can be related to feature deployment, security patches, or any change on demand or business-related.

- The following are the focus points for this pillar:

  - **Workload Resources Monitoring**

    Continuous monitoring logs and metrics of various workload resources are important to gain insight into the health of your workload. Configuration can be done to monitor logs and metrics, and an alert is sent when thresholds are crossed or significant events occur. Monitoring is important for failure detecting failures and recovering from them automatically.

  - **Workload Design to Adapt to In-demand Changes**

    Workloads that are dependable and scalable provide flexibility to add, modify, or remove resources as needed to accommodate variations in demand at any given time. This makes workload architecture reliable for handling consistent changes efficiently.

  - **Changes Implementation**

    Deploying new functionality on successfully running operating systems, system workloads, and patched software requires controlled changes. It is challenging to anticipate the impact of these changes and to deal with problems that result from them if they become uncontrollable.

- **Failure Recovery Management**

  Although we have taken all the measures, MLOps systems have the potential for low-level and high-level failures that can impact workload. As a result, to construct a reliable workload, a few actions must be taken to implement a resilient ML system that can be recoverable from failures.

The following are the focus points for this pillar:

- **Data Back-up**

  Data backup along with applications and configuration
  backup is crucial for failure recovery management.

- **Workload Designing to Handle Component Failures**

  Workloads must be designed to withstand component failures
  with low recovery time and should be able to fulfill the high
  availability needs.

- **Reliability Test**

  For the live deployment environment, it is critical to ensure
  workload-resilient testing for reliability. Reliability testing is
  the way to ensure that the workload is designed, operates, and
  delivers the resiliency as per functional and nonfunctional
  requirements.

- **Disaster Recovery (DR) Planning**

  Disaster recovery planning is crucial and actions need
  to be taken in advance. Make a backup of your data and
  workload resources, and arrange for any redundant tasks to
  be completed beforehand. Disaster recovery focuses on time
  recovery with the recovery cost in check as per business value.

Importance of Reliability in MLOps

In today's modern era, machine learning operations (MLOps) is a crucial aspect of
machine learning. MLOps involves developing, deploying, managing, and monitoring
machine learning models in production environments. Every MLOps system requires
the implementation of a reliable machine learning system. In this article, we will discuss
the importance of reliability in MLOps.

- **Continuous Improvement**

  Implementing a reliable ML system leads to resilient workload architecture and disaster recovery is possible. It set up the foundation for continuous improvement in MLOps. Organizations can gain valuable insights by analyzing historical data, trends, and patterns and converting them into the long-term performance of machine learning models. This information can guide model retraining, feature engineering, and overall system enhancements to enhance accuracy, efficiency, and robustness continuously.

- **Early Fault Detection and Debugging**

  Continuous monitoring is required to detect anomalous activities. With proactive system monitoring, faults can be detected at early stages. If a malicious activity occurs, engineers lead incident response actions to lessen the effects, mitigate it, and stop it from happening again.

  For a reliable system's functionality, a proactive approach is required to predict challenges, address issues, and identify bottlenecks before they affect the system. Instead of reacting to problems, proactive monitoring and debudding the issue is instrumental in ensuring the early detection of issues, allowing for swift, reliable, and efficient resolution.

- **Performance Optimization**

  Reliable machine learning systems provide valuable insights into the performance of the ML models by analyzing logs, data, output, and configuration parameters. Thorough analysis helps in identifying system bottlenecks and providing resolution to them. Optimizing resource utilization with the best configurations can lead to improvement in the speed and overall efficiency of the models. This performance optimization is essential to achieve service-level agreements (SLAs) and guarantee seamless, reliable, and responsive user experiences.

- **Operational Resilience**

  Reliability in the MLOps system contributes to the operation resilience of machine learning models by monitoring critical performance configurations, efficient resource usage, and maintaining logs of relevant information. In the case of proactive anomaly detection and service interruption prevention, operational resiliency helps in maintaining high system uptime even in the face of changing environmental conditions or data patterns.

- **System Health Assurance**

  The ultimate responsibility of a reliable MLOps system is to safeguard the health of the entire machine learning operations ecosystem. With the efficient management of workload resources, planning for disaster recovery, and troubleshooting issues in real time, a reliable MLOps system contributes to the stability, scalability, and efficiency of data pipelines, models, and the underlying infrastructure.

CAP Theorem for MLOps Reliability

We can design a reliable MLOps system by understanding the CAP theorem that balances consistency, availability, and partition tolerance in a distributed ML system.

MLOps system must maintain model consistency and model availability across distributed nodes and clusters. An MLOps system needs to ensure good model performance despite the model being deployed across multiple environments or regions. Achieving a high-performing and reliable MLOps system is possible with the implementation of CAP theorem components in MLOps systems.

Three components need to be followed for the CAP theorem in MLOps for reliability:

1. Strong consistency

2. High availability

3. Partition tolerance

Pillars of MLOps Reliability

Availabilty

Availability means the percentage of time that a workload is available for use. and performs its agreed function successfully when required.

Resilience

Resiliency is the ability of a workload to recover from infrastructure or service disruptions like misconfiguration, component failure, software bugs, or network issues.

Disaster Recovery

Disaster Recovery (DR) is based on strategies to restore workload in the event of a disaster, such as a natural disaster, a significant technical failure, or human threats

There are three pillars of MLOps reliability.

1. **Availability**

    Availability, also known as *service availability*, is the percentage of time that a workload is available for use and performs its agreed-upon function as required successfully. Availability is calculated as the percentage of usage time availability over total time, such as a month or a year. In scheduled and unscheduled interruptions, availability is reduced anytime if the application is not operating normally. Availability is defined as follows:

$$Availability = \frac{Usage\ time\ availability}{Total\ time}$$

2. **Resiliency**

In general terms, resilience is the ability to recover from unanticipated accidents or change. In MLOps resiliency means a workload ability that can recover from infrastructure or service disruptions like misconfigurations, component failures, software bugs, or network issues by dynamically acquiring computing resources.

In MLOps, a resilient strategy is required to monitor workload resources and consider all the elements of business and technical metrics, such as notifications, automation, analysis, etc. With resilience, MLOps can produce a scalable, agile, robust, and reliable ML production model.

3. **Disaster Recovery (DR)**

The last pillar of a reliable MLOps system is disaster recovery strategies to recover your workload in case of a disaster event. Disaster recovery is the process of responding to one-time events such as natural catastrophes, significant technological malfunctions, or human hazards like mistakes or attacks.

Disaster recovery is not the same as availability, which calculates the average resilience across time to deal with software problems, load spikes, and component failures. It is based on strategies to restore workload in a disaster event, such as a natural disaster, a significant technical failure, or a human threat.

Best Practices to Ensure a Reliable ML System

Seven best practices need to be implemented to ensure reliability in a complete ML/AI system.

1. **Data Management Automation**

    During the MLOps lifecycle, data is managed, processed, and transformed in many ways to make it ready for machine learning modeling. All of the data-related management needs to be automated to make the system fast and reliable.

    The following are the key features of data management automation:

    - Automated data pipeline

    - Automatic check for data schema for concept drift

    - Automation of input data processing to convert it into needed format

    - Automation of input data transformation

    - Feature pipeline automation

2. **CI/CD Automation with Traceability**

CI/CD pipeline automation with traceability ensures reliable deployment. Automated CI/CD of the pipeline includes tasks for building, testing, and validating data, models, and components of the ML pipeline and the deployment of the model artifact into production.

The following are the key of CI/CD pipeline automation with traceability:

- Automated model training pipeline and tracing at all steps

- Automation tests running before deploying the ML model and related artifacts

- Automatically maintained centralized repository of models

- Automated testing and deployment of ML models

- Automatic testing of the model before going to production

- Reducing the development cycle time

3. **Feature Consistency**

Feature consistency needs to be maintained to reach the desired model output. If the input features to the model differ at training and serving time, it leads to training or serving skew. To avoid feature skew, features need to be kept tracked for consistency.

The following are the key features of feature consistency:

- Check for input features at training and inference time.

- Maintain a log of training and serving feature value.

- When it comes to the same feature, the values should be the same throughout training and serving.

- Check the feature for skewed values.

4. **Model Validation**

   Model validation needs to be done before deploying any ML model. It ensures good model performance on unknown data.

   The following are the key features of model validation:

   - Model validation is done through model pipeline automation.

   - Test data needs to be independent of training and validation data.

   - Validate the model performance for bias, variance, inclusion, and fairness.

   - Validate the model for error detection before deployment.

5. **Data Bias Detection and Mitigation**

   Keep a check on data bias to avoid data drift. When detecting biasing in data and mitigating, it is important to reach to desired model outputs.

   The following are the key features of data bias detection and mitigation:

   - Bias, variance, and fairness testing for the ML model performance.

   - Models should try to reach nearly zero bias.

   - Every change in data and ML model should be tracked.

   - Mitigate data bias during data gathering using different strategies.

6. **Deployment and Testing Strategy**

   After the model is developed, its deployment and testing strategy need to be executed so that the user can leverage the benefits of the ML model.

The following are the key features of the deployment and testing strategy:

- Continuous testing of critical infrastructure.

- Checking for biased system behavior.

- Checking for stability for data, code, and ML model.

- Testing for ML algorithms decisions aligned with business objectives.

- CI/CD automated pipelines are used for fast and reliable model deployment in production.

- The integration of the full ML pipeline should be tested.

7. **Version Control Management**

Version control management is crucial to track versions of data, code, and ML models. Versioning helps in keeping track of data, code, and model and also helps in reproducing the same result by rolling back quickly to previous versions.

The following are the key features of version control management:

- Keep track of different versions of data metadata, datasets, and features.

- Even slight changes in hyperparameters or configurations are tracked.

- There is an easy-to-meet client demand based on the previous set of features.

- All the experiments with the ML model can be tracked easily.

How to Implement Reliability in AWS

Reliability is the third key pillar of AWS's Well-Architected Framework. Reliability is crucial for every organization to run a consistent and reliable system. Throughout the machine learning lifecycle, the reliability pillar guarantees that a workload executes as expected, accurately and reliably, for the intended purpose.

There are five design principles for reliability to perform accurately: automatic failure recovery, recovery procedures testing, scaling horizontally to increase aggregate workload availability, capacity management, and automated change management.

This section will discuss the best practices that need to be followed to implement the reliability pillar in AWS.

Reliability Best Practices by ML Lifecycle Phase

The machine learning lifecycle consists of six phases. All the reliability best practices for AWS are divided among these phases. Let's discuss each best practice in detail.

1. **Business Goal Identification**

   Business goal identification is the first phase of the ML lifecycle. During the identification of business goals, there is no best practice to follow for reliability. Reliability best practices start for the ML problem-framing phase of the lifecycle.

2. **ML Problem Framing**

In this phase of the ML lifecycle, the machine learning problem is framed. In this phase, decisions are taken on which data must be observed, how to describe the target variables, and what needs to be predicted. Performance metrics are defined as this stage to optimize the ML model's performance.

The reliability best practice under ML problem framing is detailed here:

a. **Implementing API to Track Changes from Model-Consuming Applications**

There is a need to track changes introduced in applications from model consumption. These changes are tracked using flexible APIs. The main agenda is to introduce a model with no or minimal interruption to existing workload capabilities. This flexible API design helps minimize changes across all downstream ML applications. Its implementation plan is detailed here:

Adopt Best Practices for APIs

To introduce model changes without interfering with upstream interactions, expose your ML endpoints via APIs. Ensure that calling services quickly comprehend your API's routes and flags. It is necessary to document your API services in a common repository or documentation website. Ensure in case of any calling services or any changes you make to your API, it should be informed.

Model Deployment in Amazon SageMaker

Amazon SageMaker is a low-cost, fully managed infrastructure with tools (IDEs for data scientists and no-code interface for business analysts), and automated deployment of trained machine learning (ML) models to get accurate predictions. It also incorporates human feedback across the ML lifecycle to reach a high-performance ML system.

The features offered by Amazon SageMaker are as follows:

- SageMaker hosting services to get one prediction at a time for persistent real-time endpoints

- SageMaker batch transform to get predictions for an entire dataset

- Serverless Inference for workloads that have cold starts

- Tools for resource management and inference performance optimization while implementing machine learning models

Use Amazon API Gateway to create APIs

Amazon API Gateway is a fully managed AWS service that builds, publishes, maintains, monitors, and secures APIs at any scale. RESTful APIs and WebSocket APIs that allow for real-time two-way communication apps can be made with API Gateway. API Gateway supports all types of web apps and containerized and serverless workloads.

Figure 5-1 shows the API Gateway architecture, showing APIs built through Amazon API Gateway, which provides developers with an integrated and consistent developer experience for building AWS serverless applications.

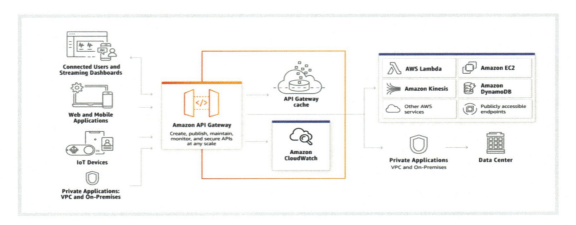

Figure 5-1. *Amazon API Gateway architecture*

The features offered by Amazon API Gateway are as follows:

- Effective API development because it allows for rapid testing, iteration, and version release

- High performance at any scale

- High-cost optimization

- Easy monitoring services

- Flexible security controls

The following Python code example demonstrates how to deploy API by using the AWS SDK for Python with API Gateway:

```python
class ApiGatewayToService:

    def __init__(self, apig_client):
        self.apig_client = apig_client
        self.api_id = None
        self.root_id = None
        self.stage = None

    def deploy_api(self, stage_name):
        try:
            self.apig_client.create_deployment(
                restApiId=self.api_id, stageName=stage_name
            )
            self.stage = stage_name
            logger.info("Deployed stage %s.", stage_name)
        except ClientError:
            logger.exception("Couldn't deploy stage %s.",
            stage_name)
            raise
        else:
            return self.api_url()
```

This code initializes an API Gateway client that deploys a REST API, which can be called from any REST client, such as the Python Requests package or Postman. It takes the parameter stage_name as input and returns the base URL of the deployed REST API.

b. **Implementing Microservice Strategy for ML**

Sometimes, there is a requirement to decompose a large complex business problem into multiple small problems with a loosely coupled implementation. This can be achieved by implementing a microservice strategy for machine learning models instead of a monolithic architecture. This approach facilitates dispersed development, enhances scalability, and simple change management, and reduces the impact of a single failure on the overall workload. Its implementation plan is detailed here:

Adopting a Microservice Strategy

To adopt a microservice strategy, service-oriented architecture (SOA) is implemented where the application is broken into separate components. These components are well connected via APIs and can be run as per usage unlike a monolithic application, where all functionality is contained in a single runtime. See Figure 5-2.

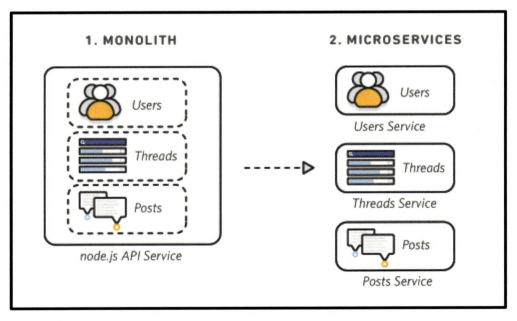

Figure 5-2. *Distributing a monolith application into microservices*

In monolithic architectures, all application operations operate as a single service because they are tightly coupled as a single unit. In a microservices architecture, each service is built as an independent component where each process runs independently. Communication between these independent services is done using lightweight APIs. Each service can be updated, launched, and expanded to match the demand for particular functions of an application, with no need to scale the entire application like monolithic architecture.

Use AWS Services in Developing Microservices

AWS offers two services for developing microservices for ML.

1. **AWS Lambda**

   With AWS Lambda, applications can be run virtually without worrying about servers or clusters. It is a very cost-effective service as developers pay only for the consumed computing time.

   The main features of AWS Lambda are as follows:

   - It is a cost-effective and serverless computing service.

   - It quickly processes data and workflows at scale automatically.

   - Code can easily be run without any infrastructure management and provisioning.

   - Performance and code execution time can be optimized with AWS Lambda.

   The following Python code example demonstrates how to create a Lambda function using AWS SDK included in the Python:

```python
import boto3
import botocore

def lambda_handler(event, context):
    print(f'boto3 version: {boto3.__version__}')
    print(f'botocore version: {botocore.__version__}')
```

The previous Python code creates AWS Lambda that runs in an environment that includes the SDK for Python (Boto3) to provide runtimes to process events.

2. **AWS Fargate**

AWS Fargate is a serverless container management service that can run these containers without provisioning, configuring, and scaling clusters of virtual machines. AWS Fargate's complete focus is on building applications and accelerating the process to production.

Figure 5-3 shows who the AWS Fargate architecture contains an image that defines the required memory and compute resources to run and manage applications.

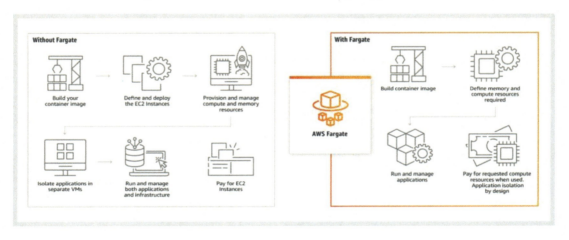

Figure 5-3. *AWS Fargate architecture*

The main features of AWS Fargate are as follows:

- It deploys and manages your applications, not infrastructure.

- It monitors your application to gain insights into it.

- It improves security through workload isolation by design.

- It optimizes cost by removing operational overhead.

3. **Data Processing**

Data processing is the third stage of the ML lifecycle that comes before model development. Data needs to be processed to get it ready for model development. It contains various steps like data collection, data preparation, data cleaning, missing data imputation, data scaling, and feature engineering. Two best practices come under data processing for the reliability pillar as detailed here:

a. **Implementing a Data Catalog Usage**

A Data Catalog is an essential component of a data lake built on Amazon S3 that discovers, prepares, moves, integrates, and processes data across multiple data sources in data lake S3 buckets. It enables ETL process integration with data tracking and version management, thus offering more reliability and efficiency. Its implementation plan is detailed here:

Use AWS Glue Data Catalog

AWS Glue Data Catalog is used to keep track of the data assets that have been added to your machine-learning task. Furthermore, data catalogs describe the transformations made to the data as it is fed into warehouses and data lakes. Extract, transform, and load (ETL) services are entirely managed by AWS Glue. It makes it possible to organize your data, clean it up, enrich it, and transfer it reliably between different data sources and repositories easily and affordably.

Figure 5-4 shows the building of the AWS Glue Data Catalog, which is a database that stores metadata in tables consisting of data schema, data location, and runtime metrics.

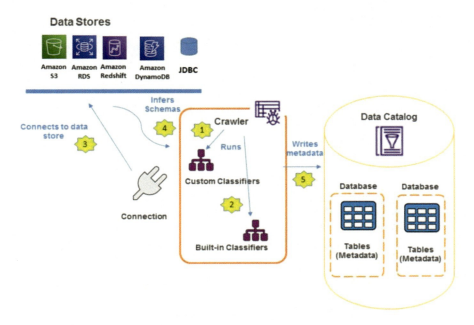

Figure 5-4. *AWS Glue Data Catalog*

The main features of the AWS Glue Data Catalog are as follows:

- Automatically discover data and organize it to build a data lake.

- Automatically extract, transform, prepare, clean, and load data for analysis.

- Complex ETL pipelines are built with simple job scheduling.

- Automatically build and scale data pipelines and monitor jobs.

b. **Implementing a Data Pipeline Usage**

A data pipeline is used to automate the process of data processing, movement, transformation, integration, and delivery between different computing and storage services. Because of this, the data processing is highly available, reproducible, and fault-tolerant. Its implementation plan is detailed here:

Use Amazon SageMaker Data Wrangler and Pipelines

Two steps are followed in implementing an automatic data pipeline to automate data processing and deployment.

1. **Amazon SageMaker Data Wrangler**

   SageMaker Data Wrangler is the easiest and simplest method to select data, clean, process, explore, and visualize it before exporting it to SageMaker Pipelines. It is scaled to process petabytes of data through a visual and natural language interface.

   Figure 5-5 shows Amazon SageMaker Data Wrangler Architecture, which visually aggregates and prepares data for ML.

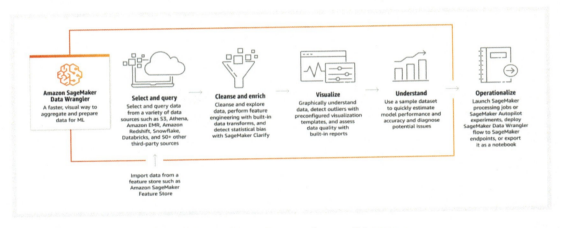

Figure 5-5. *Amazon SageMaker Data Wrangler architecture*

   The key features of SageMaker Data Wrangler are as follows:

   - It prepared data within minutes for machine learning modeling.

   - Diagnosing data anomalies before models are deployed ensures high-accuracy models.

   - It works with no or minimal code.

2. **Amazon SageMaker Pipelines**

   Amazon SageMaker Pipelines is an automated way to move and transform processed data from SageMaker Data Wrangler in your ML workload workflows. It automates the process of model deployment and management. Inaccuracies and inconsistencies may arise when data is moved and transformed manually. It helps reduce errors and save time as well.

The key features of SageMaker Pipelines are as follows:

- Automate the model development lifecycle.

- Build and automate the end-to-end MLOps workflows.

- Easily manage ML workloads at scale as per organizational needs.

c.   **Implementing Automated Data Change Management**

In the data processing phase, automated data change management to track changes in training data is implemented. Training data changes are tracked via version control technology. In the event of failure, rolling back to the exact model version is possible to reproduce the desired results. Its implementation plan is detailed here:

MLOps Workload Orchestrator on AWS

MLOps Workload Orchestrator on AWS provides a standard interface for managing automation tools and ML pipelines to simplify machine learning model development and production. The solution's template allows you to upload your trained models, often known as bring your model (BYOM). It sets up the pipeline's orchestration and monitors its operations. It keeps track of model versions, artifacts, lineage, and metadata using SageMaker Model Registry. This solution makes it possible to replicate effective procedures at a large scale, which boosts agility and efficiency.

4.   **Model Development**

After data processing comes the model development stage where a model is built, trained, fine-tuned, and evaluated. In model development, all the model building, training, and release to staging and production environment processes are automated using the CI/CD pipeline. The reliability best practice under model development is detailed here:

a. **Implementing CI/CD/CT Automation with Traceability**

The first best practice for model development for reliability is implementing CI/CD/CT automation with traceability to ML workload operations. It offers version control of the ML workload's source code, data, and artifacts. This makes rollback to a specific version easy. Its implementation plan is detailed here:

Use Amazon SageMaker Pipelines

Amazon SageMaker Pipelines is the first purpose-built service for machine learning workflows. It includes continuous integration (CI), continuous delivery (CD), and continuous training (CT) services that help in creating, automating, and managing end-to-end ML workflows at scale. Automated SageMaker Pipelines are cost and time-optimized and offer reproducibility by rollback to the required version in case of failure.

b. **Implementing Feature Consistency across Training and Inference**

For model development, it is necessary to have scalable, consistent, and highly available features across training and inference. This can be implemented using the Amazon SageMaker feature store which helps in reducing training-serving skew by keeping consistency in features between training and inference. Its implementation plan is detailed here:

Use Amazon SageMaker Feature Store

Amazon SageMaker Feature Store is used to create, share, and manage features for machine learning development. It is a centralized store that stores features and their related metadata for both training and inference, so that features can be easily discoverable. The key features of the feature store are as follows:

- An online feature store is used for low latency, real-time inference use cases.

- An offline feature store is used for training and batch inference.

- Reduce the repetitive data processing work.

- Reduce the training-serving skew.

- It offers feature storage, feature consistency, feature reuse, feature catalog, and feature standardization.

- It integrates with Amazon SageMaker Pipelines that support MLOps practices and speed time to model deployment.

c. **Implementing Model Validation Assurance**

In the model development phase, the model is also validated and assured with relevant data. Data that is included for validation needs to be real and representative. Data needs to include all possible scenarios and patterns that will result in failures once the model is in production. Always examine the inference data and the training, validation, and test data for any discrepancies in distribution. Its implementation plan is detailed here:

Use Amazon SageMaker Experiments

Amazon SageMaker Experiments are used to organize, track, compare, and evaluate machine-learning experiments. It helps in efficient experimentation with the foundation model, its testing, and validation using data with all possible patterns they will encounter in production. Data used for validation at this stage consists of both real-world and engineered data to avoid errors and failures when the model is deployed in production. Using the Amazon SageMaker Experiments, the models seamlessly transit from experimentation to production without failures.

Use Amazon SageMaker Model Monitor

Amazon SageMaker Model Monitor is used to test and monitor endpoints periodically for any deviation in model performance. It also monitors the quality of machine learning models in production. With Amazon SageMaker Model Monitor:

- It is easy to detect deviation at early stages and corrective actions are taken accordingly.

- Alerts are raised in case of deviation in model quality.

- Continuous monitoring with a real-time endpoint and batch transform job runs regularly.

- On-schedule monitoring for asynchronous batch transform jobs.

d. **Implementing Data Bias Detection and Mitigation**

Data bias detection and mitigation are important to avoid inaccurate model results. Data bias detection methodologies must be established at the data preparation stage long before model training. Once the model is in production, continuously monitor, detect, and mitigate bias. Create feedback loops to monitor the drift over time and start the retraining process. Its implementation plan is detailed here:

Use Amazon SageMaker to Clarify

Amazon SageMaker Clarify detects potential bias to improve machine learning models and explains how these models make predictions. The fairness and explainability functionality provided by SageMaker Clarify takes a step toward enabling you to build trustworthy and understandable ML models. The Amazon SageMaker Clarify helps in the following tasks:

- Evaluate the foundation model in minutes and evaluate the model predictions.

- Assess biases that could arise at every phase of the machine learning life cycle. Data gathering, model training, model tuning, and model monitoring are some of these phases.

- Generate model governance reports targeting potential risk, compliance terms, and external regulators.

5. **Model Deployment**

Once a model has undergone training, tuning, evaluation, and validation, it can be deployed into production. After that, conclusions, predictions, forecasts, and inferences can be made against the model. The reliability best practice under model deployment is detailed here:

a. **Implementing Endpoint Changes through Automated Pipeline**

Endpoint changes can be implemented through the automated pipeline as manual changes are error-prone and high in cost and effort. Automated pipelines are integrated with a change management tracking system to deploy changes to your model endpoints. As we discussed earlier, the versioned pipeline artifacts and inputs let you keep track of modifications and immediately roll back them when they don't work. Its implementation plan is detailed here:

Use Amazon SageMaker Pipelines

Amazon SageMaker Pipelines lets you design, automate, and oversee end-to-end machine learning processes at scale with easy-to-build, user-friendly continuous integration, and continuous delivery (CI/CD) service. Deploying changes through the SageMaker Pipelines is a safe engineering method with consistent MLOps process automation.

b. **Implementing Appropriate Deployment and Testing Strategy**

Implementing an appropriate deployment and testing strategy is crucial. Deployment and testing strategies must be selected according to business needs.

A performance metric is used to evaluate model performance to identify when a rollback or roll-forward is required. Take into consideration the following factors for each model when designing for rollback or roll forward:

- Where is the model artifact stored?

- Are model artifacts versioned?

- What changes are included in each version?

- For a deployed endpoint, which model version is deployed?

Its implementation plan is detailed here:

Deployment/Testing in Amazon SageMaker

There are two options available in Amazon SageMaker to test and deploy updated models in production and real-world scenarios.

1. **Blue/green deployments using Amazon SageMaker**

   When updating a SageMaker real-time endpoint, Amazon SageMaker automatically employs a blue/green deployment to maximize the availability of your endpoints. The key features of blue/green deployments in SageMaker are as follows:

   - Traffic shifting modes to give more granular control over shifting traffic between the blue and green fleet.

   - The baking period is a predetermined amount of time to monitor the green fleet before proceeding to the next deployment stage.

   - Auto-rollbacks are initiated to the blue fleet to maintain availability thereby minimizing risk.

213

2. **Canary Deployment using Amazon SageMaker**

Amazon SageMaker offers the canary deployment option,
which lets you shift one small portion of your traffic (a
canary) to the green fleet and monitor it for a baking
period. The remaining traffic is moved from the blue
fleet to the green fleet if the canary on the green fleet is
successful, and then the blue fleet is stopped.

The following section is the Python code example that
demonstrates how to update an endpoint with canary
traffic shifting using an API named UpdateEndpoint.

```python
import boto3
client = boto3.client("sagemaker")

response = client.update_endpoint(
    EndpointName="<your-endpoint-name>",
    EndpointConfigName="<your-config-name>",
    DeploymentConfig={
        "BlueGreenUpdatePolicy": {
            "TrafficRoutingConfiguration": {
                "Type": "CANARY",
                "CanarySize": {
                    "Type": "CAPACITY_PERCENT",
                    "Value": 30
                },
                "WaitIntervalInSeconds": 600
            },
            "TerminationWaitInSeconds": 600,
            "MaximumExecutionTimeoutInSeconds": 1800
        },
        "AutoRollbackConfiguration": {
            "Alarms": [
                {
                    "AlarmName": "<your-cw-alarm>"
                }
            ]
```

```
            }
        }
    )
```

When updating your endpoint, instead of giving DeploymentConfig here, you can use the RetainDeploymentConfig option to retain the deployment configuration that was specified at the time of endpoint creation. Set RetainDeploymentConfig to True to keep the original endpoint deployment configuration.

Linear Deployment using Amazon SageMaker

You can progressively move traffic from your old fleet (blue fleet) to your new fleet (green fleet) by using linear traffic shifting. By using many steps to transfer traffic, linear traffic shifting reduces the possibility of an endpoint disruption. You have the most precise control over traffic shifting with this blue/green deployment option.

The following Python code example demonstrates how to update an endpoint with linear traffic shifting using an API named UpdateEndpoint:

```python
import boto3
client = boto3.client("sagemaker")

response = client.update_endpoint(
    EndpointName="<your-endpoint-name>",
    EndpointConfigName="<your-config-name>",
    DeploymentConfig={
        "BlueGreenUpdatePolicy": {
            "TrafficRoutingConfiguration": {
                "Type": "LINEAR",
                "CanarySize": {
                    "Type": "CAPACITY_PERCENT",
                    "Value": 30
                },
```

```
                    "WaitIntervalInSeconds": 600
                },
                "TerminationWaitInSeconds": 600,
                "MaximumExecutionTimeoutInSeconds": 1800
            },
            "AutoRollbackConfiguration": {
                "Alarms": [
                    {
                        "AlarmName": "<your-cw-alarm>"
                    }
                ]
            }
        }
    }
)
```

Set RetainDeploymentConfig to True to preserve the original
endpoint settings while updating.

A/B Testing Using Amazon SageMaker

A useful last step in the validation process for a new model
is to run A/B testing with production traffic between the new
model and the old model. A/B testing entails evaluating several
versions of the model and comparing each iteration to how well
each performs. If a newer version of the model performs better
than an earlier version, the earlier version should be replaced in
production with the updated version.

6. **Model Monitoring**

   Model monitoring is the last stage of the machine learning
   lifecycle. A model monitoring system uses early detection and
   mitigation to ensure model performance at an optimum level. The
   reliability best practice under model monitoring is detailed here:

   a. **Implementing Automatic Scaling of the Model Endpoint**

      In the environment of changing workloads, capabilities
      need to be implemented that ensure reliable processing
      and automatic scaling of model endpoints. Incorporate

endpoint monitoring to find the threshold at which resources are added or removed to meet demand. In case of scaling request is received, a solution is placed to scale backend resources supporting that endpoint. Its implementation plan is detailed here:

Configure Automatic Scaling for Amazon SageMaker Endpoints

Automatic scaling is configured using Amazon SageMaker for your hosted models. Auto scaling ensures your SageMaker endpoints maintain the same level of service, in case of traffic increase in your application. It is a key feature in cloud services that automatically provision new resources to handle the increase in system loss or user demand. In a distributed system, auto-scaling removes unnecessary instances when the workload decreases, so customers don't have to pay for provisioned instances that are not in use.

Use Amazon Elastic Inference

With Amazon Elastic Inference, the CPU instance in AWS is chosen based on the overall computing and memory needs of the application. By configuring the appropriate amount of GPU-powered inference acceleration separately, you may effectively use resources and reduce inference costs by up to 75%.

The key benefits of Amazon Elastic Inference are as follows:

- The inference cost is redacted by 75%.

- Amazon Elastic Inference provides trillion floating point operations per second (TFLOPS) of inference acceleration as per the requirements.

- Scale the amount of inference to meet the application demands without over-provisioning capacity.

Use Amazon Elastic Inference with EC2 Auto Scaling

EC2 Auto Scaling is used in Amazon Elastic Inference to virtually create a secure and autoscale compute capacity for any workload in the cloud. Amazon EC2 is a service offered by Amazon known as the Amazon Elastic Compute Cloud web service.

The key features of EC2 Auto Scaling are as follows:

- It is reliable, accessible, and scalable on-demand within minutes.

- It offers secure computing for your applications.

- Its performance can be optimized and cost-effective with flexible options.

b. **Implementing a Managed Version Control Strategy.**

All data, models, artifacts, container images, metadata, and endpoint configuration need to be version-controlled. Implementing a managed version-controlled strategy is crucial for data monitoring and rollback to the required version in case of failures. Ensure that every component that goes into creating the endpoint that hosts the model predictions, as well as the endpoint itself, is fully recoverable, version-controlled, and traceable in a lineage tracker system. Its implementation plan is detailed here:

Implement MLOps Best Practices with Amazon SageMaker Projects

Amazon SageMaker Projects with CI/CD pipelines are used to implement MLOps best practices. Amazon SageMaker Projects enable teams of data scientists and MLOps engineers to collaborate on machine learning business problems. It is a Service Catalog–provisioned product that helps in the easy creation of an end-to-end ML solution. Pipeline executions, registered models, endpoints, datasets, dependency management, build reproducibility, and code repositories are examples of entities found in SageMaker projects.

Every SageMaker project is assigned a unique name and ID, which serve as tags for all the AWS and SageMaker resources that are generated within the project. With the name and ID, all the entities associated with your project can be viewed as mentioned here:

- SageMaker Pipelines

- Registered models

- Deployed models (endpoints)

- Model Registry

- Datasets

- Service Catalog products

- CodePipeline and Jenkins pipelines

- CodeCommit and third-party Git repositories

Use Infrastructure as Code (IaC) Tools

Use IaC tools like Amazon CloudFormation are used to create and build your infrastructure, including your model endpoints. To version control your infrastructure code, save your CloudFormation code in Git repositories like AWS CodeCommit.

Use Amazon Elastic Container Registry (Amazon ECR)

Use Amazon ECR, a Docker container artifact repository, to store your containers. As you change your containers, Amazon ECR automatically generates a version hash for them, enabling you to revert to earlier versions.

There are five components of Amazon ECR as mentioned here:

1. **The Amazon ECR Private Registry** is provided to each AWS account in which one or more repositories are created.

2. **An authorization token** authenticates an Amazon ECR private registry as an AWS user before it can push and pull images.

3. **A repository** contains Docker images, Open Container Initiative (OCI) images, and OCI-compatible artifacts.

4. **Repository policies** are used to control access to repositories and their content.

5. **Container images** can be pushed or pulled into your repositories.

Final Thoughts

In conclusion, MLOps empowers machine learning engineers to build robust and reliable models with ensured sustained performance by seamlessly integrating smart workload availability, resiliency, and disaster recovery processes.

The reliable MLOps system revolutionizes the way machine learning projects are implemented and optimized to reach new heights of its potential performance. Nowadays, organizations strive to offer completely deployed MLOps solutions at scale while preserving agility and reliability.

References

- https://docs.aws.amazon.com/wellarchitected/latest/reliability-pillar/welcome.html

- https://docs.aws.amazon.com/wellarchitected/latest/machine-learning-lens/best-practices-by-pillar.html#bp-rel

- https://docs.aws.amazon.com/wellarchitected/latest/machine-learning-lens/best-practices-by-ml-lifecycle-phase.html#ml-problem-framing-phase

- https://aws.amazon.com/sagemaker/

- https://aws.amazon.com/api-gateway/

- https://docs.aws.amazon.com/code-library/latest/ug/
  python_3_api-gateway_code_examples.html

- https://aws.amazon.com/microservices/

- https://docs.aws.amazon.com/lambda/latest/dg/lambda-
  python.html

- https://aws.amazon.com/fargate/

- https://docs.aws.amazon.com/whitepapers/latest/building-
  data-lakes/data-cataloging.html

- https://aws.amazon.com/sagemaker/data-wrangler/

- https://aws.amazon.com/solutions/implementations/mlops-
  workload-orchestrator/

- https://docs.aws.amazon.com/sagemaker/latest/dg/deployment-
  guardrails-blue-green-canary.html

- https://docs.aws.amazon.com/sagemaker/latest/dg/deployment-
  guardrails-blue-green-linear.html

- https://docs.aws.amazon.com/sagemaker/latest/dg/sagemaker-
  projects-whatis.html

- https://pixabay.com/

- https://aws.amazon.com/api-gateway/

- https://www.wellarchitectedlabs.com/reliability/

- https://aws.amazon.com/microservices/

- https://aws.amazon.com/fargate/

- https://docs.aws.amazon.com/whitepapers/latest/building-
  data-lakes/data-cataloging.html

- https://aws.amazon.com/sagemaker/data-wrangler/

CHAPTER 6

Performance Efficiency in MLOps

Performance efficiency is a critical aspect of any well-architected machine learning operations (MLOps) framework. It is one of the foundational pillars of the AWS Well-Architected Framework, underscoring the importance of efficiently utilizing computing resources to meet evolving requirements. This principle is essential not only for managing current demands but also for adapting to future technological advancements.

Performance efficiency is defined as the optimal use of computing resources to meet system requirements, ensuring that these resources are used effectively as demand fluctuates and new technologies emerge. The focus areas for achieving performance efficiency include selecting appropriate resources, continuously reviewing and monitoring system performance, and making informed trade-offs to balance various aspects of performance.

In the context of MLOps, performance efficiency is paramount for several reasons. First, it ensures that machine learning models and pipelines operate smoothly and reliably, providing consistent and accurate results. Second, efficient resource utilization helps to reduce operational costs, which is crucial for the scalability and sustainability of ML initiatives. Finally, maintaining high-performance efficiency is essential for delivering real-time predictions and insights, which can significantly enhance decision-making processes and overall business value.

To effectively measure and manage performance efficiency in MLOps, it is important to track key performance metrics. These metrics provide insights into various aspects of system performance and help identify areas for improvement. The primary metrics include the following:

© Neel Sendas and Deepali Rajale 2024
N. Sendas and D. Rajale, *The Definitive Guide to Machine Learning Operations in AWS*,
https://doi.org/10.1007/979-8-8688-1076-3_6

- **Throughput:** This measures the amount of data processed by the system over a given period, indicating the system's capacity to handle large volumes of data.

- **Latency:** This measures the time taken to process a single data point or request, highlighting the system's responsiveness.

- **Resource Utilization:** This tracks the usage of computing resources such as CPU, GPU, and memory, ensuring that resources are used optimally without wastage.

- **Scalability:** This evaluates the system's ability to scale up or down in response to changing demands, ensuring consistent performance under varying workloads.

The objective of this chapter is to provide a comprehensive guide on improving performance efficiency in MLOps. It will explore best practices for selecting and managing resources, techniques for continuous monitoring and performance review, and strategies for making effective trade-offs to balance performance with other operational requirements. By the end of this chapter, readers will have a thorough understanding of how to enhance the performance efficiency of their MLOps workflows, ensuring robust, cost-effective, and scalable machine learning operations.

Understanding Performance Efficiency Drivers for ML Lifecycle

The ML lifecycle is the cyclic iterative process with instructions and best practices to use across defined phases while developing an ML workload (see Figure 6-1). It includes the following phases:

- Business goal identification

- ML problem framing

- Data processing (data collection, data preprocessing, feature engineering)

- Model development (training, tuning, evaluation)

- Model deployment (inference, prediction)

- Model monitoring

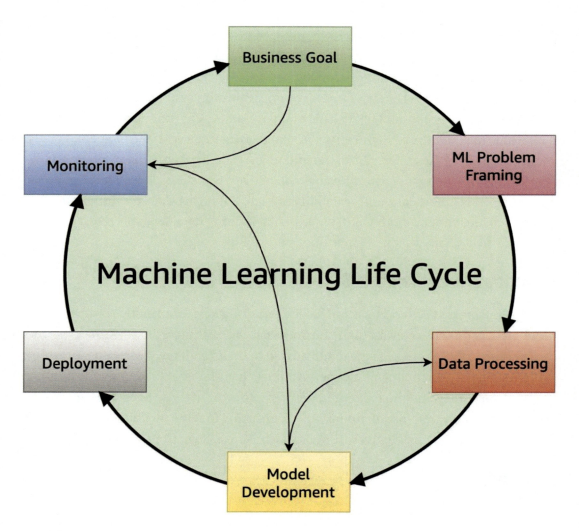

Figure 6-1. *Machine learning lifecycle*

Source: https://docs.aws.amazon.com/wellarchitected/latest/machine-learning-lens/well-architected-machine-learning-lifecycle.html

Each phase of the ML lifecycle has the potential to implement best practices to optimize performance.

Defining Business Goals and Framing the Machine Learning Problem

Identifying business goals is the most crucial phase of the ML lifecycle. Organizations must have a clear understanding of the problem they aim to solve and the business value they expect to gain. It's essential to measure this value against specific objectives and success criteria. This step is particularly challenging for ML solutions due to the constantly evolving nature of the technology.

After defining success criteria, assess your organization's capacity to achieve these goals. The target should be realistic and pave the way to production. Engaging all relevant stakeholders from the outset is vital to align them with the target and any new business processes arising from the initiative. Begin by evaluating whether ML is the right approach to meet your business objectives. Consider all available options, assessing the accuracy, cost, and scalability of each. For an ML-based solution to be effective, ensure you have sufficient, high-quality training data. Evaluate data sources thoroughly to confirm their relevance and accessibility.

Guidance from Business Stakeholders

Involving business stakeholders is crucial for capturing key performance indicators (KPIs) that are directly relevant to the business use case. By incorporating their insights, you can ensure that these KPIs are tightly linked to the overall business value, providing clear guidance on acceptable model performance. It is essential to identify the minimum acceptable accuracy and the maximum permissible error in these KPIs. This approach helps manage the variability in model results, ensuring that the machine learning solutions align with and effectively support the business objectives.

Quantify Business Value

Identifying business goals is the most crucial phase of the ML lifecycle. Organizations must have a clear understanding of the problem they aim to solve and the business value they expect to gain. It's essential to measure this value against specific objectives and success criteria. This step is particularly challenging for ML solutions due to the constantly evolving nature of the technology. Follow these best practices:

1. Define a success criteria and assess your organization's capacity to achieve these goals. The target should be realistic and pave the way to production. Engaging all relevant stakeholders from the outset is vital to align them with the target and any new business processes arising from the initiative.

2. Consider evaluating if ML is the right approach to meet your business objectives. Consider all available options, assessing the accuracy, cost, and scalability of each. For an ML-based solution to be effective, ensure you have sufficient, high-quality training data. Evaluate data sources thoroughly to confirm their relevance and accessibility.

Align ML Problems with Business Challenges

Organizations must have a clear understanding of the problem they aim to solve and the business value they expect to gain. It's essential to measure this value against specific objectives and success criteria. After defining success criteria, assess your organization's capacity to achieve these goals. The target should be realistic and pave the way to production. Engaging all relevant stakeholders from the outset is vital to align them with the target and any new business processes arising from the initiative.

Begin by evaluating whether ML is the right approach to meet your business objectives. Consider all available options, assessing the accuracy, cost, and scalability of each. For an ML-based solution to be effective, ensure you have sufficient, high-quality training data. Evaluate data sources thoroughly to confirm their relevance and accessibility.

To effectively frame an ML problem, clearly define the inputs, desired outputs, and the key performance metric to optimize. Ensure model performance aligns with business expectations by using metrics that capture the business's tolerance for error. Develop custom metrics tailored to specific business goals, and utilize standard metrics such as precision, recall, accuracy, F1 score, RMSE, and MAPE to comprehensively evaluate and validate the model's performance.

Data Processing

In the evolving landscape of machine learning operations (MLOps), the efficiency of data processing is paramount. Modern data architectures are designed to handle the exponential growth of data by integrating various data storage and processing technologies seamlessly. These architectures enable the fluid movement of data between data lakes and purpose-built data stores, such as data warehouses, relational and nonrelational databases, and big data processing platforms.

Modern Data Architecture for MLOps

A modern data architecture is the backbone of effective data processing in MLOps. It provides a flexible and scalable environment where data can be ingested, stored, processed, and analyzed. Key components of this architecture include the following.

Centralized Data Lakes

A data lake serves as a centralized repository that can store vast amounts of structured, semi-structured, and unstructured data. It provides a unified platform for running analytics and machine learning workflows across diverse data structures, enabling organizations to extract valuable insights from disparate data sources efficiently. The flexibility of a data lake is crucial for MLOps, as it supports the collection and processing of the varied data types needed for model training and evaluation.

Figure 6-2 shows an example lake house architecture with five logical layers, where each layer is composed of multiple purpose-built components that address specific requirements.

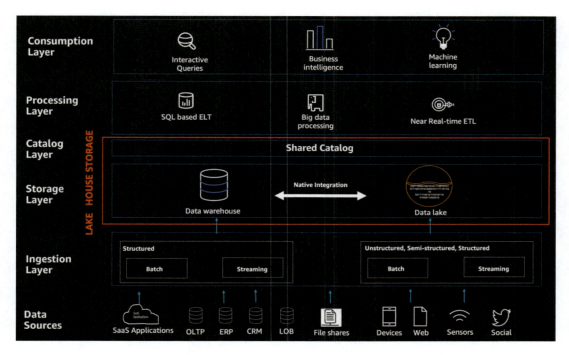

Figure 6-2. *Data Lake House architecture*

Source: `https://aws.amazon.com/blogs/big-data/build-a-lake-house-architecture-on-aws/`

- **Data Sources Layer:** This layer is responsible for collecting data from a wide array of sources, both structured (e.g., ERP, CRM applications) and unstructured (e.g., web apps, IoT devices, social media). These data sources provide continuous streams or batched data, depending on the nature of the application.

- **Data Ingestion Layer:** The ingestion layer manages the flow of data from various sources into the lakehouse storage. It supports both batch processing and real-time streaming, ensuring that data is efficiently ingested into the system for further processing. The flexibility to connect to a range of data sources over multiple protocols is key to maintaining a continuous and reliable data flow.

- **Data Storage Layer:** At the core of the Lake House architecture, the storage layer integrates a data lake with a data warehouse, enabling the storage of structured, semi-structured, and unstructured data.

The storage is cost-efficient and scalable, handling everything from raw data to processed, trusted datasets. It allows for the organization of data into zones based on its readiness for consumption, such as raw, trusted, and curated data.

- **Data Processing Layer:** This layer transforms raw data into actionable insights through validation, normalization, transformation, and enrichment. It utilizes a combination of SQL, big data processing, and real-time ETL tools. The processing layer is designed to handle diverse data formats and can scale effectively to meet varying workload demands.

- **Data Consumption Layer:** The final layer provides access to the processed data for various use cases, including business intelligence (BI), machine learning (ML), and analytics. It democratizes data access across the organization, allowing different user personas to interact with and derive insights from the data. This layer supports a unified interface, ensuring seamless access to data stored across the Lake House architecture.

Together, these layers provide a comprehensive framework that integrates diverse data sources, processes them efficiently, and makes them accessible for a wide range of analytical applications, enabling organizations to derive meaningful insights and drive business outcomes.

Purpose-Built Data Stores

Modern data architectures incorporate purpose-built stores tailored to specific use cases. For instance, data warehouses are optimized for large-scale query processing, making them ideal for aggregating and analyzing large datasets. Relational and non-relational databases offer high performance for transactional and real-time processing needs, respectively. In the context of MLOps, these specialized data stores allow for the rapid retrieval and processing of data required for different stages of the machine learning lifecycle, from data preprocessing to real-time model inference.

Enhancing Data Movement and Integration

Efficient data processing in MLOps requires seamless movement and integration of data across various storage solutions and processing engines. This involves the following:

- **Data Pipelines:** Automated data pipelines are essential for moving data between data lakes and purpose-built stores. These pipelines ensure that the right data is available at the right time for model training, validation, and inference, reducing latency and improving processing performance.

- **ETL Processes:** Extract, transform, load (ETL) processes play a crucial role in preparing data for machine learning tasks. By optimizing ETL processes, organizations can reduce the time and resources required to clean, transform, and load data into the desired format, ensuring that models are trained on high-quality data.

Leveraging Real-Time Analytics and Processing

Real-time analytics is becoming increasingly important in MLOps, particularly for applications that require immediate insights and decision-making.

- **Streaming Data Processing:** Streaming data processing technologies allow organizations to process data in real-time as it is ingested. This is particularly useful for applications such as real-time dashboards, anomaly detection, and log analytics, where timely data processing is critical.

- **In-Memory Computing:** In-memory computing solutions enhance data processing speed by storing data in memory rather than on disk. This reduces the time needed for data retrieval and processing, leading to faster model training and inference in MLOps.

Exploratory Data Analysis (EDA)

Effective data processing ensures that raw data is transformed into a format that models can efficiently use for training and inference. This process includes exploratory data analysis (EDA), data preparation, and feature engineering, each of which plays a critical role in optimizing data processing performance.

EDA is the foundational step in data processing where data scientists explore and understand the structure, patterns, and relationships within the dataset. The iterative nature of EDA allows for the creation of reproducible, editable, and shareable datasets. By leveraging tools that support visualization and statistical analysis, data teams can identify key features, outliers, and correlations that inform subsequent stages of the ML lifecycle. Optimizing EDA involves automating repetitive tasks, enabling collaboration across teams, and ensuring that insights can be easily shared and revisited as the project evolves.

Data Preparation and Feature Engineering

Data preparation is the process of cleaning, transforming, and structuring data for machine learning models. This step often involves handling missing values, normalizing data, and aggregating information from multiple sources. Feature engineering, on the other hand, involves creating new features or refining existing ones to enhance model performance. The visibility and reusability of features across teams are critical for efficiency; hence, the use of a centralized feature store becomes essential. This not only standardizes feature engineering practices but also reduces redundancy and ensures consistency across models.

Feature stores are specialized systems that manage the entire lifecycle of features, from creation to consumption. They enable teams to share and reuse features across different projects, ensuring that best practices are maintained and that models benefit from well-engineered features. Feature stores also support versioning and tracking, allowing teams to monitor how features evolve over time and how they impact model performance.

To optimize data processing performance, it's crucial to automate data preparation and feature engineering tasks as much as possible. This includes using distributed computing frameworks to handle large datasets, employing parallel processing to speed up computations, and caching intermediate results to avoid redundant calculations. Additionally, adopting a schema-on-read approach can allow for more flexibility in handling diverse data formats without the need for upfront schema definitions.

Optimizing Resource Utilization

Efficient data processing in MLOps also depends on optimizing the use of computational resources. Strategies include the following:

- **Autoscaling:** Implementing autoscaling for data processing workloads ensures that computational resources are allocated dynamically based on demand. This helps to optimize cost and performance by scaling resources up or down as needed.

- **Serverless Architectures:** Serverless computing offers a flexible and cost-effective approach to managing data processing tasks. By leveraging serverless architectures, organizations can eliminate the need for manual infrastructure management, allowing data processing workloads to scale automatically.

Monitoring and Continuous Improvement

Finally, continuous monitoring of data processing workflows is essential for maintaining and improving performance. The following techniques are beneficial:

- **Performance Metrics:** Regularly monitor key performance metrics such as data throughput, processing latency, and resource utilization. This enables early detection of bottlenecks and performance issues.

- **Feedback Loops:** Implement feedback loops to capture insights from data processing performance and use them to refine and optimize workflows. This iterative approach ensures that data processing remains efficient as data volumes grow and new technologies emerge.

Improving data processing performance in MLOps is a multifaceted challenge that requires a strategic approach to data architecture, resource management, and real-time analytics. By adopting modern data architectures and leveraging advanced technologies, organizations can enhance the efficiency and scalability of their MLOps pipelines, ultimately driving better outcomes for their machine learning initiatives.

Model Development

Performance optimization in ML model development is crucial for ensuring that models are both efficient and effective in real-world applications. This involves carefully managing computing resources during model training, tuning, and evaluation to meet specific performance requirements. Best practices include selecting the right model architectures, fine-tuning hyperparameters, and using techniques like early stopping or regularization to prevent overfitting. As technologies evolve and demands change, maintaining this efficiency is key, requiring continuous monitoring and adjustments to optimize resource utilization without compromising model accuracy.

Instance Type Selection

The type of instance used for training and inference significantly impacts the model's performance. Models that are memory-intensive require instance types with high memory capacity, while compute-intensive models benefit from instances with high processing power, such as GPUs. For real-time inference, instance types with low latency and high throughput are essential. Generally, GPUs are preferred for training deep learning models due to their parallel processing capabilities, while CPUs are often sufficient for inference tasks, particularly when the model complexity is lower.

Model Complexity and Inference Speed

The complexity of a model directly affects its inference speed. High compute instances can be used to accelerate inference, but optimizing model complexity through pruning or simplifying architectures can also lead to faster inferences without requiring high-end hardware. Balancing model accuracy with computational efficiency is key to achieving optimal performance.

Benchmarking and Performance Evaluation

Benchmarking is a critical step in evaluating and comparing different ML workloads. It involves testing various algorithms, features, and architectures to identify the combination that offers the best performance. During benchmarking, it is essential to use a broad dataset to improve the model's success metric, ensuring that it performs well across different scenarios.

Feature Engineering

Feature engineering is the process of extracting important signals from data, which can significantly enhance model performance. By carefully selecting and transforming features, the model can better understand the underlying data patterns, leading to improved accuracy and efficiency.

Algorithm Selection and Hyperparameter Tuning

Choosing the right algorithm that fits the specifics of the data is crucial. Sometimes, using an alternative algorithm or combining multiple models through ensemble methods can provide better results. Additionally, hyperparameter tuning is necessary to calibrate the model to the data, optimizing its performance.

Enhancing Model Training with Ensemble Learning

Ensemble learning is a powerful machine learning technique that involves combining multiple models to improve overall prediction accuracy. By aggregating different learners, such as regression models or neural networks, ensemble learning harnesses the strengths of each model, leading to better generalization and reduced error rates compared to relying on a single model. This approach is based on the principle that a group of diverse models can outperform individual models by compensating for each other's weaknesses.

Bias-Variance Trade-Off

The bias-variance trade-off is a key challenge in machine learning. Bias refers to errors due to overly simplistic models that fail to capture the underlying data patterns, leading to poor performance on training data. Variance, on the other hand, refers to errors due to models being too complex, causing them to overfit the training data and perform poorly on new, unseen data. Ensemble learning helps balance this tradeoff by combining models with varying levels of bias and variance, resulting in a model that generalizes better to new data.

Advantages of Multiple Models

Each machine learning algorithm is influenced by factors such as training data and hyperparameters, which can lead to different models with varying performance. By combining these models, ensemble learning reduces the overall error rate while preserving the unique strengths of each individual model. Research shows that greater diversity among the models in an ensemble leads to more accurate predictions, making ensemble learning an effective strategy for addressing problems like overfitting without sacrificing model bias.

Diversity in Ensembles

The success of ensemble learning largely depends on the diversity of the models used. Diverse models are less likely to make the same errors, allowing the ensemble to cover a broader range of data patterns. This diversity is particularly useful in high-dimensional data scenarios, where traditional dimensionality reduction techniques may not be sufficient. Ensemble learning can therefore be seen as an alternative approach to handling complex datasets, ensuring robust and reliable model performance.

In the literature, ensemble learning methods in machine learning are generally divided into two main categories: parallel and sequential (Figure 6-3).

- **Parallel methods**: These involve training each base learner independently of the others. As the name suggests, parallel ensembles train these base learners simultaneously without any interaction between them during the training process.

- **Sequential methods**: In this approach, a new base learner is trained to correct the errors made by the previously trained model. Sequential methods build base models one after another in a step-by-step manner.

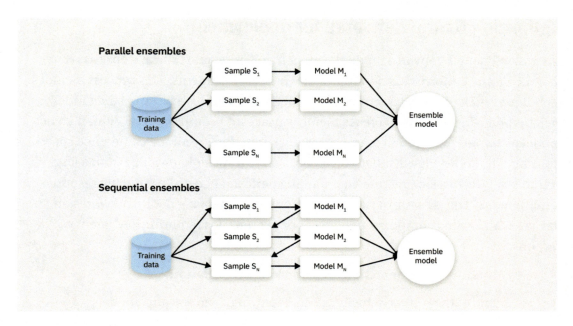

Figure 6-3. *Ensemble learning techniques*

Source: https://www.ibm.com/topics/ensemble-learning

In conclusion, ensemble learning is a valuable technique in machine learning that improves model accuracy and robustness by combining multiple models. Its ability to balance the bias-variance trade-off and leverage the strengths of diverse models makes it an essential tool for enhancing model training and deployment in various applications.

Model Deployment

Deploying a machine learning model can be a daunting task, even for experienced engineers. There are many challenges to overcome, from choosing the right deployment platform to ensuring your model is optimized for production. As AI models transition from controlled environments to large-scale deployment, issues like model robustness and slow inference times emerge. Addressing these gaps is essential for the effective deployment of AI models.

Here are some effective strategies to optimize ML models for deployment.

Optimizing Neural Networks for Deployment

Optimizing neural networks for deployment involves several critical steps to ensure that the model performs efficiently in real-world environments. This process includes techniques such as model quantization, which reduces the precision of the model's weights and activations to decrease memory usage and computational demand, and model pruning, which removes unnecessary parameters to enhance inference speed. Additionally, knowledge distillation can be used to transfer knowledge from a large, complex model to a smaller one, maintaining performance while reducing resource requirements. These optimizations are essential for deploying neural networks on devices with limited computational power or in scenarios requiring low-latency responses.

- **Memory Management with Knowledge Distillation**

    One of the primary challenges in deploying deep learning models is managing memory. Knowledge distillation is a technique that transfers the knowledge from a larger, complex model (teacher) to a smaller, more efficient one (student). This method reduces the model's memory footprint while maintaining performance, making it suitable for deployment on less powerful hardware.

- **Model Quantization for Faster Inference**

    Model quantization reduces the precision of model parameters, leading to faster inference times without significant loss in accuracy. Techniques like Post-Training Quantization (PTQ) and Quantization Aware Training (QAT) can be employed to optimize models for real-time applications.

- **Layer Fusion for Enhanced Efficiency**

    Layer fusion is another method to improve model efficiency. By identifying and merging similar layers within a neural network, the model's computational load can be reduced, leading to faster inference times.

Deployment Strategies

Deploying machine learning models efficiently is crucial for their successful integration into real-world applications. The deployment strategy chosen can significantly impact a model's performance, scalability, and accessibility across various environments. This section explores key strategies for optimizing model deployment, including the use of ONNX for cross-framework compatibility, selecting the appropriate mode of deployment based on specific application needs, and implementing model pruning to enhance efficiency, particularly on resource-constrained devices. Understanding these strategies is essential for ensuring robust and efficient model deployment.

- **ONNX for Cross-Framework Compatibility:**

  The Open Neural Network Exchange (ONNX) framework is designed to convert models between various machine learning libraries, facilitating seamless deployment across diverse platforms. This cross-framework compatibility is vital for ensuring that models can operate effectively in different environments, from cloud to edge.

- **Modes of Model Deployment:**

  Selecting an appropriate deployment strategy hinges on the application's requirements. Real-time applications benefit from single-sample inference, which provides immediate responses. Batch processing, on the other hand, is more suitable for analyzing large datasets in scheduled intervals. For applications that demand minimal latency, edge deployment is preferred, although it may necessitate simplifying the model to suit hardware constraints.

- **Model Pruning for Efficiency:**

  Model pruning is a technique that enhances deployment efficiency by eliminating unnecessary parameters in a neural network. This reduction in model size leads to faster inference times and lower computational requirements, making it particularly useful for deploying models on devices with limited resources. Pruning is a critical step in optimizing models for environments where computational power and memory are constrained, such as mobile or IoT devices.

Choosing the Right Deployment Platform

Selecting an appropriate deployment platform is crucial for meeting the specific requirements of your model. Popular platforms like AWS offer various tools and services tailored to different needs. Consider factors such as budget, model complexity, and deployment environment when choosing a platform. Evaluate the level of control each platform offers and balance it against cost considerations to find the best fit for your project.

Optimizing Model Performance for Deployment

After selecting the deployment platform, the next crucial step is to optimize the model for production. This involves simplifying the model architecture to reduce resource consumption and enhance deployment efficiency. It's essential to ensure data consistency by preprocessing input data, which helps maintain high-quality model performance. Additionally, fine-tuning hyperparameters can further optimize the model's performance while minimizing deployment time. Finally, testing and validating the model in a production-like environment is vital to preemptively address any potential issues.

To achieve smooth and efficient model deployment, several best practices should be followed. Containerizing the model and its dependencies ensures consistency across different environments. Implementing version control allows tracking of code and model changes, facilitating easy rollbacks when necessary. Additionally, robust security measures, including authentication and encryption, are crucial to protecting models and data. Continuous monitoring of the model's performance in production helps identify and resolve issues, ensuring the model remains reliable and accurate over time.

Continuous Optimization Post-Deployment

Once machine learning models are deployed, ensuring their ongoing relevance and accuracy is crucial, as data patterns can change over time. Continuous optimization of these models is essential to maintain their effectiveness in real-world applications. Two key strategies in this ongoing process are online deep learning and federated learning.

- **Online Deep Learning for Adaptation:** In dynamic environments, data evolves, and models must adapt to these changes. Online deep learning facilitates this by enabling models to continuously learn from new data. Unlike traditional batch learning, where models are updated periodically, online deep learning updates models incrementally as new data arrives. This continuous learning approach ensures that the model remains accurate and aligned with current data patterns, reducing the risk of model degradation over time.

- **Federated Learning for Privacy-Preserving Optimization:** Federated learning offers a solution for optimizing models in scenarios where data privacy is a concern, particularly when dealing with sensitive or distributed data across edge devices. In federated learning, models are trained locally on edge devices, and only the model updates are shared with a central server. This method allows the model to be optimized across various devices without transmitting raw data, thereby preserving privacy. Federated learning is especially beneficial in applications such as mobile devices, where data security and privacy are paramount. By leveraging this approach, organizations can ensure that their models remain up-to-date and relevant, while also addressing privacy concerns.

Model Monitoring

The model monitoring system is designed to track and analyze data, comparing it with the original training set to identify issues such as data quality, model performance, bias drift, and feature attribution drift. It uses explainability to assess the reliability of model predictions. When the system detects significant data or concept drift, which indicates changes in data distribution or target properties, it triggers an alert. If the alert reveals a violation, the system automatically initiates a model update pipeline, involving data preparation, continuous integration, and feature pipelines for retraining. The following are some of the areas that could contribute to performance optimization for model monitoring.

Evaluating Model Explainability

One of the critical aspects of performance efficiency during the model monitoring phase is ensuring that the model meets the explainability requirements dictated by business and compliance needs. Depending on the application, model inferences may need to be transparent and easily interpretable. Evaluating these needs early allows for selecting the appropriate model type or evaluation metrics that balance explainability with complexity, ensuring that the reasons behind a model's predictions are clear.

Monitoring and Adapting to Data Drift

Data drift—when the statistical properties of input data change over time—can significantly impact model performance, leading to inaccurate predictions. A robust monitoring strategy is essential for detecting data drift. By continuously evaluating model outputs and comparing them against baseline metrics, teams can identify when data drift occurs. Implementing a strategy for adaptive re-training, where the model is periodically updated or retrained when drift is detected, ensures that the model remains accurate and relevant.

Continuous Model Quality Monitoring

Model performance can degrade over time due to various factors such as declining data quality, evolving model bias, or changing explainability needs. Continuous monitoring is necessary to maintain model quality. This involves setting up real-time alerts to notify teams of any significant performance drops, allowing for quick intervention. Additionally, understanding the right time and frequency to retrain the model is crucial. Automated retraining triggered by specific thresholds, such as variance or data availability, can mitigate performance degradation.

Integrating Human-in-the-Loop Monitoring

Despite advances in automation, human oversight remains valuable in ensuring model performance efficiency. Human-in-the-loop (HITL) monitoring involves comparing human-labeled data against model predictions to estimate performance degradation accurately. This approach not only validates the model's decisions but also identifies areas where the model may need retraining. By integrating HITL monitoring into the workflow, teams can maintain high model accuracy while ensuring that automated decisions align with human expectations.

Automating Model Retraining

Automation plays a pivotal role in maintaining model performance over time. By establishing a framework for automated model retraining, teams can address issues like data and concept drift efficiently. This process involves regularly analyzing model predictions against predefined performance metrics, with automated triggers for retraining when the model's variance exceeds acceptable thresholds. Additionally, automating data exploration and feature engineering ensure that new features are incorporated into the model training process, further optimizing performance.

Maintaining Data and Model Integrity

Ensuring the integrity of both data and model predictions is vital for maintaining performance efficiency. Regular analyses should be conducted to assess the quality of incoming data and the accuracy of model predictions. By implementing automated checks and alerts, any deviations from expected performance can be quickly identified and corrected, minimizing the risk of performance degradation. This proactive approach helps maintain the model's reliability and accuracy throughout its lifecycle.

Achieving MLOps Performance Efficiency with AWS

Achieving machine learning efficiency with AWS involves a strategic approach to optimizing various aspects of your cloud architecture. By carefully selecting the right architecture, compute resources, and data management practices, organizations can enhance the performance and scalability of their ML workloads. AWS provides a suite of tools and services that facilitate this, enabling continuous monitoring and optimization. Regularly reviewing architectural decisions and leveraging advanced features such as caching, compression, and network optimization are essential to maintain and improve ML model performance in the cloud.

For MLOps, AWS provides a comprehensive suite of tools, particularly through Amazon SageMaker, to support the entire machine learning lifecycle—from data preparation to model deployment. By leveraging SageMaker's automated pipelines, experiment tracking, and model registry features, businesses can enhance their MLOps maturity, ensuring models are not only well-trained but also efficiently deployed and maintained, all within a fully managed infrastructure.

Let's take a deeper look into each phase of ML model development lifecycle and discuss best practices to optimize performance.

Defining Business Goals and Framing the Machine Learning Problem

Using prebuilt AWS ML services can significantly enhance performance efficiency in MLOps by leveraging pre-optimized components that are designed to handle specific tasks more effectively than bespoke solutions. By integrating managed AI services like those offered through Amazon SageMaker, organizations can offload much of the complexity associated with training and maintaining ML models. This allows teams to focus on fine-tuning custom models for their specific use cases while relying on the robust infrastructure provided by AWS to manage routine tasks such as data preprocessing, model training, and deployment.

Additionally, AWS services such as SageMaker JumpStart provide access to pre-trained models and algorithms, which can accelerate the development process and reduce the time to market. These prebuilt components are optimized for various problem types and can be easily integrated into existing workflows. Furthermore, by utilizing resources from the AWS Marketplace, businesses can access third-party tools and services that complement their custom ML models, ensuring a balanced approach between efficiency and solution specificity. This strategic use of AWS ML services not only improves performance but also simplifies the overall management of ML workloads.

Data Processing

In MLOps, data processing on AWS is crucial for building efficient machine learning workflows. The data, which includes both input and output pairs, plays a vital role in defining the system's objectives, training models, and monitoring performance against data drift. AWS services offer comprehensive tools for data processing, including collection, preprocessing, and feature engineering, ensuring that the same transformations applied during training are consistently applied during inference.

Data processing on AWS involves several critical steps, beginning with data collection and preparation. Data preparation, which encompasses preprocessing and feature engineering, is essential for transforming raw data into a format suitable for model training. AWS provides advanced data wrangling tools for interactive analysis and visualization, which are particularly useful for exploratory data analysis (EDA). EDA allows data scientists to understand the dataset, perform sanity checks, and validate data quality, ensuring that the models are built on reliable data. This robust data processing pipeline is key to maintaining model performance and accuracy, especially as data distributions change over time.

As we discussed in an earlier section, to gain performance efficiency, it is crucial to have a strategy to obtain valuable insights from rapidly expanding datasets by leveraging a modern data architecture. This approach facilitates seamless data movement between a centralized data lake and specialized data stores, including data warehouses, relational and nonrelational databases, and platforms for machine learning, big data processing, and log analytics. A data lake serves as a unified repository for diverse data structures collected from various sources, enabling comprehensive analytics. Purpose-built analytics services within this architecture offer the necessary speed and efficiency for specialized tasks such as real-time dashboards and log analytics.

Accelerating MLOps with AWS's Comprehensive Analytics Ecosystem

AWS provides a comprehensive suite of analytics services tailored to extract maximum insights from your data. These services enable organizations to innovate faster by leveraging AI and ML capabilities directly on the data lake. With the ability to run complex analytics and machine learning tasks using tools like Amazon EMR, Amazon Athena, and AWS Glue, organizations can perform queries, process unstructured data, and build predictive models without the need to move data to separate systems. Furthermore, AWS Glue's centralized data catalog simplifies data management by allowing users to crawl, catalog, index, and secure data efficiently. This centralized approach to data governance and security ensures that diverse users across the organization, such as data scientists, data developers, and business analysts, can access and analyze data with confidence, driving faster innovation and improved customer experiences.

Data Lake on AWS

Data lakes on AWS, particularly those built on Amazon S3, offer a robust foundation for breaking down data silos and maximizing end-to-end insights in MLOps. Amazon S3's unmatched durability, availability, scalability, and security make it the optimal choice for creating data lakes that can handle massive datasets from various sources. These data lakes support a wide range of analytics services, including big data processing, machine learning, and real-time analytics, all at a cost-effective scale. AWS Lake Formation simplifies the creation and management of secure data lakes, allowing organizations to build them in days rather than months. By integrating with AWS Glue, seamless data movement between data lakes and purpose-built analytics services is achieved, ensuring that all data, regardless of its source or format, is readily available for analysis.

Figure 6-4 shows an example architecture for querying an Amazon S3 data lake using the AWS Glue Data Catalog. AWS Glue crawlers scan your data lake and keep the Glue Data Catalog synchronized with the underlying data, enabling direct queries through Amazon Athena or Amazon Redshift Spectrum. Additionally, the AWS Glue Data Catalog can serve as your external Apache Hive Metastore for big data applications on Amazon EMR.

Figure 6-4. *Querying an Amazon S3 data lake using AWS Glue Data Catalog*

Source: https://docs.aws.amazon.com/whitepapers/latest/big-data-analytics-options/example-1-queries-against-an-amazon-s3-data-lake.html

Lake House Architecture on AWS

Earlier, we discussed the five logical layers of lake house architecture. Figure 6-5 illustrates the lake house reference architecture on AWS.

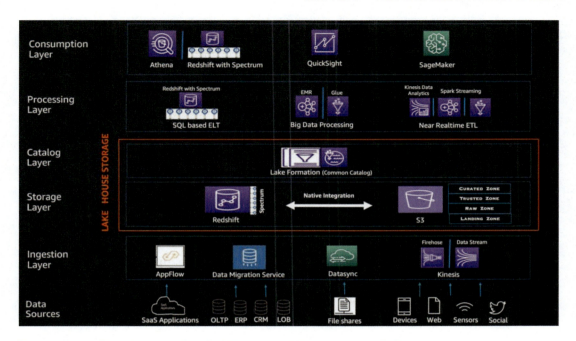

Figure 6-5. *Five layers of Lake House architecture on AWS*

Source: https://aws.amazon.com/blogs/big-data/build-a-lake-house-architecture-on-aws/

1. **Data Ingestion Layer:** The data ingestion layer is the entry point for all data entering the lakehouse architecture on AWS. This layer integrates various AWS services like AWS Data Migration Service (DMS) and Amazon Kinesis Data Firehose, enabling the seamless transfer of data from multiple sources, including databases, SaaS applications, and streaming data. The layer efficiently manages data ingestion into Amazon S3 (for data lakes) and Amazon Redshift (for data warehousing), handling both batch and real-time streaming data.

2. **Data Storage Layer:** This layer serves as the backbone of the lakehouse architecture, unifying Amazon S3 and Amazon Redshift to store structured, semi-structured, and unstructured data. Amazon S3 provides scalable, durable storage for vast amounts of data, while Amazon Redshift offers high-performance storage for curated, conformed data. The data is organized in various zones within the S3 data lake—landing, raw, trusted, and curated—ensuring proper data management throughout its lifecycle.

247

3. **Data Processing Layer:** The data processing layer is responsible for transforming and preparing data for analysis. AWS services like Amazon EMR, AWS Glue, and Redshift Spectrum enable data processing through SQL queries, Spark jobs, and other processing frameworks. This layer allows seamless access to both structured and unstructured data stored in the lakehouse, ensuring data is ready for downstream analytics and machine learning tasks.

4. **Data Catalog and Governance Layer:** This layer manages metadata and ensures data governance across the lakehouse architecture. AWS Glue Data Catalog plays a crucial role in organizing, discovering, and securing data across the lakehouse. By maintaining a centralized repository of metadata, this layer enables efficient data discovery, schema management, and security enforcement, supporting a unified view of data for various analytics and machine learning use cases.

5. **Data Consumption Layer:** The data consumption layer democratizes data access, enabling different personas within an organization to leverage AWS services for analytics, business intelligence, and machine learning. This layer provides tools like Amazon Athena and Amazon Redshift Spectrum for SQL-based queries, Amazon SageMaker for machine learning, and various other AWS services for real-time dashboards and advanced analytics. The unified interface ensures that all data within the lakehouse is accessible and usable, fostering data-driven decision-making.

AWS Compute Options for Data Processing

Selecting the right compute resources in AWS is essential for achieving performance efficiency while optimizing costs. AWS provides flexible compute options, including instances, containers, and functions, each tailored to meet varying performance needs.

Instances:

AWS instances are virtual servers that offer a range of capabilities, from general-purpose to specialized configurations like GPUs and SSDs. These instances are easily scalable, allowing you to experiment with different types and sizes to match workload requirements. The flexibility of these virtual machines makes them suitable for a wide range of applications, especially those that require specific hardware configurations or sustained performance.

Containers:

Containers provide a lightweight virtualization method, enabling you to run applications and their dependencies in isolated environments. AWS offers serverless compute for containers through AWS Fargate, which abstracts away the underlying infrastructure management. For those needing more control over their environment, Amazon EC2 can host containerized applications with full customization. Orchestration platforms like Amazon ECS and Amazon EKS further enhance performance by automating the deployment, scaling, and management of containerized applications.

Functions:

For highly dynamic workloads, AWS Lambda allows you to execute code without managing servers. This serverless compute option abstracts the entire execution environment, making it ideal for applications that need to scale automatically based on demand. By leveraging Lambda, you can focus solely on writing code while AWS handles the infrastructure, ensuring efficient performance for event-driven applications.

Performance Optimization Considerations:

When optimizing for performance, it's crucial to align your compute choices with your workload's specific requirements. Whether you choose instances for their configurability, containers for their isolation, or functions for their simplicity, each option can be tuned to meet performance goals. Additionally, AWS's elasticity mechanisms enable you to scale resources dynamically, ensuring that your application maintains high performance even as demand fluctuates. The key to maximizing efficiency lies in

selecting the appropriate compute resources, tailoring them to
your workload, and leveraging AWS's powerful scaling features to
meet your performance needs effectively.

SageMaker Processing Jobs

As organizations grapple with the surge in data generation, the need for efficient data
processing, analysis, and visualization has never been more critical. Amazon SageMaker
Processing, combined with the power of Apache Spark, offers a robust solution for
managing and optimizing big data workloads. This integration is particularly valuable
when scaling machine learning (ML) workflows and embedding data processing within
complex pipelines. Amazon SageMaker Processing simplifies the process of running
data processing tasks within a managed ML environment. It allows data scientists and
engineers to preprocess data, evaluate models, and perform other essential tasks on
large datasets without the overhead of managing underlying infrastructure. The service
seamlessly integrates with other AWS services, ensuring that processing tasks can be
automated, scaled, and monitored efficiently.

- **Apache Spark for Distributed Processing:**

    Apache Spark, an open-source distributed computing system, is
    designed to handle large-scale data processing with high speed and
    efficiency. Spark's ability to work in both stand-alone mode and
    on clusters managed by tools like Apache Mesos or Hadoop YARN
    makes it versatile. Its compatibility with multiple programming
    languages such as Java, Scala, Python, and R, along with its support
    for batch and real-time data processing, positions Spark as a key
    component in any data processing architecture.

- **Optimizing with HDFS:**

    For managing large datasets, the Hadoop Distributed File System
    (HDFS) provides a fault-tolerant and scalable storage solution. In
    HDFS, data is divided into blocks and distributed across various
    nodes in a cluster, ensuring that processing tasks can be performed
    in parallel, enhancing efficiency. The system's architecture, which
    includes NameNodes managing metadata and DataNodes handling
    actual data blocks, ensures robust data storage and retrieval, critical
    for any large-scale data processing task.

By integrating Apache Spark with SageMaker Processing, organizations can build scalable and efficient data pipelines. This combination allows them to leverage the power of distributed computing for ML workloads, ensuring that data processing is not just fast but also scalable and resilient, thus optimizing performance across the entire data lifecycle (see Figure 6-6).

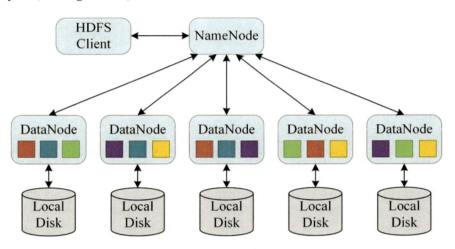

Figure 6-6. *HDFS architecture*

Source: `https://www.researchgate.net/figure/The-overview-of-the-Hadoop-Distributed-File-System-HDFS_fig4_348387085`

When running distributed processing jobs with Apache Spark, it's essential not only to write efficient code but also to choose the appropriate instance types and correctly size the cluster. Amazon SageMaker offers a variety of instance types categorized by memory, compute, acceleration, and general-purpose needs. By consulting the official documentation, you can select the most suitable instance for your workload. After selecting the instance type and cluster size, further optimization is necessary for large-scale jobs. SageMaker Processing with Spark provides preconfigured Spark settings, which can be customized to match your instance configurations for better performance.

Model Development

Amazon SageMaker is a powerful tool for enhancing model training performance, especially when dealing with large-scale machine learning (ML) workloads. It offers a variety of instance types, including GPUs and specialized accelerators like AWS Trainium and Inferentia, which are crucial for memory-intensive or compute-intensive tasks.

By selecting the right instance type based on the model type and data velocity, SageMaker helps in achieving faster inference speeds and more efficient training processes.

SageMaker also supports distributed training through its HyperPod feature, designed for large-scale distributed training, including foundation models. This capability allows for the automatic splitting of models and datasets across multiple instances, accelerating the training process. Additionally, SageMaker integrates easily with third-party libraries such as DeepSpeed, Horovod, and Megatron, providing flexibility and scalability. With automated scaling, real-time dataset refinement, and continuous monitoring, SageMaker not only reduces the time and cost of training but also ensures the robustness of ML models during production deployment.

Optimizing Model Training with Amazon SageMaker Debugger

Amazon SageMaker Debugger is a powerful tool designed to optimize and troubleshoot machine learning model training by providing real-time insights into model behavior. As models grow increasingly complex, with millions or even billions of parameters, ensuring stable convergence during training becomes critical. Debugger facilitates this by allowing you to access and analyze model parameters, activations, and gradients during the optimization process.

Debugger offers built-in rules to detect common training issues such as overfitting, vanishing gradients, and saturated activation functions. These rules can be integrated with Amazon CloudWatch Events and AWS Lambda to automate responses to detected issues, such as triggering retraining or adjusting hyperparameters. This proactive approach helps prevent issues before they degrade model performance, ensuring more reliable and efficient training.

One of the key features of SageMaker Debugger is its ability to register hooks that extract model output tensors during training and save them to Amazon S3. These tensors can be analyzed to identify non-converging issues in real time, enabling you to take corrective actions quickly. Moreover, SageMaker Debugger supports a variety of popular machine learning frameworks, including Apache MXNet, PyTorch, TensorFlow, and XGBoost, making it a versatile tool for optimizing a wide range of models.

By visualizing collected metrics and tensors, SageMaker Debugger not only aids in identifying the root causes of training anomalies but also provides a comprehensive understanding of the model's training dynamics. This capability is essential for refining models, improving their performance, and ultimately achieving faster and more stable convergence in complex training scenarios.

To integrate SageMaker Debugger into your workflow, follow these steps:

1. Update your training script with the `sagemaker-debugger` Python SDK if necessary.

2. Configure a SageMaker training job using the SageMaker Estimator API, the `CreateTrainingJob` request (via Boto3 or CLI), or custom training containers with Debugger.

3. Launch the training job and monitor it in real time using Debugger's built-in rules.

4. Set up alerts for training issues and take prompt action, using built-in actions or custom setups with CloudWatch Events and AWS Lambda.

5. Perform deep analysis of any detected issues using tools like TensorBoard.

6. Address the issues and iterate on your model until you achieve the desired performance.

The SageMaker Debugger developer guide provides a detailed walk-through of these steps.

SageMaker Debugger includes profiling features that help identify computational inefficiencies, such as system bottlenecks and underutilized resources, to optimize hardware usage across large-scale deployments. While the profiling aspect focuses on performance optimization, Debugger's core functionality addresses model optimization by analyzing issues that prevent training convergence, such as problems in minimizing loss functions through optimization algorithms like gradient descent. The architecture of SageMaker Debugger highlights the key components it manages to analyze and optimize your training jobs. See Figure 6-7.

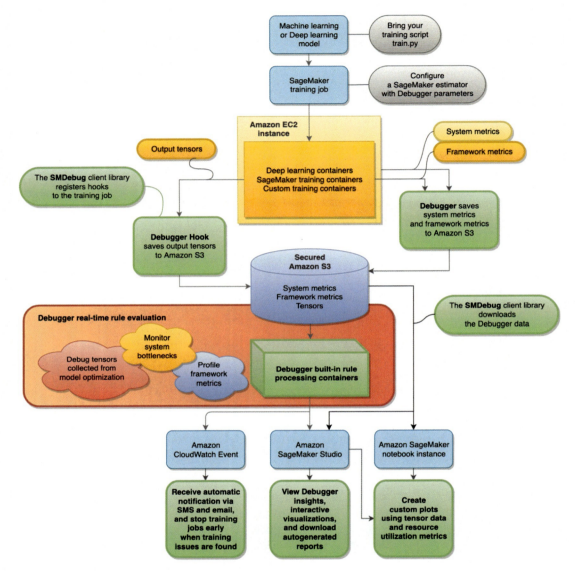

Figure 6-7. *SageMaker debugger architecture*

Source: https://docs.aws.amazon.com/sagemaker/latest/dg/debugger-how-it-works.html

Distributed Training for Performance Efficiency

Amazon SageMaker's distributed training capabilities significantly enhance model training performance by leveraging both data-parallel and model-parallel strategies. It combines software and hardware technologies to improve inter-GPU and inter-node communications.

It extends SageMaker's training capabilities with built-in options that require only small code changes to your training scripts. Additionally, SageMaker supports distributed training across multiple instances, ensuring scalability for training complex models.

When using multiple instances in a distributed training setup, it's essential to optimize how these nodes communicate and access data. Efficient networking between instances and seamless data transfer are key to maximizing compute resource utilization and speeding up training. Critical factors include ensuring that the instances, VPC subnets, and data storage (e.g., Amazon S3 or Amazon FSx for Lustre) are all configured within the same AWS Region and Availability Zone. This configuration minimizes communication overhead, leading to faster and more efficient training performance.

For distributed training, while various instances can technically be used, certain cases, like training large models such as large language models (LLMs) and diffusion models, benefit significantly from specialized instances. SageMaker recommends using EFA-enabled GPU instances, particularly the P4d and P4de instances with NVIDIA A100 GPUs. These instances are designed for optimal performance, offering high-throughput, low-latency storage, and faster intra-node communication. Additionally, using Amazon FSx for Lustre is advised for efficient storage and retrieval of training datasets and model checkpoints.

Amazon SageMaker offers two key strategies for distributed training: SageMaker Distributed Data Parallel (SDP) and SageMaker Distributed Model Parallel (SMP).

- **SageMaker Distributed Data Parallel (SDP)**: SDP enhances SageMaker's training capabilities by optimizing the job for AWS infrastructure and EC2 instance topology, achieving near-linear scaling with minimal code changes. It efficiently manages gradient updates across nodes using a custom AllReduce algorithm, making it ideal for reducing training time on large datasets by scaling across multiple instances and GPUs.

- **SageMaker Distributed Model Parallel (SMP)**: SMP addresses the challenge of training large models constrained by GPU memory limits by automatically partitioning models across multiple GPUs and instances. This approach allows for the creation of larger, more accurate models by efficiently coordinating training across distributed resources. SMP integrates seamlessly with TensorFlow and PyTorch workloads, requiring minimal adjustments to existing code, and can be accessed via the SageMaker SDK.

These distributed strategies significantly improve training performance, enabling faster, scalable, and efficient deep learning model training on AWS.

Explore Alternatives for Performance Improvement

Benchmarking is crucial for enhancing machine learning model performance by evaluating and comparing various algorithms, features, and architectural choices. Through benchmarking, you can identify the optimal combination that delivers the best performance for your specific workload. This process involves several strategies: increasing data volume to improve model metrics, applying feature engineering to capture key data signals, experimenting with different algorithms, utilizing ensemble methods, and tuning hyperparameters.

To implement these strategies effectively, you can use Amazon SageMaker Experiments to track and organize your experiments. Start with a basic model using simple features and algorithms to establish a baseline. Gradually introduce more complex algorithms and features, testing their impact on performance. Consider ensemble methods for higher accuracy, but weigh the trade-offs in efficiency. Finally, automate the hyperparameter tuning process using Amazon SageMaker's Hyperparameter Optimization to find the best settings for your model, ensuring optimal performance.

Perform a Performance Trade-Off Analysis

In machine learning, the balance between accuracy and model complexity is crucial. Simpler models are more interpretable and explainable but may sacrifice some accuracy. On the other hand, complex models like deep learning can deliver superior accuracy but at the cost of interpretability. Evaluating this trade-off helps in selecting a model that aligns with both performance goals and business needs.

Bias vs. Fairness Trade-Off

Managing bias and fairness in machine learning models is essential, especially when dealing with historically biased data. Business value often aligns with models that minimize bias while maintaining fairness, particularly in sensitive applications affecting underrepresented groups. Implementing processes to monitor and mitigate bias ensures that models deliver equitable outcomes.

Bias vs. Variance Trade-Off (Supervised ML)

Balancing bias and variance is a key objective in supervised learning. Techniques like cross-validation, regularization, and early stopping can help optimize this trade-off, resulting in models that generalize well to new data. The goal is to achieve the lowest possible bias and variance for a given dataset.

Precision vs. Recall Trade-Off (Supervised ML)

In many applications, the trade-off between precision and recall must be carefully analyzed. Precision is critical when reducing false positives is the priority, while recall is vital when minimizing false negatives. This trade-off should be aligned with the specific business objectives and the consequences of different types of errors.

To optimize business value, it is important to construct workflows that balance these trade-offs effectively. Use tools like Amazon SageMaker Experiments to track and evaluate different model configurations, and use SageMaker Clarify to assess bias and fairness throughout the model lifecycle. For models requiring deployment at the edge, Amazon SageMaker Neo can be employed to optimize them for performance and efficiency across cloud and edge devices. This systematic approach ensures that the chosen model delivers both the performance and ethical standards required by the business.

Model Deployment

When deploying machine learning models, it's essential to assess the need for near-real-time inference results, especially in scenarios where network connectivity is limited or unavailable. For applications like predictive maintenance in factories, minimizing latency by eliminating roundtrips to remote servers is crucial. This can be achieved by running inference directly on edge devices, ensuring rapid response to local events.

Optimize Edge Deployment

Training machine learning models typically demands significant computational resources, making the cloud a natural fit. However, once trained, models can be optimized for inference directly on edge devices, which require less computing power and offer real-time processing capabilities. This approach ensures that IoT applications respond quickly to local events, meeting business requirements for low-latency results.

Amazon SageMaker Edge is designed to facilitate this process by optimizing, securing, and deploying machine learning models to edge devices. It supports a variety of frameworks, such as TensorFlow, PyTorch, and XGBoost, and allows for the continuous monitoring of model performance across a fleet of devices. The SageMaker Edge Compiler further enhances model efficiency by optimizing them for edge deployment, while the SageMaker Edge Agent enables the execution of multiple models on the same device, collecting prediction data for periodic retraining.

Amazon SageMaker Neo and AWS IoT Greengrass

Amazon SageMaker Neo extends this capability by enabling models to be trained once and deployed anywhere, whether in the cloud or at the edge. It uses a compilation process that optimizes models for specific hardware, ensuring maximum performance without sacrificing accuracy. AWS IoT Greengrass complements this by enabling machine learning inferences on edge devices using models trained in the cloud. These models can be stored in Amazon S3 and deployed to edge devices, allowing for efficient and scalable edge AI solutions.

By leveraging these tools, organizations can optimize their machine learning models for edge deployment, reducing latency and improving performance, which is critical for applications that require real-time decision-making in environments with limited or no network connectivity.

Optimizing Cloud Deployment for Machine Learning Models

To achieve optimal performance efficiency when deploying models in the cloud, it is essential to match deployment options with the specific requirements of frequency, latency, and runtime for your use cases.

- **Amazon SageMaker Real-time Inference** is ideal for scenarios requiring a persistent endpoint for near-instantaneous responses. This managed service supports HTTPS endpoints and autoscaling, ensuring your models are always available for incoming requests.

- **Amazon SageMaker Serverless Inference** is suited for workloads with unpredictable, spiky inference requests. This serverless option automatically scales up and down without the need to manage infrastructure, making it perfect for applications with sporadic traffic and idle periods.

- **Amazon SageMaker Asynchronous Inference** is designed for cases involving large payloads (up to 1GB) and long processing times (up to 15 minutes). It handles requests asynchronously using an internal queuing system, making it suitable for workloads with substantial latency and processing time requirements.

- **Amazon SageMaker Batch Transform** is best for batch processing needs where real-time responses aren't necessary. This service efficiently handles large datasets by distributing the workload across multiple instances and automatically managing resources to avoid out-of-memory issues. This is ideal for scenarios where you can group data points and process them in scheduled batches.

By carefully selecting the appropriate deployment option, you can optimize both performance and cost efficiency for your machine learning workloads in the cloud.

Optimize model inference with Amazon SageMaker

Amazon SageMaker provides a suite of inference optimization techniques to enhance the performance and cost-efficiency of generative AI models. By applying these techniques—such as quantization, speculative decoding, and compilation—you can achieve better latency and throughput while controlling costs. SageMaker also offers pre-optimized versions of many models, tailored for different performance needs, allowing you to deploy optimized models without manual adjustments.

- **Speculative Decoding:** This technique accelerates the decoding process in large language models (LLMs) by using a faster "draft" model to generate candidate tokens, which the slower "target" model then verifies. The process enhances latency without sacrificing text quality. SageMaker provides a prebuilt draft model, but you can also use custom ones.

- **Quantization:** This technique reduces a model's hardware requirements by utilizing lower precision data types for weights and activations. SageMaker supports Activation-aware Weight Quantization (AWQ) for GPUs, balancing efficiency and accuracy while enabling deployment on less expensive hardware. While quantization can lead to minor accuracy reductions, it significantly improves resource utilization.

- **Compilation:** Compilation optimizes models for specific hardware, like AWS Trainium and AWS Inferentia, ensuring peak performance without accuracy loss. This technique reduces deployment time and autoscaling latency by compiling model weights ahead of time.

These techniques collectively offer a powerful set of tools to refine model performance, ensuring that your applications can handle real-world demands efficiently.

Amazon SageMaker's inference optimization toolkit significantly reduces the cost and latency of deploying large language models (LLMs). The toolkit simplifies the implementation of techniques like speculative decoding, quantization, and compilation, which previously required extensive developer time and effort. By providing prebuilt optimization recipes and the ability to stack various techniques efficiently, SageMaker allows users to deploy models with enhanced performance quickly. The platform also supports popular models like Llama 3 and Mistral with preset configurations for optimized inference.

Optimize Model Performance with SageMaker Neo

Amazon SageMaker Neo is a powerful capability within SageMaker that enables machine learning models to be trained once and then optimized for deployment across various environments, including both cloud instances and edge devices. This flexibility is particularly beneficial for organizations looking to deploy models on diverse hardware without the need for manual tuning.

Traditionally, optimizing machine learning models for different platforms requires a deep understanding of hardware-specific details, such as architecture, instruction sets, memory access patterns, and input data configurations. This complexity often leads to a manual and error-prone process of trial and error, which can be both time-consuming and inefficient.

SageMaker Neo automates this optimization process by converting models from popular frameworks such as TensorFlow, PyTorch, MXNet, and others into a framework-agnostic intermediate representation. Neo then performs a series of optimizations tailored to the specific hardware and generates optimized binary code that can be executed efficiently on various platforms. These platforms range from cloud instances, including those powered by AWS Inferentia chips, to edge devices running on processors from ARM, Intel, Nvidia, and others.

How SageMaker Neo Works

The core of SageMaker Neo's functionality lies in its compiler and runtime. The Neo compiler reads the model exported from various frameworks, converts framework-specific operations into an intermediate representation, and applies multiple optimizations to enhance performance. Afterward, it generates binary code and stores it in a shared object library, while the model's definition and parameters are saved in separate files. The Neo runtime is then used on the target platform to load and execute the compiled model, ensuring optimal performance regardless of the deployment environment.

Using SageMaker Neo, organizations can achieve significant improvements in performance without needing to manually tailor models for each hardware configuration. By automating the optimization process, Neo not only accelerates the deployment of machine learning models but also ensures that they run efficiently across different environments, from cloud-based instances to edge devices, providing a scalable solution for modern AI applications.

Model Monitoring

A robust model monitoring system is essential for ensuring the ongoing accuracy and reliability of machine learning models. This system continually captures new data, compares it against the training data, and applies predefined rules to detect any issues. If anomalies are found, such as deviations in data quality, model performance, bias drift, or changes in feature attribution, the system generates alerts.

Key Components of Model Monitoring

These are the key components:

1. **Model Explainability:** The monitoring system assesses whether the model's predictions are sound and trustworthy. This involves examining how well the model's outputs align with expectations and business requirements.

2. **Drift Detection:** The system monitors for data and concept drift, both of which can lead to model degradation. Data drift occurs when the statistical properties of input data change over time, while concept drift refers to changes in the relationships between input features and the target variable.

3. **Model Update Pipeline:** If significant issues are detected, the system triggers an automated pipeline to update and retrain the model. This process involves refreshing data preparation, continuous integration/continuous deployment (CI/CD), and feature engineering pipelines to maintain the model's performance.

This continuous monitoring and updating cycle is crucial for maintaining the effectiveness of machine learning models in dynamic environments.

Enhance Model Explainability with SageMaker Clarify

When deploying machine learning models, it's crucial to ensure that their predictions are explainable, especially when compliance or business objectives require transparent decision-making. To achieve this, it's important to evaluate the trade-offs between model complexity and the need for explainability. Selecting appropriate models and evaluation metrics that align with these requirements provides clarity on how predictions are derived from input data.

SageMaker Clarify is a powerful tool that helps detect potential biases and explains how machine learning models make predictions. It identifies biases during both training and production phases, using a feature attribution approach to clarify the influence of each input feature on the predictions. This transparency not only improves fairness but also aids in creating more understandable models. Additionally, SageMaker Clarify provides tools for generating governance reports, assisting in compliance with regulatory requirements and informing risk management processes.

Evaluate Data Drift with SageMaker Model Monitor

Data drift can significantly affect the accuracy of machine learning models, leading to inaccurate predictions if not properly managed. Data drift occurs when the distribution of data changes over time, which can result in a model's outputs becoming less reliable. To address this, it's essential to implement a strategy that continuously monitors data drift and adapts through model re-training.

Amazon SageMaker Model Monitor plays a critical role in detecting both model and concept drift in real-time, helping to maintain high-quality ML models by alerting you to deviations that require immediate attention. It tracks the quality of models by analyzing changes in independent variables (features) and dependent variables (outputs).

SageMaker Model Monitor is also integrated with Amazon SageMaker Clarify, which aids in identifying potential biases within models, further ensuring the reliability and fairness of your predictions. Regular monitoring and prompt adaptation through re-training when drift is detected can help sustain model performance over time.

Monitoring and Managing Model Performance Degradation

Model performance can degrade over time due to factors like data quality, model quality, bias, and explainability. To prevent this, it's crucial to monitor the model continuously and detect any signs of performance degradation. By setting up real-time monitoring, you can identify the right time and frequency for retraining and updating the model, ensuring it remains effective in production.

Once you've deployed your model, Amazon SageMaker Model Monitor enables continuous real-time monitoring of its quality. You can set up alerts to trigger actions if any performance drift is detected. This proactive detection allows you to take corrective actions like collecting new training data or retraining models without needing to manually monitor the system. Figure 6-8 illustrates the high-level workflow of Model Monitor.

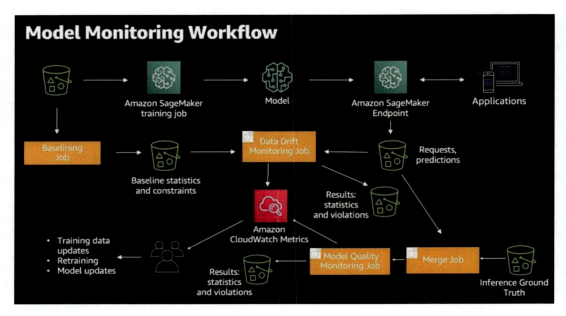

Figure 6-8. *SageMaker Model Monitor workflow*

Source: https://aws.amazon.com/blogs/machine-learning/monitoring-in-production-ml-models-at-large-scale-using-amazon-sagemaker-model-monitor/

The workflow begins with monitoring an endpoint and capturing inference data in real time, which is stored in an Amazon S3 bucket. Model Monitor captures both input data and predictions, then generates a baseline to create statistical rules. You can define and schedule monitoring jobs that automatically analyze model prediction data over time. For accuracy and precision monitoring, Model Monitor merges ground truth labels with prediction data to compute performance metrics, providing real-time insights into your model's effectiveness.

Model Monitor offers four different types of monitoring capabilities to detect and mitigate model drift in real time.

- **Data quality:** This helps detect change in statistical properties of independent variables and alerts you when a drift is detected.

- **Model quality:** This monitors model performance characteristics such as accuracy and precision in real time and alerts you when there is a degradation in model performance.

- **Model bias:** This helps you identify unwanted bias in your ML models and notify you when a bias is detected.

- **Model explainability:** Drift detection alerts you when there is a change in the relative importance of feature attributions.

Monitor Model Performance

Amazon SageMaker Model Monitor helps you track model quality by establishing a baseline during training and comparing it with production data. This allows you to detect data drift or changes in model inferences, indicating when retraining might be necessary. Additionally, SageMaker Clarify can be used to identify potential bias in the model.

Configure Alerts

Use Amazon CloudWatch to set up alerts that notify you of unexpected changes in model performance, bias, or data quality. This proactive approach helps initiate actions to address issues before they significantly impact operations.

Automatic Scaling

Amazon SageMaker supports automatic scaling, adjusting compute resources dynamically based on demand. This feature ensures your hosted model can handle fluctuating workloads without compromising performance, reducing operational overhead.

Monitor Endpoint Metrics

SageMaker provides endpoint metrics that can be monitored for usage and health. These metrics can be aggregated and analyzed using Amazon OpenSearch Service, which supports Kibana for visualization. This traceability allows you to analyze the impact of changes in inputs on the model's operational performance.

Use Human-in-the-Loop Monitoring

To monitor model performance effectively, integrating human oversight into the process is crucial. When automating decisions, human labeling of model outputs serves as a robust quality check. By comparing these human labels with model predictions, you can identify performance degradation and determine when model retraining is necessary.

Human Review with Amazon Augmented AI (A2I): Design a quality assurance system using Amazon A2I to involve human reviewers, particularly for low-confidence predictions or random samples. This approach leverages IAM, SageMaker, and Amazon S3 to create and manage human review workflows, ensuring that the model's performance remains reliable and accurate over time. Establish a team of subject-matter experts to audit model outputs, providing a safety net for automated decision processes and facilitating timely interventions when issues are detected.

SageMaker Clarify provides ML developers with greater visibility into their data and models so they can identify potential bias and explain predictions. SHAP (SHapley Additive exPlanations), based on the concept of a Shapley value from the field of cooperative game theory, works well for both aggregate and individual model explanations. The Kernel SHAP algorithm is model agnostic, and Clarify uses a scalable and efficient implementation of Kernel SHAP.

Amazon A2I makes it easy to build the workflows required for human review at your desired scale and removes the undifferentiated heavy lifting associated with building human review systems or managing large numbers of human reviewers. You can send model predictions and individual SHAP values from Clarify for review to internal compliance teams and customer-facing employees via Amazon A2I.

Together, Clarify and Amazon A2I can complete the loop from producing individual explanations to validating outcomes via human review and generating feedback for further improvement.

Conclusion

Performance efficiency is vital in MLOps, requiring careful selection and optimization of resources throughout the ML lifecycle. From defining business goals to model deployment and monitoring, each phase offers opportunities to enhance efficiency. The following are the key takeaways:

>**Resource Optimization:** Selecting appropriate compute resources, optimizing data pipelines, and leveraging cloud and edge solutions are crucial to meeting performance goals.

>**Continuous Monitoring:** Implementing robust monitoring and alerting mechanisms ensures that models remain performant and aligned with business objectives.

>**Adaptation and Scalability:** Embracing scalability and automated processes, like model retraining and human-in-the-loop reviews, helps maintain model accuracy and relevance in changing environments.

By applying these strategies, organizations can achieve a well-architected MLOps framework that supports efficient, scalable, and robust machine learning operations, ultimately driving better business outcomes.

References

- https://www.tensorflow.org/model_optimization

- https://aws.amazon.com/blogs/machine-learning/mlops-foundation-roadmap-for-enterprises-with-amazon-sagemaker/

- https://aws.amazon.com/blogs/machine-learning/achieve-up-to-2x-higher-throughput-while-reducing-costs-by-50-for-generative-ai-inference-on-amazon-sagemaker-with-the-new-inference-optimization-toolkit-part-1/

- https://docs.aws.amazon.com/wellarchitected/latest/machine-learning-lens/machine-learning-lens.html

## CHAPTER 7

Cost Optimization in MLOps

In the rapidly evolving landscape of machine learning operations (MLOps), cost optimization has emerged as a critical practice for ensuring sustainability and efficiency. As organizations increasingly rely on ML models to drive business outcomes, the financial implications of developing, deploying, and maintaining these models have become a significant concern. Effective cost optimization in MLOps not only reduces operational expenses but also maximizes resource utilization, enhances model performance, and accelerates innovation. By implementing strategic cost management practices, businesses can achieve a balance between budget constraints and the pursuit of cutting-edge ML solutions. This chapter delves into the vital role of cost optimization in MLOps, exploring methodologies, tools, and best practices that enable organizations to harness the full potential of their ML investments while maintaining fiscal responsibility.

Overview of ML Model Lifecycle

The ML lifecycle is the cyclic iterative process with instructions and best practices to use across defined phases while developing an ML workload (see Figure 7-1). It includes the following phases:

- Business goal identification

- ML problem framing

- Data processing (data collection, data preprocessing, feature engineering)

© Neel Sendas and Deepali Rajale 2024
N. Sendas and D. Rajale, *The Definitive Guide to Machine Learning Operations in AWS*,
https://doi.org/10.1007/979-8-8688-1076-3_7

- Model development (training, tuning, evaluation)

- Model deployment (inference, prediction)

- Model monitoring

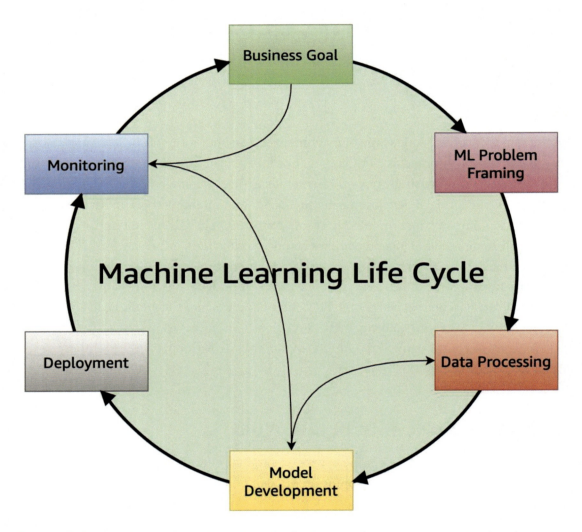

Figure 7-1. *Machine Learning Lifecycle (https://docs.aws.amazon.com/ wellarchitected/latest/machine-learning-lens/well-architected- machine-learning-lifecycle.html)*

Each phase of the ML lifecycle has the potential to implement best practices to optimize cost.

From the initial design of your first proof of concept to the continuous operation of production workloads, embracing these practices allows you to develop and manage cost-efficient systems. This approach helps achieve business goals while minimizing expenses, ultimately maximizing your business's return on investment.

Understanding Cost Drivers for ML Lifecycle

Understanding the cost drivers for the machine learning (ML) lifecycle is crucial for organizations seeking to optimize their AI investments. From data collection and preprocessing to model training, deployment, and ongoing maintenance, each stage of the ML lifecycle incurs costs that can significantly impact a project's overall budget. Identifying these cost drivers and understanding their implications helps businesses make informed decisions, ensuring they allocate resources efficiently and achieve the best return on investment. This section explores the key factors influencing costs throughout the ML lifecycle, offering insights into how organizations can manage expenses while maintaining the quality and performance of their ML solutions.

Business Goal Identification

When setting your business goals, it is crucial to also define the overall return on investment (ROI) and consider the opportunity costs. Thoroughly evaluate the potential benefits and drawbacks of applying machine learning to each use case to address specific business problems. This comprehensive assessment ensures that you make cost-effective decisions regarding long-term resource allocation.

Assessing Opportunity Cost and ROI

Here's how to assess:

1. **ROI Definition**: Clearly outline the expected financial and strategic returns from your ML projects. This includes direct revenue impacts, cost savings, and intangible benefits like improved customer satisfaction.

2. **Opportunity Cost Evaluation**: Weigh the benefits of implementing ML solutions against the costs and benefits of alternative approaches. For example, consider if a rule-based system might achieve similar results with lower complexity and cost.

3. **Specialized Resources**: Recognize that resources such as data scientists and model deployment times are among the most constrained and expensive. Allocate these resources judiciously to maximize their impact.

Ensuring Cost-Effective Resource Allocation

Follow these steps:

1. **Comprehensive Understanding**: Gain a thorough understanding of the ML development process, including data requirements, computational needs, and potential pitfalls. This knowledge helps in planning and avoids unforeseen expenses and delays.

2. **Long-Term Planning**: Develop a long-term resource allocation strategy that aligns with your business goals and ensures sustainable growth. Consider the scalability of your infrastructure and the ability to support ongoing ML operations.

Automation and Optimization Strategies

Follow these steps:

1. **Adopt Automation**: Leverage automation tools and frameworks to streamline repetitive tasks in the ML pipeline, such as data preprocessing, model training, and deployment. This reduces manual effort and errors, leading to cost savings and faster time-to-market.

2. **Optimization Techniques**: Implement optimization strategies to enhance model performance and reduce computational costs. Techniques like hyperparameter tuning, model pruning, and efficient data processing can lead to significant cost reductions.

Reducing Total Cost of Ownership (TCO)

Follow these steps:

1. **Cost Control Measures**: Implement measures to minimize the total cost of ownership of your ML infrastructure. This includes optimizing cloud resource usage, adopting cost-effective storage solutions, and using scalable compute options.

2. **Regular Audits**: Conduct regular audits of your ML operations to identify areas where costs can be reduced without compromising performance or quality. This proactive approach helps in maintaining a lean and efficient ML environment.

By meticulously planning and executing these strategies, you can ensure that your machine learning initiatives are both effective and economical, driving substantial value for your organization while managing associated costs and risks.

ML Problem Framing

When planning machine learning (ML) projects, it is important to assess whether simpler alternatives, such as rule-based systems, might be more effective. Balancing the cost of implementing ML solutions against the opportunity cost of not pursuing ML transformation is crucial for making informed decisions.

Evaluating Alternatives

Follow these steps:

1. **Rule-Based Systems**: Consider if a straightforward rule-based approach can achieve the desired outcomes with less complexity and cost. Rule-based systems can be effective for tasks with clear, definable rules and may offer faster implementation and easier maintenance.

2. **Hybrid Solutions**: Explore the possibility of combining rule-based systems with ML models to leverage the strengths of both approaches. This can provide a more balanced solution, optimizing both performance and cost.

Balancing Costs and Benefits

Follow these steps:

1. **Opportunity Cost of ML**: Evaluate the benefits of ML transformation against the costs involved. Consider the potential for improved accuracy, automation, and scalability that ML can offer compared to traditional methods.

2. **Long-Term Gains**: Assess the long-term benefits of ML adoption, such as enhanced data-driven decision-making capabilities, competitive advantages, and the ability to handle complex and evolving tasks.

Specialized Resources

Follow these steps:

1. **Data Scientist Time**: Recognize that data scientists are among the most valuable and scarce resources in ML projects. Efficiently allocating their time to tasks that maximize their impact is essential for project success.

2. **Time-to-Market**: Consider the importance of rapid development and deployment. The time-to-market for ML models can be a critical factor in staying competitive. Delays can lead to missed opportunities and increased costs.

Hardware and Infrastructure Choices

Follow these steps:

1. **Cost-Effective Hardware**: While selecting hardware, consider the trade-offs between cost and performance. The most affordable option may not always be the best if it hampers experimentation and slows down development.

2. **Scalability and Flexibility**: Choose hardware and infrastructure that can scale with your needs and support fast iterations and experimentation. This ensures that the development process is agile and can adapt to new requirements and challenges.

Strategic Decision-Making

Follow these steps:

1. **Comprehensive Evaluation**: Conduct a thorough analysis of all available options, including traditional methods and ML, to make well-informed decisions that align with your business goals.

2. **Continuous Assessment**: Regularly review and assess the performance and cost-effectiveness of your chosen approach. Be prepared to pivot if necessary to ensure optimal results.

By carefully considering these factors, you can make strategic decisions that balance the cost and benefits of ML adoption, optimize the use of specialized resources, and select the most appropriate hardware and infrastructure for your projects. This approach will help you achieve your business objectives while managing costs and maintaining flexibility in your ML initiatives.

Data Processing

In machine learning workloads, data is paramount. The process of ML involves extensive data exploration, cleaning, and transformation, which can quickly lead to the creation of multiple redundant copies of data. This redundancy can cause exponential growth in storage costs. Therefore, it is crucial to implement a robust cost control strategy at both the storage and data processing levels.

Data Storage Management

Follow these steps:

1. **Deduplication**: Implement data deduplication techniques to reduce redundant copies and save storage space.

2. **Compression**: Use data compression methods to minimize the storage footprint of large datasets.

3. **Tiered Storage**: Leverage tiered storage solutions that store less frequently accessed data in cheaper, lower-performance storage while keeping frequently accessed data on high-performance storage.

4. **Lifecycle Policies**: Apply data lifecycle policies that automatically move or archive data based on its age or access patterns.

Data Processing Optimization

Follow these steps:

1. **Efficient Data Transformation**: Streamline data transformation processes to avoid unnecessary replication and processing of data.

2. **Batch Processing**: Utilize batch processing techniques to handle large volumes of data more cost-effectively compared to real-time processing.

3. **Incremental Updates**: Implement incremental data processing where only the changed or new data is processed, reducing overall computation and storage needs.

4. **Cost-Aware Data Pipeline Design**: Design data pipelines with cost-awareness, ensuring that each step in the pipeline is optimized for both performance and cost efficiency.

By addressing these areas, organizations can significantly reduce the costs associated with data storage and processing in ML workloads, ensuring that the machine learning initiatives remain both effective and economical.

Model Development

The process of developing, training, maintaining, and fine-tuning ML models is iterative and demands continuous improvement. Identifying the optimal model state involves experimenting with various permutations and combinations of model parameters and data dependencies. However, optimizing ML costs extends beyond algorithm performance and model adjustments. It also requires efforts to integrate the developed models into applications effectively to fully realize their benefits.

Successfully managing the costs associated with ML model training requires a comprehensive understanding of the various factors that contribute to these expenses. Optimizing model development costs involves two main strategies: selecting the appropriate infrastructure and optimizing the training process itself. Training instances can generally be categorized into two types: accelerated GPU-based instances for deep learning models and CPU-based instances for standard ML frameworks.

The following are some of the key cost drivers.

Infrastructure Costs

These are infrastructure costs:

- **Compute Resources**: The choice between CPUs and GPUs significantly impacts costs. While GPUs offer superior performance for deep learning tasks, they are also more expensive. Selecting the right compute resources tailored to the specific needs of the ML task is essential for cost optimization.

  a. **CPUs**: Ideal for handling complex calculations sequentially. They are sufficient for many machine learning tasks, particularly those involving smaller datasets or less computationally intensive models.

  b. **GPUs**: Excellent for executing multiple simple calculations in parallel, offering a high price/performance ratio when used efficiently. However, GPUs are more expensive and should be selected only when necessary. For many scenarios, current-generation CPU instances (such as the `ml.m*` family) provide adequate computing power, memory, and network performance for Jupyter notebooks and other ML tasks. It is advisable to start with the minimum required instance specifications and gradually scale up to determine the optimal instance type and family for the mode

- **Instance Types and Sizes**: Different instance types and sizes come with varying cost structures. Optimizing the choice of instance types (such as P2, P3 for GPUs, or C5 for CPUs) and adjusting the instance size based on the workload requirements can help manage costs.

- **Scalability and Elasticity**: Leveraging scalable infrastructure that can dynamically adjust based on the workload can prevent over-provisioning and reduce costs. Tools like AWS Auto Scaling can automatically scale resources up or down as needed.

Model Training and Optimization

These are the costs in this area:

1. **Algorithm Complexity**: More complex algorithms and models typically require more computational power and time, leading to higher costs. Simplifying models where possible without sacrificing performance can lead to cost savings.

2. **Hyperparameter Tuning**: The process of hyperparameter tuning can be resource-intensive. Utilizing automated hyperparameter optimization tools and techniques can help in finding optimal parameters more efficiently, reducing costs.

Development and Experimentation

These are the costs in this area:

1. **Iterative Testing and Experimentation**: The iterative nature of developing and testing ML models involves multiple cycles of training and evaluation, each incurring costs. Efficiently managing and scheduling these experiments can help in reducing the overall expenditure.

2. **Versioning and Experiment Tracking**: Keeping track of different versions of models and experiments ensures that redundant work is minimized, which can lead to cost savings in the long run.

Performance Monitoring

It is crucial to consistently monitor the performance of your training jobs to identify and address inefficiencies. By doing so, you can optimize resource utilization and manage costs more effectively. Regular performance monitoring allows you to pinpoint areas where resources may be underutilized or overextended, enabling timely adjustments that enhance overall efficiency. This proactive approach not only helps in maintaining budget control but also ensures that your machine learning models are trained in the most resource-efficient manner. Moreover, consistent monitoring can provide valuable insights into the training process, helping to refine and improve future training strategies and workflows.

Licensing and Software Costs

These are the costs in this area:

- **Software Licenses**: Some ML tools and frameworks require paid licenses. Understanding and managing these software costs is essential for overall cost optimization.

- **Open Source Alternatives**: Where feasible, leveraging open-source tools and frameworks can help in reducing software costs.

By thoroughly evaluating these factors, you can effectively optimize both your infrastructure and the training process. This approach ensures that resources are utilized efficiently and costs are managed effectively while still achieving high-performance training results. A comprehensive assessment allows you to select the most appropriate compute resources, balance the use of CPUs and GPUs and implement strategies such as distributed training to handle large datasets. Additionally, by continuously monitoring performance and making data-driven adjustments, you can eliminate inefficiencies and enhance overall productivity. This careful planning and ongoing optimization not only control expenses but also contribute to the development of robust and scalable machine learning models.

Model Deployment

Model deployment is a critical step in the ML lifecycle, where the trained model is deployed to generate predictions and integrated into the application to meet both functional and non-functional requirements. Optimizing costs during this phase is essential to ensure that the deployment is both efficient and sustainable. Effective cost control can be achieved through several strategies.

Using the Right Inference Option

Depending on your requirements, determine whether you need real-time, high-throughput inference or offline, batch inference that can be scheduled as needed. Real-time inference is necessary for applications that require immediate predictions and responses, but it incurs ongoing compute costs for the entire duration that the inference endpoint is active. This can be more expensive due to the continuous resource allocation required to maintain the endpoint's availability and responsiveness.

In contrast, batch inference is more cost-effective when real-time predictions are not essential. Batch processing allows you to schedule inference tasks at specific times, such as during off-peak hours, reducing the need for constant resource utilization. This approach can significantly lower costs, as compute resources are only used during the scheduled inference runs. By evaluating your specific needs and choosing the appropriate inference strategy, you can optimize both performance and cost-efficiency. For instance, batch inference might be ideal for scenarios like generating reports or processing large datasets overnight, while real-time inference would be essential for applications like live chatbots or real-time recommendation systems.

Selecting the Optimal Infrastructure

The growing complexity of machine learning models driving AI applications has led to significant increases in the costs of the underlying compute infrastructure. In fact, up to 90% of the infrastructure expenditure for developing and running ML applications is often attributed to inference operations. Therefore, it is crucial to seek cost-effective infrastructure solutions for deploying ML applications in production. Selecting the appropriate compute infrastructure for your model ensures you are using the most efficient instance that offers optimal performance at the lowest possible cost.

To maximize cost-efficiency, it is essential to monitor and understand the utilization metrics of your chosen infrastructure. By regularly checking CPU, GPU, and other resource utilization metrics, you can determine if the instance is being underutilized. Underutilization indicates that you might be paying for more resources than necessary, which can lead to unnecessary expenses. Conversely, overutilization can suggest that your infrastructure may need scaling to handle the workload more effectively.

Implementing a strategy for continuous monitoring and adjustment based on these metrics can help you optimize resource allocation. This involves scaling up or down as needed, switching to more cost-effective instance types, or even exploring serverless or container-based deployment options that can offer dynamic resource management. By staying vigilant and proactive in managing infrastructure utilization, organizations can significantly reduce their ML operational costs while maintaining high performance and scalability for their AI applications.

Autoscaling

Unless the traffic to your model is consistent throughout the day, there will be periods of inactivity that result in excess unused compute capacity. This leads to low utilization and wasted resources, driving up costs without corresponding benefits. To address this inefficiency, implement autoscaling mechanisms that monitor your workloads and dynamically adjust capacity. This approach ensures steady and predictable performance while minimizing costs.

With autoscaling, the system automatically scales the number of active instances based on real-time demand. When the workload increases, additional instances are brought online to handle the increased load, maintaining optimal performance. Conversely, when the workload decreases, autoscaling deactivates unnecessary instances, preventing the waste of compute resources and reducing overall costs.

By leveraging autoscaling, you can optimize resource utilization, ensuring that your infrastructure is right-sized to meet current demands without over-provisioning. This not only enhances the cost-efficiency of your operations but also ensures that your applications remain responsive and reliable regardless of fluctuations in traffic. Implementing autoscaling as part of your deployment strategy allows you to maintain high availability and performance while keeping compute costs as low as possible.

Model Monitoring

Effective ML model monitoring is essential for ensuring the accuracy, reliability, and fairness of machine learning models in production. However, this process incurs costs that need to be managed carefully to maintain efficiency. Understanding the cost drivers for ML model monitoring can help organizations optimize their monitoring strategies and reduce unnecessary expenses.

Data Collection and Storage

The following are the primary cost drivers to consider in this area:

- **Volume of Data**: The amount of data generated and collected for monitoring purposes can be substantial. This includes not only the input data fed into the model but also the output predictions, metadata, and logs.

- **Storage Solutions**: The choice of storage solution (e.g., on-premises, cloud storage, or hybrid) affects costs. Cloud storage services often charge based on the volume of data stored and the frequency of access, so efficient data management is crucial.

- **Data Retention Policies**: How long data is retained can impact storage costs significantly. Organizations need to balance the need for historical data for long-term analysis against the costs of storing large volumes of data over time.

Computational Resources

The following are the primary cost drivers to consider in this area:

- **Processing Power**: Monitoring systems require computational resources to process and analyze data continuously. This includes running comparison algorithms, detecting anomalies, and generating reports.

- **Scalability**: The ability to scale computational resources up or down based on demand is essential for cost efficiency. Autoscaling features can help manage costs by allocating resources dynamically.

- **Real-time vs. Batch Processing**: Real-time monitoring systems provide immediate insights but are often more resource-intensive compared to batch processing systems, which analyze data at scheduled intervals.

Monitoring Infrastructure

The following are the primary cost drivers to consider in this area:

- **Infrastructure Setup**: The initial setup of the monitoring infrastructure, including hardware, software, and integration with existing systems, can be a significant up-front cost.

- **Maintenance and Upgrades**: Ongoing maintenance, updates, and upgrades to the monitoring system are necessary to ensure its effectiveness and adapt to changing requirements, contributing to operational costs.

- **Cloud Services**: Leveraging cloud-based monitoring services can provide flexibility and scalability but may also introduce variable costs based on usage patterns.

Model Performance and Drift Detection

The following are the primary cost drivers to consider in this area:

- **Performance Metrics**: Continuously monitoring model performance metrics, such as accuracy, precision, recall, and F1 score, requires computational resources.

- **Drift Detection**: Detecting changes in data distribution (data drift), model performance (model drift), bias drift, and feature attribution drift involves sophisticated algorithms and regular computation, which can drive up costs.

Compliance and Security

The following are the primary cost drivers to consider in this area:

- **Regulatory Compliance**: Ensuring that monitoring systems comply with relevant regulations and standards (e.g., GDPR, HIPAA) can add to the costs due to the need for secure data handling and audit trails.

- **Security Measures**: Protecting the monitoring infrastructure and data from unauthorized access and breaches requires investment in security measures and tools.

By understanding these cost drivers, organizations can implement strategies to optimize their ML model monitoring processes. This includes selecting cost-effective storage solutions, leveraging scalable cloud services, implementing efficient data retention policies, and investing in automation and real-time processing where necessary. Additionally, balancing the need for comprehensive monitoring with cost considerations can help ensure that the benefits of ML model monitoring are realized without unnecessary financial burdens.

Strategies for MLOps Cost Optimization in AWS

Having identified the cost drivers for each phase of the ML lifecycle, it is crucial to explore strategies that organizations can implement to optimize costs across the entire ML pipeline. These strategies aim to ensure that every stage, from data preparation to model deployment and monitoring, is managed efficiently to achieve significant cost savings while maintaining high performance and scalability.

Business Goal Identification

When setting a business goal, it is important to assess the entire data pipeline, the machine learning models, and the expected quality of production inferences. This evaluation helps estimate the costs associated with data handling, processing, and potential errors. Identify potential risks that could impact the project. Evaluate these risks and implement monitoring systems to track them throughout the project lifecycle. Understanding risks allows for proactive management and mitigation, reducing unexpected costs.

- **Develop a cost-benefit model**: Create a detailed cost-benefit model to understand the financial implications of your ML project. Continuously reassess this model as changes occur, such as shifts in the external business environment or the integration of expensive data sources. This ongoing reassessment ensures that the model remains accurate and relevant.

- **Estimate Resource Costs**: Calculate the cost of the resources required to maintain a production model. This includes salaries for data engineers, data scientists, and other technical staff. Ensuring an accurate estimation helps in budgeting and prevents resource-related cost overruns.

- **Reduce Total Cost of Ownership (TCO) with Managed Services**:
  Optimizing the Total Cost of Ownership (TCO) can be achieved by
  leveraging managed services and pay-per-usage models. Managed
  services allow organizations to operate more efficiently, requiring
  fewer resources and reducing overall costs. Managed services
  enable organizations to focus on their core business functions while
  outsourcing the management and maintenance of infrastructure.

- **Amazon SageMaker for Cost-Effective Machine Learning**:

  Amazon SageMaker is a fully managed machine learning service that
  facilitates building, training, and deploying models at scale. It offers
  significant cost savings compared to self-managed cloud-based ML
  solutions like Amazon Elastic Compute Cloud (EC2) and Amazon
  Elastic Kubernetes Service (EKS). Over a three-year period, the TCO
  of using SageMaker is substantially lower, providing an economical
  alternative for large-scale ML operations.

- **Amazon Managed AI Services for Out-of-the-Box Intelligence**:

  AWS offers a suite of pre-trained AI services designed to integrate
  seamlessly with applications and workflows. These managed
  AI services cater to common use cases such as personalized
  recommendations, modernizing contact centers, enhancing safety
  and security, and boosting customer engagement. These services
  are fully managed, require no up-front commitment, and follow
  a pay-as-you-go pricing model, making them accessible even for
  organizations without extensive machine learning expertise.

- **Perform Pricing Model Analysis**:

  Conduct a thorough analysis of the pricing models for each
  component of your workload. Determine if the components and
  resources will be used for extended periods, making them eligible
  for commitment discounts like AWS Savings Plans. Savings Plans
  allow you to save on AWS usage by committing to a consistent
  amount of usage. Amazon SageMaker Savings Plans offer flexible
  options for instance family, instance size, AWS region, and
  component usage, providing further opportunities to reduce costs.

By leveraging these strategies, organizations can significantly reduce their TCO, enhance operational efficiency, and achieve substantial cost savings while maintaining high performance and scalability.

ML Problem Framing

After determining that machine learning is the appropriate solution for your problem, it is essential to conduct a thorough cost trade-off analysis between custom-built models and pre-trained models. This analysis should consider various factors such as security, performance efficiency, and cost, ensuring they remain within acceptable thresholds.

Custom Models vs. Pre-Trained Models

1. **Custom Models**:

    - **Development Costs**: Building custom models from scratch often requires significant investment in terms of data collection, preprocessing, and model training. This process necessitates specialized resources, including skilled data scientists and engineers, which can drive up costs.

    - **Tailored Solutions**: Custom models offer the advantage of being tailored specifically to the unique requirements of your business problem, potentially yielding higher accuracy and relevance.

    - **Security Considerations**: Custom models can be developed with security measures that align with your organization's specific needs, providing greater control over data handling and compliance.

    - **Flexibility to Fine-Tune**: The benefit of a custom model lies in its flexibility, allowing you to fine-tune it to meet the specific requirements of your business use case. In contrast, a pre-trained model can be challenging to modify, often requiring you to use it as is.

2. **Pre-Trained Models**:

- **Lower Initial Costs**: Pre-trained models, such as those provided by AWS AI services, significantly reduce initial development costs by leveraging models already trained on vast datasets.

- **Faster Deployment**: These models can be quickly integrated into your applications, accelerating the time to market and reducing the time spent on development and training.

- **Scalability and Maintenance**: Managed pre-trained models often come with built-in scalability and maintenance, reducing ongoing operational costs and resource requirements.

Amazon SageMaker Built-in Algorithms

Amazon SageMaker offers a comprehensive suite of built-in algorithms designed to help data scientists and machine learning practitioners quickly get started with training and deploying machine learning models.

AWS Marketplace offers ready-to-use pre-trained ML models that can be swiftly deployed using SageMaker, significantly reducing the time and effort required to implement AI and ML solutions

This allows organizations to deliver AI- and ML-powered features faster and at a lower cost.

SageMaker Jumpstart for Pre-trained Models

SageMaker JumpStart offers an extensive array of pre-trained models, prebuilt solution templates, and examples for various common problem types. These resources are designed to help data scientists and machine learning practitioners quickly initiate the training and deployment of machine learning models.

SageMaker provides built-in algorithms that can be categorized into the following sections:

- Supervised learning

- Unsupervised learning

- Textual analysis

- Image processing

Figure 7-2 provides a quick cheat sheet that shows how you can start with an example problem or use case and find an appropriate built-in algorithm offered by SageMaker that is valid for that problem type.

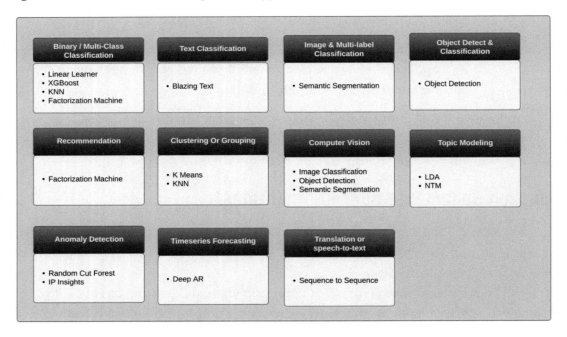

Figure 7-2. *SageMaker built-in algorithms*

When deciding between developing a custom model and using a pre-trained model, it is crucial to evaluate the costs involved. This includes considering the time and resources required for your data scientists to develop a custom model versus the convenience and speed of deploying a pre-trained model on SageMaker for inference.

When making a decision, consider the following:

- **Business Needs**: Determine whether the specific requirements of your business use case necessitate a custom model or if a pre-trained model can adequately meet those needs.

- **Resource Availability**: Assess the availability and cost of resources, including the time of data scientists and the computational power required for training custom models.

- **Project Timeline**: Consider the urgency of deployment. Pre-trained
  models offer faster integration, which can be crucial for projects with
  tight deadlines.

By carefully evaluating these factors, organizations can make informed decisions
about whether to develop custom models or leverage pre-trained models on Amazon
SageMaker. This strategic approach ensures that the chosen solution aligns with
business goals, resource constraints, and desired outcomes.

Data Processing

Data processing is crucial in a data-centric AI approach. However, preparing raw data for
machine learning training and evaluation can be a tedious and resource-intensive task,
requiring significant compute power, time, and human effort. This process often involves
integrating data from multiple sources and addressing issues such as missing values,
noisy data, and outliers.

Moreover, beyond the typical extract, transform, and load (ETL) tasks, machine
learning teams sometimes need more advanced capabilities. These can include creating
quick models to evaluate data and generate feature importance scores or performing
post-training model evaluation as part of an MLOps pipeline.

As shown in Figure 7-3, data processing consists of data collection and data
preparation.

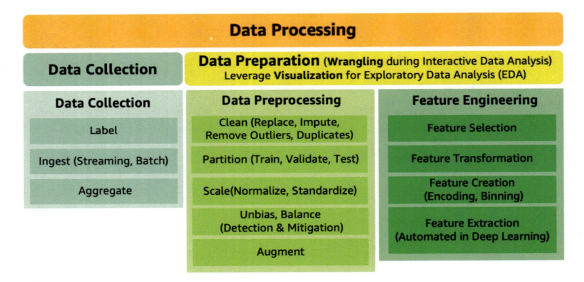

Figure 7-3. *Data preprocessing for machine learning*

Data collection is a critical phase in the machine learning lifecycle identifying the necessary data and evaluating various methods for collecting it to train your model. Key components of the data collection phase include labeling, ingesting, and aggregating data. Labeled data consists of samples tagged with one or more labels, and if labels are missing, they must be added manually or automatically. Data collection involves gathering data from multiple sources, such as time-series, events, sensors, IoT devices, and social networks, and storing it using various technologies like transactional (SQL) databases, data lakes, and data warehouses. Data ingestion can occur in real time with streaming technologies or in historical mode with batch technologies, often utilizing ETL pipelines to capture and store the data.

Data preprocessing shapes and refines data for training through various strategies, including cleaning, balancing, replacing, imputing, partitioning, scaling, augmenting, and unbiasing. Feature engineering involves selecting and transforming variables to create a predictive model, encompassing feature creation, transformation, extraction, and selection.

SageMaker GroundTruth for Managed Data Labeling

Amazon SageMaker Ground Truth is designed to help you build high-quality training datasets for your machine learning models. Ground Truth allows you to leverage machine learning along with human annotators from Amazon Mechanical Turk, a vendor company of your choice, or your internal workforce to create a labeled dataset. The labeled dataset generated by Ground Truth can be used to train your own models or serve as a training data set for an Amazon SageMaker model.

Amazon SageMaker Ground Truth offers two options: a self-service and an AWS-managed offering.

The AWS-managed option, known as SageMaker Ground Truth Plus, takes care of everything for you. This includes selecting and managing the appropriate workforce, designing and customizing an end-to-end workflow with detailed workforce training and quality assurance steps, and providing a skilled team managed by AWS. This team is trained on your specific tasks and ensures data quality, security, and compliance requirements are met. Ground Truth Plus is an advanced, turnkey service that uses an expert workforce to deliver high-quality training datasets quickly and cost-effectively, reducing expenses by up to 40 percent. This service allows you to focus on your core tasks without requiring deep ML expertise or extensive knowledge of workflow design and quality management. You only need to provide the data and specify the labeling requirements, and Ground Truth Plus will handle the data labeling workflows and manage the process to meet your specifications.

Figure 7-4 shows the AWS managed SageMaker GroundTruth Plus workflow.

Figure 7-4. *AWS managed SageMaker GroundTruth Plus workflow*

In the self-service option, your team of data annotators, content creators, and prompt engineers (whether in-house, vendor-managed, or public crowd) can utilize a low-code user interface to streamline human-in-the-loop tasks and manage custom workflows.

Figure 7-5 shows the self-managed SageMaker GroundTruth Plus workflow.

Figure 7-5. *Self-managed SageMaker GroundTruth Plus workflow*

As part of the AWS Free Tier, you can get started with SageMaker Ground Truth for free.

SageMaker Processing for Managed Data Preprocessing

With managed data processing, you can utilize a streamlined, managed environment to execute your data processing tasks, including feature engineering, data validation, model evaluation, and model interpretation.

With Amazon SageMaker Processing, you can execute processing jobs for various data processing steps in your machine learning pipeline. These jobs take input data from Amazon S3 and store the output back into Amazon S3. You can use either an Amazon SageMaker built-in container image or a custom image you provide for the processing container. Amazon SageMaker fully manages the underlying infrastructure for a processing job, provisioning cluster resources for the job's duration and cleaning them up upon completion, thereby unlocking compute cost savings for you. SageMaker Processing simplifies running ML preprocessing and postprocessing tasks, supporting popular frameworks such as scikit-learn, Apache Spark, PyTorch, TensorFlow, Hugging Face, MXNet, and XGBoost. See Figure 7-6.

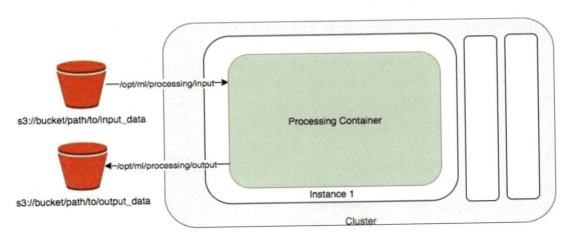

Figure 7-6. *Amazon SageMaker processing container*

The benefit of using SageMaker Processing is that you pay only for the processing instances while the job is running. Therefore, you can take advantage of powerful instances without worrying too much about the cost. For example, as a general recommendation, you can use an ml.m5.4xlarge for medium jobs (megabytes to gigabytes of data), ml.c5.18xlarge for workloads requiring heavy computational capacity, or ml.r5.8xlarge when you want to load multiple gigabytes of data in memory for processing, and pay only for the time of the processing job. Sometimes, you may consider using a larger instance to get the job done quicker and end up paying less in total cost of the job.

SageMaker Data Wrangler for Data Preparation

With SageMaker Data Wrangler, you can streamline data preparation and feature engineering, completing each step of the data preparation workflow—from data selection and cleansing to exploration, visualization, and processing at scale—from a single visual interface. You can use SQL to efficiently select and import data from various sources. The data quality and insights report allows you to automatically verify data quality and detect anomalies, such as duplicate rows and target leakage. SageMaker Data Wrangler offers more than 300 built-in data transformations, enabling you to quickly transform data without needing to write any code. The no-code/low-code, automation, and visual capabilities help improve productivity and reduce the cost for interactive analysis.

SageMaker Feature Store to Enable Feature Reusability

Using Amazon SageMaker Feature Store offers significant cost benefits by streamlining the management of machine learning features. It reduces duplication and the need to rerun feature engineering code across teams and projects, leading to more efficient use of resources. The fully managed, purpose-built repository allows data scientists and ML engineers to create, share, and manage features effortlessly. Its online storage supports low-latency retrieval for real-time inference, while its offline storage maintains a historical record of feature values for training and batch scoring, ensuring both efficiency and cost-effectiveness in ML development.

Model Development

Model training and tuning involves choosing a machine learning model that fits the use case, followed by the training and fine-tuning of the model. As previously discussed, optimizing model development costs relies on two key strategies: selecting the right infrastructure and optimizing the training process.

General guidance is to right-size the training instances to match the specific machine learning algorithm for optimal efficiency and cost savings. Utilize debugging tools to identify the most suitable resources for training. Simple models may not benefit from larger instances, as they might not utilize the additional compute resources effectively. In some cases, they may even train slower due to increased GPU communication overhead. It is advisable to begin with smaller instances and scale up as needed. AWS provides tools and services for cost efficient model development while maintaining the performance as outlined next.

Right-Sizing the Training Instance

Using fully managed Amazon SageMaker Training allows you to send all necessary components for a training job, such as code, containers, and data, to a separate compute infrastructure, ensuring your training jobs are not constrained by the resources of the SageMaker notebook instance. The SageMaker Training Python SDK enables you to launch training and tuning jobs as needed. Since ML training is often compute-intensive and time-consuming, these jobs run asynchronously on remote infrastructure, allowing you to shut down the notebook instance for cost savings if starting a training job is your last task of the day.

When selecting instances for training, consider the following cost-optimization factors:

- **Instance Family**: Determine the most suitable type of instance for your training. Optimizing overall training costs might sometimes mean choosing a larger instance, which can result in faster training and reduced total cost. Assess whether the algorithm can utilize a GPU instance.

- **Instance Size**: Identify the minimum compute and memory capacity required for your algorithm to run the training. Evaluate if distributed training is feasible.

- **Instance Count**: For distributed training, decide on the type of instances (CPU or GPU) needed for the cluster and the number of instances required.

When selecting the instance family and type, base your decision on the specific algorithms or frameworks used for the workload. Figure 7-7 provides a brief overview of the instance families available on SageMaker. For more detailed information on pricing and instance sizes, please refer to Amazon SageMaker Pricing.

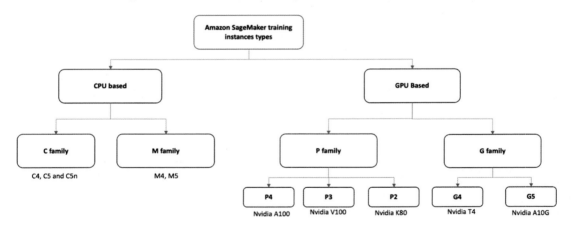

Figure 7-7. *Amazon SageMaker Training instance types*

The instance types are as follows:

- **CPU-based instances**:

    - **M Family**: These instances offer a balanced mix of compute, memory, and network resources, making them an excellent initial choice for most CPU-based training jobs. They provide a well-rounded ratio of CPU and memory, with higher memory sizes available as the number of CPU cores increases.

    - **C Family**: Optimized for compute-intensive workloads, these instances deliver high performance at a cost-effective price per compute unit. They are ideal for training jobs that require substantial processing power but have lower memory requirements.

- **GPU-based instances**:

    - **P3 Family**: Utilizing NVIDIA V100 GPUs, the P3 family includes the top-performing single GPU instance (P3.2xlarge), ideal for high-memory workloads that do not require multiple GPUs. Additionally, P3 instances come in configurations with 4 and 8 GPUs, suitable for training large models.

    - **P4 Family**: The most powerful GPU instance in the cloud, based on NVIDIA A100 GPUs, is ideal for distributed training on large models and datasets. Each P4 instance includes 8 A100 GPUs, each with 40 GB of memory, and features third-generation NVLink for fast multi-GPU training.

    - **G4 Family**: These instances offer lower performance compared to P3 and P4 but are more cost-effective for model development and training. G4 instances, equipped with NVIDIA T4 GPUs with 16 GB GPU memory, are based on the previous generation NVIDIA Turing architecture. For additional vCPUs and higher system memory, consider g4dn.(2/4/8/16)xlarge, especially if more preprocessing or postprocessing is required.

- **G5 Family**: Providing a low-cost alternative to P3 and P4, G5 instances offer single and multi-GPU options, delivering three times better performance than the previous generation G4 instances. Equipped with NVIDIA's latest A10G processors, G5 instances are available with 1, 4, and 8 GPUs.

- **AWS Silicon-Based Instances**:

  - **Trainium**: AWS's custom-built Trn1 instances offer a high-performance, cost-effective solution for training large deep learning models with over 100 billion parameters. The largest instance, trn1.32xlarge, features 16 Trainium accelerators with 512 GB of accelerator memory, providing up to 3.4 petaflops of FP16/BF16 compute power. These 16 Trainium accelerators are connected via ultra-high-speed NeuronLinkv2, facilitating efficient collective communications.

Recommended Best Practices for Instance Right-Sizing

These are some best practices:

- If you utilize SageMaker's built-in algorithms, each one comes with recommendations for which instance type to use for training. For instance, XGBoost is currently only compatible with CPUs and is a memory-bound algorithm rather than compute-bound. Therefore, a general-purpose compute instance (such as M5) is more suitable than a compute-optimized instance (like C4). Conversely, for the SageMaker image classification algorithm, a GPU instance such as P3 or G5 is advised.

- When using your own algorithms with script mode or custom containers, it's important to determine whether the framework or algorithm supports CPU, GPU, or both, to select the appropriate instance type. For example, since Scikit-learn does not support GPU, using GPU instances like G5 or P3 would be inefficient and costly, providing no runtime benefit. For GPU-based training, you should profile your jobs to find the optimal balance between the number of instances and runtime to minimize costs. Amazon SageMaker

Debugger can help profile training jobs in real-time, optimize resource utilization by identifying and eliminating bottlenecks, improve training times, and reduce costs for your ML models.

- It is advisable to begin with a small number of instances and gradually increase them based on your needs. SageMaker supports training large models using multiple instances.

Selecting the Appropriate Data Source for Training

Up to this point, we have covered instances and right-sizing. Another crucial aspect to consider during training is the data source and its handling. SageMaker supports three different data sources for training: Amazon EFS, Amazon S3, and Amazon FSx for Lustre. Depending on the size of your data and its current location, you can use the flowchart in Figure 7-8 to determine the most suitable data source for your training job.

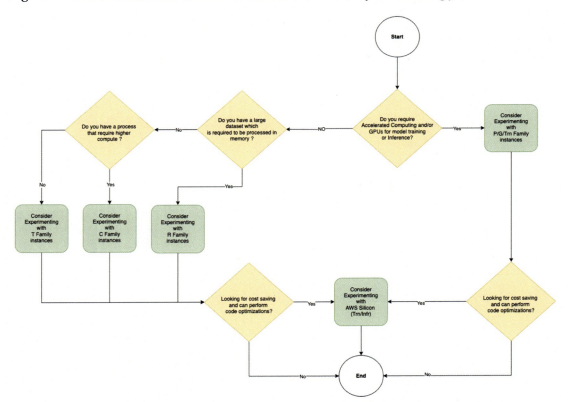

Figure 7-8. *Selecting appropriate data source for training*

Use Managed Spot Training

Another important consideration for training is the choice between On-Demand Instances and Spot Instances. On-Demand ML Instances allow you to pay for compute capacity based on usage time at standard rates. However, for jobs that can tolerate interruptions and do not require specific start and stop times, Managed Spot Training is a cost-effective alternative. SageMaker can reduce training costs by up to 90% compared to On-Demand Instances and manages Spot interruptions on your behalf.

Managed Spot Training utilizes Amazon EC2 Spot instances to run training jobs instead of On-Demand instances. You can specify which training jobs should use Spot instances and set a stopping condition to determine how long SageMaker will wait for a job to run using Spot instances. Metrics and logs generated during training are available in CloudWatch.

Additionally, Amazon SageMaker automatic model tuning, or hyperparameter tuning, can leverage Managed Spot Training. Spot instances can be interrupted, potentially delaying job completion. To mitigate this, you can configure your managed Spot training job to use checkpoints. SageMaker will copy checkpoint data from a local path to Amazon S3. If the job is interrupted, it can resume from the last checkpoint by retrieving the data from S3, avoiding the need to restart from the beginning.

Reduce Training Time

As deep learning models become more complex, the time required to optimize and train them also increases. For instance, training an NLP model such as RoBERTa can take thousands of GPU hours. Although there are techniques and optimizations available to reduce training time, implementing these strategies requires significant time and specialized skills, which can hinder innovation and the broader adoption of artificial intelligence (AI).

There are three primary methods to accelerate training:

- Using more powerful, individual machines to handle calculations

- Distributing compute tasks across a cluster of GPU instances to enable parallel model training

- Optimizing model code to run more efficiently on GPUs by reducing memory and compute usage

Optimizing machine learning (ML) code is challenging, time-consuming, and requires specialized expertise. To address this, SageMaker Training Compiler can automatically compile your Python training code and generate GPU kernels tailored to your specific model. This process reduces memory and compute usage, resulting in faster training times and reduced cost.

Model Deployment

In many instances, up to 90% of the infrastructure costs for developing and running a machine learning (ML) application are attributed to inference. This is because build and training jobs are infrequent and incur costs only for their duration, while endpoint instances must run continuously (while in service). Therefore, selecting the appropriate hosting method and instance type is crucial for minimizing the total cost of ML projects.

For model deployment, it's essential to start by understanding your specific use case. Consider the following questions:

- What is the frequency of predictions?

- Will your application experience live traffic, requiring real-time responses to clients?

- Are there multiple models trained for different subsets of data within the same use case?

- Does the prediction traffic vary significantly?

- Is inference latency a critical concern?

By addressing these questions, you can determine the most effective and cost-efficient strategy for deploying your ML models.

Select the Right Inference Option

The choice of inference and instance type has a significant impact on cost. You need to understand the latency requirements, synchronous versus asynchronous needs, traffic patterns, and real-time versus batch needs, and then choose the right inference type that meets all the requirements. Choosing the right instance for your model helps ensure you have the most performant instance at the lowest cost for your models.

- **Real-time inference**: Suitable for low-latency workloads with predictable traffic patterns requiring consistent latency and constant availability. The payload size should be less than 6 MB, and requests a timeout after 60 seconds. You pay for the instance usage.

- **Serverless inference**: Ideal for synchronous workloads with intermittent or unpredictable traffic patterns that can tolerate variations in p99 latency. Serverless inference automatically scales with your workload, so you don't pay for idle resources, only for the duration of the inference request. It supports the same models and containers as real-time inference, allowing you to switch between modes as needed. The payload size should be less than 4 MB and requests a timeout after 60 seconds.

- **Asynchronous inference**: Designed for processing asynchronous workloads up to 1 GB in size (e.g., text corpus, images, videos, and audio) that are not sensitive to latency and are cost-sensitive. Asynchronous inference includes a built-in request queue and allows for processing times of up to 15 minutes per request. You can control costs by using an auto-scaling group of instances optimized for your processing rate and scale down to zero to save additional costs.

- **Batch inference**: Best for processing large sets of data offline, where a persistent endpoint is not required. You pay for the instance usage only for the duration of the batch inference job.

Figure 7-9 provides a decision tree to help you select the appropriate deployment strategy.

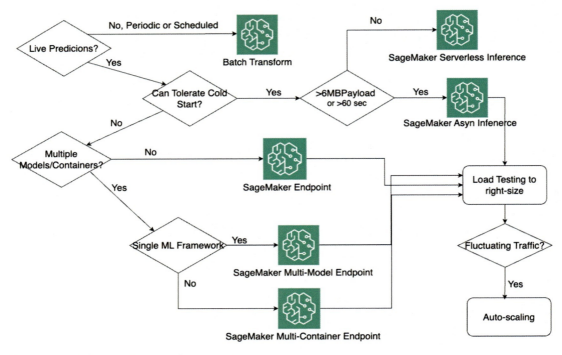

Figure 7-9. *Selecting the appropriate deployment strategy*

Right-Size the Model Hosting Instance Fleet

Amazon SageMaker Inference Recommender automatically determines the optimal compute instance type, instance count, container parameters, and model optimizations for inference, aiming to enhance performance and reduce costs. Accessible via SageMaker Studio, the AWS Command Line Interface (AWS CLI), or the AWS SDK, it provides deployment recommendations for your ML model within minutes. You can deploy your model to a recommended instance or conduct a fully managed load test on selected instance types without managing the testing infrastructure. Results from the load test can be reviewed in SageMaker Studio, allowing you to evaluate trade-offs between latency, throughput, and cost to choose the best deployment configuration.

You can access these recommendations via CloudWatch and also view them in SageMaker Studio. Keep in mind that integration with the SageMaker model registry is required to use Inference Recommender.

When considering CloudWatch metrics:

- If your priority is overall price-performance with a focus on throughput, you should pay attention to the `CostPerInference` metric.

- If you need a balance between latency and throughput, you should monitor the `ModelLatency` and `MaxInvocations` metrics. Note that `MaxInvocations` indicates throughput.

Recommended Best Practices for Instance Right-Sizing

Here are the best practices:

- Choosing a GPU-based instance to manage peak loads for a deep learning application might not be cost-effective if the resources are not fully utilized. Instead, consider using Elastic Inference, which enables you to add low-cost, GPU-powered acceleration to SageMaker instances, thereby reducing the cost of deep learning inference.

- Consider deploying transformer models at scale using NVIDIA Triton Inference Server on SageMaker. NVIDIA Triton Inference Server is an open-source software designed for inference serving, offering features that optimize throughput and hardware utilization while achieving ultra-low (single-digit milliseconds) inference latency.

- SageMaker includes an autoscaling feature that monitors workloads and dynamically adjusts capacity to ensure consistent performance at the lowest cost. As workload demands rise, autoscaling adds more instances, and as demands fall, it reduces the number of instances, helping to lower compute costs. SageMaker automatically distributes instances across multiple Availability Zones for high availability. Therefore, it is highly recommended to deploy multiple instances for each production endpoint. If you are using a VPC, configure at least two subnets in different Availability Zones to allow Amazon SageMaker to effectively distribute your instances.

Consolidate Multiple Models to Fewer Endpoints

If you have multiple under-utilized endpoint instances, consider these hosting options to consolidate usage into fewer endpoint instances:

- **SageMaker multimodel endpoints**: Multimodel endpoints (MMEs) allow you to deploy thousands of ML models on a single endpoint, making them ideal for models with similar size and latency requirements. Since not all models are kept in memory simultaneously, MMEs are a cost-effective solution for real-time inferencing workloads that can handle cold starts. This scalable approach uses a shared serving container to host multiple models, enhancing endpoint utilization and reducing hosting costs compared to single-model endpoints. Additionally, MMEs lower deployment overhead, as Amazon SageMaker manages model loading and scaling based on traffic patterns.

- **SageMaker multicontainer endpoints**: Multicontainer endpoints (MCEs) allow you to deploy multiple containers, each using different models or frameworks, on a single endpoint. These containers can either run sequentially as an inference pipeline or be accessed individually through direct invocation, enhancing endpoint utilization and optimizing costs. With MCEs, you can deploy up to 15 distinct containers on one endpoint, each potentially using a different ML framework. Unlike MMEs, MCEs keep containers in memory, avoiding cold start issues. Containers can be invoked either directly or in sequence, providing flexibility in deployment.

Explore Cost-Effective Hardware Options

It is recommended to look for cost-effective infrastructure solutions for deploying ML applications in production.

- **SageMaker Neo**: SageMaker Neo enhances cloud inference performance and reduces costs by creating an optimized inference container in SageMaker hosting. For edge inference, it automatically tunes the model for the specified operating system and processor, saving developers months of manual work. SageMaker Neo optimizes machine learning models for both cloud instances and edge devices by compiling them into an executable. The optimized model can then be deployed as a SageMaker endpoint or on supported edge devices for efficient predictions.

- **Amazon EC2 Inf1 Instances**: These instances offer high-performance machine learning inference at the lowest cost in the cloud, providing up to 2.3 times higher throughput and up to 70% lower cost per inference compared to current generation GPU-based Amazon EC2 instances. Specifically designed for machine learning inference applications, Inf1 instances feature up to 16 AWS Inferentia chips, which are high-performance inference chips developed by AWS. These instances also include second-generation Intel Xeon Scalable processors and up to 100 Gbps networking, ensuring high throughput for inference tasks.

Clean Up Unused Endpoints

SageMaker provides robust tools for deploying and testing models, including A/B testing with two model variants. You can deploy ML models as endpoints for real-time inference testing. However, endpoints sometimes remain active unintentionally, leading to unnecessary charges. It's essential to periodically review and delete endpoints once testing is complete or if there are no downstream consumers. Since model artifacts are stored in Amazon S3, and with an efficient MLOps pipeline, endpoints can be easily re-created when needed. Additionally, you can automate the detection and removal of idle endpoints using CloudWatch Events and Lambda functions. For instance, you can set up a system to identify endpoints with no invocations over a specified period, such as the past 24 hours, and automatically delete them.

Model Monitoring

The training process for deep learning (DL) models can be both costly and time-consuming. It's crucial for data scientists to track model metrics like training accuracy, training loss, validation accuracy, and validation loss to make informed decisions. Amazon SageMaker facilitates this by offering seamless integration with CloudWatch, which provides near-real-time metrics on the utilization of training job instances, including CPU, memory, and GPU usage.

For deployment, it is crucial to ensure that compute resources are used efficiently for running models in production by monitoring endpoint usage and optimizing the instance fleet size. Implement automatic scaling (autoscaling) for your hosted models to dynamically adjust the number of instances based on workload changes.

Automation and Tooling

Automation and tooling play a crucial role in optimizing costs for AWS MLOps. By automating repetitive tasks, such as data preprocessing, model training, and deployment, organizations can significantly reduce the manual effort and time required to manage these processes. Tools like AWS SageMaker offer built-in features for automating model tuning, deployment, and monitoring, ensuring efficient use of compute resources. Autoscaling capabilities dynamically adjust the number of instances based on workload demands, preventing over-provisioning and minimizing idle resources. Additionally, automated monitoring and alerting through services like Amazon CloudWatch help identify under-utilized instances and optimize their size and count. By leveraging these automation tools and techniques, organizations can achieve substantial cost savings while maintaining high performance and scalability in their ML operations. The following are some of the recommended best practices.

Assess the Cost Advantages of Automation

Automating the deployment of machine learning models eliminates the manual effort that is often prone to errors, enhances the productivity of data scientists and ML engineers, and accelerates the time to production. Amazon SageMaker offers a suite of purpose-built tools for ML operations, simplifying the process of deploying models. When integrated with AWS CodePipeline and AWS CodeDeploy, these tools enable the creation of a continuous delivery service for deploying endpoints seamlessly. Additionally, Amazon SageMaker Projects provides a robust platform for orchestrating and managing the entire ML lifecycle, including model deployment. By leveraging these automation tools, organizations can streamline their ML workflows, ensure consistency, reduce the likelihood of errors, and achieve faster and more efficient deployments, ultimately leading to cost savings and improved operational efficiency.

Utilize AWS Tagging for Enhanced Resource Management and Cost Tracking

Implementing AWS tagging allows you to assign labels to AWS resources, helping you organize and manage them more effectively. Each tag is composed of a unique key and a corresponding value. For each resource, the tag key must be unique, and it can have only one associated value. Tags are instrumental in organizing resources and utilizing cost allocation tags for detailed tracking of AWS expenditures. These tags enable AWS to organize resource costs in your cost allocation report, making it easier to categorize and monitor your AWS expenses. AWS offers two types of cost allocation tags: AWS-generated tags and user-defined tags. AWS-generated tags are automatically created by AWS services, while user-defined tags are created by you, providing flexibility in how you label and track your resources. This system facilitates precise cost management and helps ensure that you can easily attribute costs to specific projects, departments, or any other organizational units, thereby improving financial oversight and efficiency.

Leverage AWS Budgets for Comprehensive Cost Tracking and Management

AWS Budgets is an essential tool for monitoring and managing your Amazon SageMaker costs, covering all aspects such as development, training, and hosting. By setting up AWS Budgets, you can keep a close eye on your expenses and ensure they remain within predefined limits. One of the key features of AWS Budgets is the ability to set alerts that notify you when your actual or forecasted spending exceeds your budgeted amount. This proactive approach allows you to take corrective actions before costs spiral out of control. Once you create your budget, you can continuously track its progress through the AWS Budgets console, which provides detailed insights and visualizations of your spending patterns. This tool not only helps in maintaining financial discipline but also aids in making informed decisions to optimize resource allocation and cost efficiency across your machine learning projects. By integrating AWS Budgets into your financial oversight processes, you can ensure that your SageMaker expenditures align with your organizational goals and budgetary constraints.

Utilize AWS Savings Plans

Amazon SageMaker Savings Plans provide a flexible pricing model for SageMaker, in exchange for a commitment to a consistent amount of usage (measured in dollars per hour) for a one-year or three-year term. These plans automatically apply to eligible SageMaker ML instance usages, including Studio notebooks, SageMaker On-Demand notebooks, SageMaker Processing, Amazon SageMaker Data Wrangler, SageMaker Training, SageMaker real-time inference, and SageMaker batch transform, regardless of instance family, size, or region. For example, you can change usage from a CPU ml.c5.xlarge instance running in US East (Ohio) to an ml.Inf1 instance in US West (Oregon) for inference workloads at any time and automatically continue to pay the Savings Plan price.

Track Usage and Spend with AWS Cost Explorer

AWS Cost Explorer provides preconfigured views that display information about your cost trends and give you a head start on understanding your cost history and trends. It allows you to filter and group by values such as AWS service, usage type, cost allocation tags, EC2 instance type, and more. If you use consolidated billing, you can also filter by linked account. In addition, you can set time intervals and granularity, as well as forecast future costs based on your historical cost and usage data.

Figure 7-10 shows SageMaker costs per month for the selected date range, grouped by region.

Figure 7-10. *Analyzing Amazon SageMaker costs using AWS Cost Explorer*

Monitor and Enhance Return on Investment (ROI) for ML Models

Once a machine learning model is deployed into production, it is crucial to establish a reporting mechanism to track the value it delivers. For instance, if a model supports customer acquisition, you should measure how many new customers are acquired and their spending compared to a baseline without the model's advice. If a model predicts maintenance needs, track the cost savings from optimizing the maintenance cycle.

Effective reporting allows you to compare the value generated by the ML model against its ongoing operational costs, enabling informed decision-making. If the ROI is significantly positive, consider scaling the model to address similar challenges. If the ROI is negative, investigate potential improvements, such as reducing model latency through serverless inference or cutting runtime costs by adjusting the balance between model accuracy and complexity. Another approach could be to layer a simpler model to triage or filter cases before using the more complex model.

By continuously monitoring and refining the ROI of your ML models, you can maximize their impact and ensure that they contribute effectively to your organizational goals.

Use Comprehensive Logging and Monitoring

Amazon CloudWatch is a comprehensive monitoring and management service that provides data and actionable insights for AWS, on-premises, hybrid, and other cloud applications and infrastructure resources. It consolidates performance and operational data, such as logs and metrics, into a single platform, eliminating the need to monitor these elements in isolation (e.g., server, network, or database). CloudWatch allows you to oversee your entire stack—applications, infrastructure, network, and services—using alarms, logs, and event data to automate actions and reduce mean time to resolution (MTTR). This efficiency frees up valuable resources, enabling you to concentrate on building applications and adding business value.

CloudWatch delivers actionable insights that help optimize application performance, manage resource utilization, and assess system-wide operational health. It offers up to one-second visibility of metrics and logs data, retains metrics data for 15 months, and allows metric calculations. These features enable historical analysis for cost optimization and provide real-time insights to enhance the performance of applications and infrastructure resources.

Consider Use of Spot Instances

One of the easiest ways to reduce machine learning training costs is by using Amazon EC2 Spot instances. These instances provide access to unused EC2 compute capacity at a significant discount of up to 90% compared to on-demand rates. Amazon SageMaker simplifies this process with Managed Spot Training, allowing you to lower training costs without the need to manually set up and manage Spot instances. SageMaker automatically provisions Spot instances for your training jobs and, if a Spot instance is reclaimed, it will automatically resume training once capacity becomes available, ensuring seamless cost savings of up to 90%.

Conclusion

Cost optimization is crucial for managing ML workloads, primarily because it helps organizations stay within budget constraints and prevents overspending due to the high computational power required for training and inference. By optimizing costs, organizations can scale their ML initiatives more efficiently, enabling the handling of larger datasets, more complex models, and increased user demands without escalating expenses. Efficient resource usage, such as selecting the right instance types and using spot instances, translates to lower operational costs and better utilization of available infrastructure.

Moreover, cost optimization provides a competitive edge by lowering operational expenses, leading to more competitive pricing and higher profit margins. It aligns with environmental sustainability goals by reducing energy consumption and carbon footprints through efficient resource use. Managing costs effectively also enhances organizational flexibility and agility, allowing quicker adaptation to changing business needs. It mitigates financial risks by ensuring expenditures are justified by the value delivered and fosters innovation by lowering the financial barriers to experimentation and new idea exploration. Overall, optimizing ML workload costs is vital for maintaining financial health, scalability, efficiency, competitive advantage, sustainability, flexibility, risk management, and innovation.

References

- https://docs.aws.amazon.com/wellarchitected/latest/
  machine-learning-lens/well-architected-machine-learning-
  lifecycle.html

- https://aws.amazon.com/blogs/machine-learning/ensure-
  efficient-compute-resources-on-amazon-sagemaker/

- https://docs.aws.amazon.com/wellarchitected/latest/machine-
  learning-lens/mlcost-27.html

- https://aws.amazon.com/blogs/machine-learning/part-6-
  model-hosting-patterns-in-amazon-sagemaker-best-practices-
  in-testing-and-updating-models-on-sagemaker/

- https://aws.amazon.com/blogs/machine-learning/part-1-
  analyze-amazon-sagemaker-spend-and-determine-cost-
  optimization-opportunities-based-on-usage-part-1/

CHAPTER 8

MLOps Case Studies

We have gone through MLOps, including its evolution, principles, lifecycles, and best practices for various pillars of MLOps in AWS. It is time to reflect on MLOps implementation in real-world scenarios with some discrete case studies.

In this chapter, we will deep dive into case studies of various organizations that faced real-world challenges before implementing MLOps best practices and show how their results improved after implementing MLOps practices.

Amazon Music

Amazon Music offers unlimited access to its vast library of songs and podcasts. They have more than 100 million songs available for free steaming millions of free podcasts. Every search for a song, playlist, or podcast holds a challenge, especially if you don't know the exact title, artist, or album name.

Business Goal

In peak traffic times, when millions of active users are searching for their choice of music or podcast, a smart and responsive search is needed to deliver a good customer experience.

The business goal for Amazon Music is to implement amazing search bar capabilities and accomplish instant music and podcast results. To achieve this goal, Amazon Music implements Amazon SageMaker with NVIDIA to optimize ML training and uses the power of artificial intelligence.

313

© Neel Sendas and Deepali Rajale 2024
N. Sendas and D. Rajale, *The Definitive Guide to Machine Learning Operations in AWS*,
https://doi.org/10.1007/979-8-8688-1076-3_8

Challenges

The following were the challenges faced by Amazon Music before implementing MLOps:

- Delivering relevant and fast real-time search results were a challenge.

- During peak traffic times, the search bar's capabilities, like real-time spell-check and vector search, were difficult.

- Cost optimization for model training and inference of AI models was a challenge.

Platform Used

Amazon Music implemented Amazon SageMaker with NVIDIA Triton Inference Server and TensorRT to optimize cost and performance. Amazon SageMaker provides an end-to-end set of services for the ML lifecycle without any infrastructure issues. Amazon Music builds, trains, and deploys its ML models on the AWS Cloud with minimal effort.

Solution Overview

The following solutions were implemented by Amazon Music:

- Amazon SageMaker uses NVIDIA A10G Tensor Core GPUs, Triton Inference Server Container, and the TensorRT model format to host G5 instances for quick and cost-optimized results. It identifies optimization areas around the batch size and precision parameters to improve the speed, efficiency, and accuracy of training deep learning models.

- SageMaker implements real-time semantic search suggestions for vector search or embedding-based retrieval capabilities. Vector search is an ML technique that works using the semantics of the content to help users find the most relevant content.

- Amazon Music also implements fast and accurate search capabilities using the BART Transformer model for Spell Correction. The BART inference pipeline is developed by conducting both preprocessing (text tokenization) and post-processing (tokens to text) phases on CPUs, while the model execution step runs on NVIDIA A10G Tensor Core GPUs.

Key Outcomes

The following were the key outcomes of Amazon Music implementing AWS MLOps:

1. GPU utilization for model training is improved by 54% after optimizations with Amazon SageMaker.

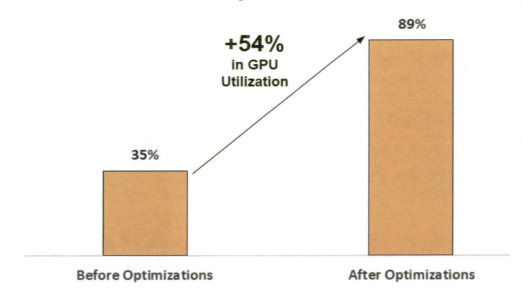

Model Training: Time To Train

2. At peak traffic, the inference latency of the spell-check model was reduced by 25 milliseconds and reduced search query latency by 63% on average using the BART spell corrector. Thus, the training time accelerated by 12x and resulted in fast and correct search results.

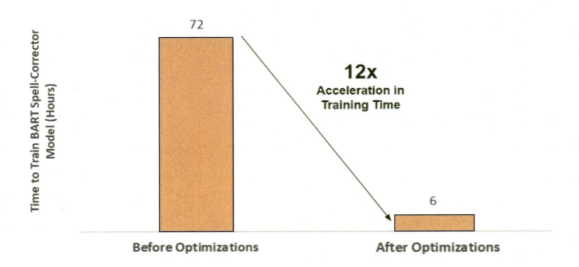

3. The inference cost of Amazon Music was reduced by 70% with
    SageMaker G5 instances with Nvidia A10G GPUs compared
    to the CPU-based baseline. It elevated the performance of
    Amazon Music.

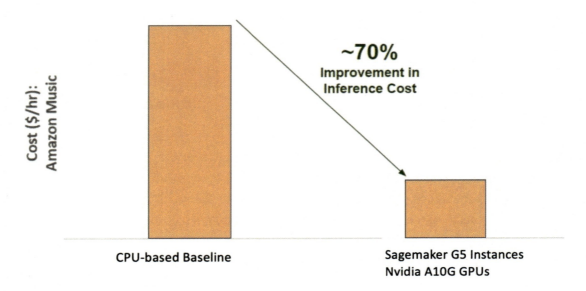

4. With deep learning neural networks, Amazon Music delivers low latency and high throughput for inference applications.

We can see significant improvement in Amazon Must search capabilities, time to result, and cost optimization by implementing Amazon SageMaker with Nvidia.

Yara

Yara is the world's leading crop nutrition company and environmental and agricultural solutions provider. Yara is focused on growing nature-positive food that creates value for customers, shareholders, and society and delivers a more sustainable food value chain. Yara is the world's largest producers of nitrate, ammonia, and NPK fertilizers.

Yara's vision is of a world without hunger, climate-friendly crop nutrition, low-carbon environmental footprint fertilizers, zero emissions energy solutions, and high-quality, and low production costs. To become a "Plant of the Future" with zero emissions and low costs is Yara's long-term target.

Business Goal of Yara

Yara's business goals include optimizing production, improving product quality, increasing production site reliability, lowering emissions, increasing worker safety and efficiency, automating manual procedures, and more. To achieve this goal, Yara established a global digital unit called Digital Production to take advantage of the vast quantity of data generated as part of their operations.

For production plants like Yara, energy consumption is the major cost component and causes an impact on probability. Yara implemented Yara's Energy Load Curve (ELC) solution to analyze their energy consumption performance. The Energy Load Curve (ELC) tool informs us when current energy consumption deviates from the historical best and gives recommendations as well to the operator to steer the energy consumption.

Now, the major goal is to implement an ELC solution across multiple sites across the globe and automate the deployment and maintenance processes.

Challenges

The following are the challenges faced by Yara before implementing MLOps:

1. Yara's Energy Load Curve (ELC) needs to be implemented across multiple sites and mines across the globe.

2. All the deployment and maintenance processes need to be automated for Yara's effective production.

Platform Used

Yara is using Amazon SageMaker features to streamline the ML lifecycle by standardizing and automating MLOps practices. Various steps of Amazon SageMaker are implemented for Yara including the Amazon framework containers, model registry, model monitor, and Amazon SageMaker Pipelines for data preparation, model training, model evaluation, and registration.

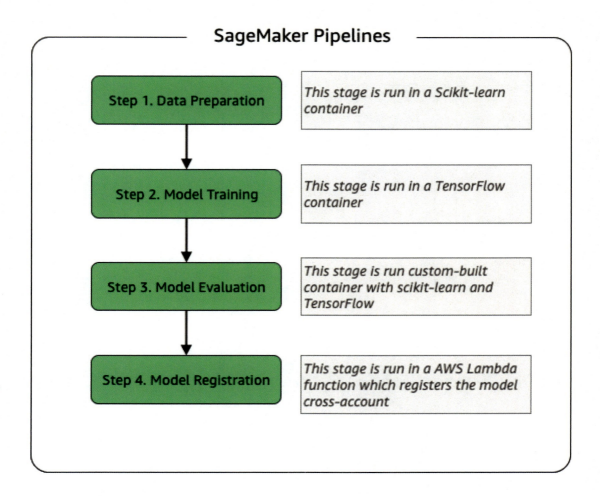

Solution Overview

Figure 8-1 shows the high-level architecture of Amazon SageMaker for Yara.

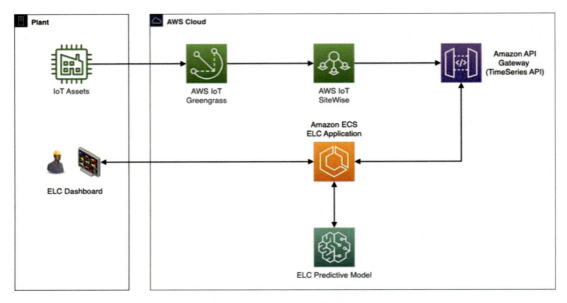

Figure 8-1. *Amazon SageMaker high-level architecture for Yara*

These were the solutions implemented by Yara:

- ELC uses Internet of Things (IoT) sensors to collect data from a plant of Yara's to measure metrics and train an energy prediction model. In the cloud, AWS IoT Greengrass was implemented to stream real-time data from a plant stream sensor.

- AWS IoT Greengrass communicates with AWS IoT Core security and exports IoT data to the AWS cloud.

- AWS IoT SiteWise is a managed service that collects, organizes, searches, and consumes data from industrial equipment on a large scale.

- Yara has used Amazon API Gateway to create APIs that expose sensor data to applications like ELC.

- The ELC application back end is delivered using Amazon ECS, and it powers ELC dashboards on the front end that will be utilized by plant operators. The ELC application is in charge of giving hourly predictions of energy consumption figures to plant operators.

Key Outcomes

The following were the major outcomes after implementing MLOps in the Yara:

- Yara's next-generation Digital Production Platform (DPP) was built with AWS to digitalize the production systems.

- DPP has been implemented on 28 production sites and two mines.

- AWS implemented DPP to serve as a secure digital core to make efficient, reliable, safe, and sustainable production to analyze new gain insights.

- For Yara, MLOps with AWS significantly reduces the effort required to on board a new plant, roll out live-stream updates to ELC, and model monitoring for quality assurance.

NatWest

National Westminster Bank, commonly known as NatWest, is a leading retail, banking, and financial services group serving 19 million people in the United Kingdom and Ireland. NatWest is considered one of the Big Four clearing banks in the United Kingdom and has a large network of more than 960 branches with online banking services. NatWest handles approximately 750 million financial transactions per month. NatWest believes in championing potential and helping people, families, and businesses.

Business Goal of NatWest

The business goal of implementing MLOps is to reduce NatWest Group's time-to-business value. NatWest group leverages analytics at scale, making it an optimized data-driven bank. But, their processes could be faster and more consistent. The fast-paced financial services industry is very competitive, and providing faster services to their 19 million customers takes a lot of work. NatWest explores its data and builds machine learning (ML) solutions that ensure a bespoke experience based on customer demands.

To accelerate its time-to-business value with ML, NatWest turned to Amazon Web Services (AWS) and adopted Amazon SageMaker as its core ML technology. Amazon SageMaker is a service that data scientists and engineers use to build, train, and deploy ML models with fully managed infrastructure, tools, and workflows for any use case virtually. NatWest group centralized its ML processes on AWS through it takes months to launch new products and services. It also introduces a more agile culture among its data science teams. Using Amazon SageMaker, an idea on a whiteboard becomes a working ML solution in production in a few months versus 1 year or more before.

Challenges

The following were the challenges faced by NatWest before implementing MLOps:

- There was a lack of current training and responsibilities for employees. The proper training of employees is itself a time-consuming and challenging task.

- Manual processes like manual handovers, and governance make progress slow and sluggish, resulting in a long time to value.

- Data, which is the first prerequisite for ML operation, is challenging to access and discover.

- Old technology and an out-of-date environment result in long development to deployment time.

Platform Used

NatWest Group collaborated with AWS Professional Services to create a scalable, secure, and long-lasting MLOps platform utilizing Amazon SageMaker. The high-level architecture diagram in Figure 8-2 shows how a NatWest business application use case is deployed on AWS to build ML solutions.

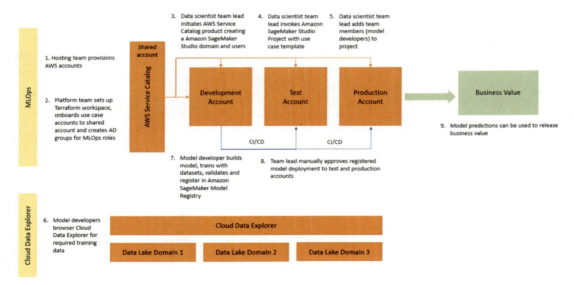

Figure 8-2. *Amazon SageMaker high-level architecture for NatWest*

Solutions Overview

The following were the solutions implemented by NatWest:

- NatWest uses Amazon Simple Storage Service (Amazon S3) for simple data storage and access. With simple and quick access to data and resources along with ML tools, it's easier and faster to build ML use cases.

- NatWest Group uses the AWS Service Catalog to create, organize, and govern infrastructure-as-code templates. It accelerates its employee's workflows from two to four weeks to a few hours.

- NatWest Group has Amazon SageMaker Studio, a single web-based visual interface where all ML development steps can be performed. As it is simple to use and configure, it is user-friendly, easy to learn, and produces effective results.

- Amazon Sage Maker integrates CI/CD pipelines workflow for production-ready use case development. It improves quality, optimized governance, and lineage tracking.

- With Amazon SageMaker Studio, NatWest's main goal of faster time to value was achieved.

Key Outcomes

Figure 8-3. *Outcomes after MLOps implementation in NatWest Group*

The following are the key outcomes after implementing MLOps in NatWest Group:

- The delivery of end-to-end ML solutions became faster as it went from 12 months to less than 3 months.

- Discovery and data access, which usually takes 5 days, is now done in a few hours.

- The ML model took more than 6 months to be deployed in a live environment; it is now done in less than 2 weeks.

- A self-service environment for end users was created that helps resolve issues within a day.

- Time to business value has been reduced significantly, which puts NatWest on top of the ladder.

Thomson Reuters

Thomson Reuters released Westlaw Is Natural (WIN), its first AI legal-related search service in 1992, and is growing continuously with more AI products and services. Thomson Reuters generated billions of machine-learning insights in various fields like legal, tax, accounts, compliance, and news services across the globe.

With the tremendous increase in AI services, Thomson Reuters needs to automate and standardize the repetitive undifferentiated engineering efforts. It also needs easy access to scalable computing resources with sensitive data security according to governance standards.

Business Goal

The business goal for Thomson Reuters is to improve ML capabilities, implementing advanced AI to extract industry insights to help navigate current and future results. Thomson Reuters wants to deliver greater value to stakeholders with higher efficiency and anticipate future challenges with premier solutions.

Challenges

These were the challenges faced by Thomson Reuters:

- Despite highly qualified engineers, the isolated techniques of Thomson Reuters did not provide sufficient visibility to establish governance over critically essential decision-making predictions.

- Business problems were not handled properly with machine learning capabilities.

- Thomson Reuters teams follow their procedures and methodologies. TR aims to provide its users with features that cover the whole ML lifecycle to accelerate the delivery of ML projects by allowing teams to focus on business goals rather than repeating undifferentiated engineering efforts.

- It was challenging to maintain governance standards across data and AI solutions.

Platform Used

Thomson Reuter's AI Platform microservices are powered by Amazon SageMaker as the core engine, AWS serverless components for workflows, and AWS DevOps services for CI/CD procedures. For experimentation and training, SageMaker Studio is implemented, and other components like the SageMaker model registry, Amazon DynamoDB table, SageMaker hosting services, SageMaker Model Monitor, and SageMaker Clarify are also implemented in the AI's platform for Thomson Reuters.

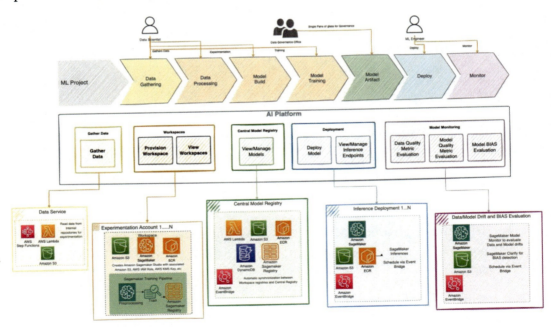

Figure 8-4. *Amazon SageMaker architecture implemented by Thomson Reuters*

Solution Overview

Thomson Reuter's Enterprise AI Platform offers simple and standardized capabilities for every stage of the ML lifecycle. All the requirements of Thomson Reuters's AI platform are modularized in five major categories:

- The data service is used to enable easy and secured access to enterprise data assets.

- SageMaker Studio is implemented to provide an experimentation workspace to experiment and train ML models.

- The SageMaker central model registry is implemented to build and register models across different business units.

- The model deployment service is implemented to follow enterprise CI/CD practices to automate the various inference deployment options.

- SageMaker Model Monitor and SageMaker Clarify have been implemented to monitor data monitoring capabilities for model bias, drift custom metric calculators, and explainability.

Key Outcomes

The following are the major outcomes after implementing MLOps via Amazon SageMaker in Thomson Reuters:

- Using AWS capabilities vast amounts of data can be processed easily and securely.

- The time taken for the ML project from ideation to production has been reduced to a few weeks, compared to the many months it took earlier.

- Thomson Reuters can register and monitor ML models for the first time, achieving compliance with their evolving model governance standards.

- Thomson Reuters enabled data scientists and product teams to effectively use their creativity to solve the most complicated problems.

Cepsa

Cepsa is a worldwide energy corporation that works in the sustainability and energy transition space. For the cruise industry, Cepsa made the first direct supply of 2G biofuels in the Port of Barcelona.

Cepsa wants to become a leader in the energy transition, sustainable mobility, and the production of green molecules and second-generation biofuels using ML capabilities.

Cepsa has implemented machine learning to solve complex challenges across all of its business lines, as well as various processes at their refineries.

Business Goal

The business goal of Cepsa is to implement MLOps architecture using the various AWS key services. The MLOps services are to be implemented from a complete ML lifecycle along with predictive maintenance for industrial equipment to monitor and enhance petrochemical processes at their refineries.

Challenges

The following are the challenges faced by Cepsa while implementing ML solutions:

- Lack of reference architecture to follow for ML implementation
- No model registry or versioning system
- Model monitoring was not implemented
- Lack of right metrics for performance evaluation

Platform Used

Cepsa data scientists and developers implemented the AWS MLOps system and its various components. AWS Cloud 9 is used to write, run, and debug code for data wrangling and ML experimentation, while GitHub is the Git code repository. Amazon SageMaker is implemented for an automatic training workflow from model training to registering output models in the model registry. SageMaker model hosting features are used to create inference endpoints to manage model deployment.

AWS Step Functions are used to develop both model training and deployment processes because they provide a versatile framework that allows us to create specific workflows for each project and easily orchestrates different AWS services and components.

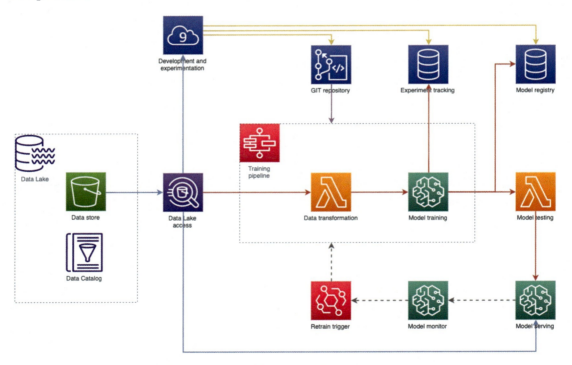

Figure 8-5. *MLOps architecture implemented by Cepsa*

Solution Overview

Cepsa implements the following AWS services for MLOps:

- Amazon SageMaker is implemented to build, train, and deploy ML models.

- The data used to train ML models is extracted from various data lakes via Amazon API Gateway.

- The API backend accesses data stored in the Amazon Simple Storage engine (Amazon S3) and cataloged in the AWS Glue Data Catalog via Amazon Athena (an interactive query engine for typical SQL data analysis).

- AWS Step Functions is a serverless low-code visual workflow service used to orchestrate and automate processes.

- Amazon EventBridge is a serverless event bus.

- AWS Lambda is a serverless computing solution that enables you to execute code without having to provision or manage servers.

- Cepsa implemented Amazon Elastic Container Registry (Amazon ECR) to store, manage, share, and deploy container images used in model training.

- The standard SageMaker Scikit-learn has been extended to include the various environment variables required for the project.

- To automate the model deployment Amazon EventBridge is implemented.

Key Outcomes

Cepsa shows tremendous improvement in ML implementation and results after implementing Amazon SageMaker and other AWS components.

- Currently, six ML models can automatically train, deploy, and track, and more than 30 versions of ML models have been deployed for each of the production models.

- This current MLOps architecture has been extended to various projects for hundreds of ML models across the company.

- With the automation pipelines and reduced bootstrapping time, the ML project mean duration was reduced by 25%.

- Quick ML projects have led to an increase in yield production thus the estimated savings turn is around €300,000 per year.

- With Amazon SageMaker for MLOps, automation of the full ML model lifecycle was implemented to ensure better model quality and faster and more frequent deployments to production.

Final Thoughts

The aim is to automate the deployment of ML systems in production seamlessly with AWS services offered by Amazon. Best practices for the AWS pillars need to be followed to achieve excellence and exceptional performance.

We have seen many big organizations improve their performance by implementing MLOps into AWS, which automates the ML lifecycle processes. Their project deploys faster to production, with better performance and efficiency, and the time to market has been reduced with an increased ROI. These are a few role models case studies for futuristic technologies, ideas, businesses, and organizations that can be followed for MLOps enhancement.

References

- https://aws.amazon.com/blogs/machine-learning/how-amazon-music-uses-sagemaker-with-nvidia-to-optimize-ml-training-and-inference-performance-and-cost/

- https://aws.amazon.com/blogs/machine-learning/how-yara-is-using-mlops-features-of-amazon-sagemaker-to-scale-energy-optimization-across-their-ammonia-plants/

- https://aws.amazon.com/blogs/machine-learning/part-1-how-natwest-group-built-a-scalable-secure-and-sustainable-mlops-platform/

- https://d1.awsstatic.com/events/Summits/reinvent2022/FSI203_NatWest-Personalizing-banking-at-scale-with-machine-learning-on-AWS.pdf

- https://aws.amazon.com/blogs/machine-learning/how-thomson-reuters-built-an-ai-platform-using-amazon-sagemaker-to-accelerate-delivery-of-ml-projects/

- https://aws.amazon.com/blogs/machine-learning/how-cepsa-used-amazon-sagemaker-and-aws-step-functions-to-industrialize-their-ml-projects-and-operate-their-models-at-scale/

CHAPTER 9

MLOps for Generative AI

Generative artificial intelligence (AI) represents one of the most fascinating and rapidly advancing fields within the broader landscape of AI. Unlike traditional AI models that focus on classification or prediction, generative AI models create new data instances. With the recent rise of generative AI, we are prompted to consider how MLOps processes should be adapted to this new class of AI-powered applications. In this chapter, we focus on the productionization of large language models (LLMs) and MLOps practices for the generative AI application lifecycle.

Understanding Generative AI

Generative AI refers to a type of artificial intelligence system that can generate new content, such as images, videos, text, or even music, that is similar to what a human might produce. This type of AI is based on deep learning algorithms that are trained on large amounts of data, such as images or text, and they use that data to generate new content. This is powered by large models that are pre-trained on a vast corpora of data and commonly referred to as *foundation models* (FMs).

These mainly include the large language models (LLMs) and large vision models (LVMs). The primary techniques in generative AI include generative adversarial networks (GANs), variational autoencoders (VAEs), and transformer-based models.

- **Generative Adversarial Networks (GANs):**

  GANs consist of two neural networks, a generator and a discriminator, that compete against each other. The generator creates fake data, while the discriminator evaluates its authenticity. Through this adversarial process, GANs produce highly realistic outputs.

© Neel Sendas and Deepali Rajale 2024
N. Sendas and D. Rajale, *The Definitive Guide to Machine Learning Operations in AWS*,
https://doi.org/10.1007/979-8-8688-1076-3_9

- **Variational Autoencoders (VAEs)**:

  VAEs encode input data into a latent space and then decode it back to reconstruct the original data. By sampling from the latent space, VAEs can generate new data instances.

- **Transformers**:

  Transformer-based models, such as GPT (Generative Pre-trained Transformer), utilize attention mechanisms to generate text and other sequential data by predicting the next item in a sequence based on the context provided by previous items.

Why Foundation Models

The size and general-purpose nature of FMs make them different from traditional ML models, which typically perform specific tasks, like analyzing text for sentiment, classifying images, and forecasting trends.

With traditional ML models, to achieve each specific task, customers need to gather labeled data, train a model, and deploy that model. With foundation models, instead of gathering labeled data for each model and training multiple models, customers can use the same pretrained FM to adapt various tasks. FMs can also be customized to perform domain-specific functions that are different from their businesses, using only a small fraction of the data and compute required to train a model from scratch. See Figure 9-1.

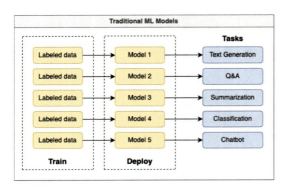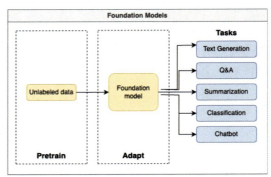

Figure 9-1. *Traditional ML models vs. foundation models*

Common tasks for foundation models include text generation, Q&A, search, text summarization, text extraction, code generation, image generation, audio generation, video generation to name a few.

Significance of Generative AI

The significance of generative AI lies in its ability to create, innovate, and augment various forms of data. This capability has far-reaching implications for creativity, efficiency, and problem-solving across multiple domains.

Creativity and Innovation

Generative AI fosters creativity by producing original content in art, music, literature, and design. Artists and creators use these models to explore new artistic directions and generate novel works.

Data Augmentation

In machine learning, generative AI helps overcome data limitations by augmenting datasets with synthetic examples and improving model training and performance.

Automation and Efficiency

Generative AI automates content creation and design processes, enhancing productivity and reducing the time and cost associated with manual creation.

Personalization

These models enable highly personalized user experiences by generating tailored content, recommendations, and interactions.

Applications of Generative AI in Various Industries

Generative AI is rapidly transforming industries by enabling new possibilities in automation, creativity, and problem-solving. By leveraging advanced machine learning models, generative AI can produce content, designs, and solutions that were once possible only through human intervention. This technology is revolutionizing processes across sectors by enhancing efficiency, driving innovation, and opening up new avenues for customization and personalization. As generative AI continues to evolve, its applications are becoming more integrated into everyday business operations, reshaping the way industries function and setting the stage for the future of work.

Healthcare

Generative AI is revolutionizing healthcare by enabling advancements in medical imaging, drug discovery, and personalized medicine.

Medical Imaging

GANs and VAEs enhance medical imaging techniques by generating high-quality images for diagnostic purposes. These models improve the resolution of MRI and CT scans and assist in creating synthetic medical images for training purposes.

Drug Discovery

Generative models accelerate drug discovery by generating potential molecular structures for new drugs. This reduces the time and cost involved in identifying viable drug candidates.

Personalized Medicine

By analyzing patient data, generative AI can create personalized treatment plans and predict individual responses to therapies, enhancing patient outcomes.

Entertainment and Media

In the entertainment and media industry, generative AI is transforming content creation, animation, and virtual experiences.

Content Creation

AI-generated text, music, and art enable creators to explore new ideas and produce content more efficiently. For instance, AI can generate script drafts, compose music, or create visual art pieces.

Animation and Visual Effects

Generative models assist in creating realistic animations and special effects for movies and video games. GANs can generate lifelike characters, landscapes, and other visual elements.

Virtual Reality (VR) and Augmented Reality (AR)

Generative AI enhances VR and AR experiences by creating immersive environments and interactive elements, making virtual experiences more engaging and realistic.

Finance

The finance industry leverages generative AI for fraud detection, algorithmic trading, and financial forecasting.

Fraud Detection

Generative models identify anomalous patterns and generate synthetic fraud scenarios to train detection systems, improving their accuracy and robustness.

Algorithmic Trading

AI-generated trading strategies analyze vast amounts of market data to identify profitable trading opportunities and optimize investment portfolios.

Financial Forecasting

Generative AI models predict market trends and financial outcomes by analyzing historical data and simulating various scenarios, aiding decision-making for investors and financial institutions.

Retail and E-commerce

Generative AI enhances the retail and e-commerce sector through personalized recommendations, virtual try-ons, and inventory management.

Personalized Recommendations

AI-generated recommendations provide customers with tailored product suggestions based on their preferences and browsing behavior, enhancing the shopping experience.

Virtual Try-Ons

Generative models create virtual fitting rooms where customers can try on clothing and accessories digitally, improving online shopping satisfaction and reducing returns.

Inventory Management

Generative AI predicts demand patterns and optimizes inventory levels, ensuring efficient stock management and reducing wastage.

Manufacturing

In manufacturing, generative AI optimizes design processes, predictive maintenance, and supply chain management.

Design Optimization

AI-generated designs create innovative product prototypes and optimize existing designs for performance, cost, and manufacturability.

Predictive Maintenance

Generative models analyze equipment data to predict maintenance needs and generate maintenance schedules, reducing downtime and improving operational efficiency.

Supply Chain Management

Generative AI predicts supply chain disruptions and generates optimal strategies for inventory management, logistics, and demand forecasting.

Conceptualizing MLOps for Generative AI

As generative AI models evolve in complexity and become central to numerous applications, the need to meticulously manage their lifecycle—from development to deployment and maintenance—becomes paramount. The multifaceted lifecycle of generative AI applications introduces significant challenges, demanding robust management and scalable solutions across various stages.

In today's data-driven landscape, businesses depend on AI to drive innovation, deliver customer value, and maintain a competitive edge. The widespread adoption of machine learning (ML) has necessitated the development of tools, processes, and organizational principles to manage code, data, and models reliably, cost-effectively, and at scale. This comprehensive approach is known as *machine learning operations* (MLOps). Extending MLOps to generative AI encompasses both LLMOps and GenAIOps, for addressing the challenges of developing and managing generative AI and LLM-powered apps in production.

Lifecycle of a Modern Generative AI Application

The development of a modern generative AI application begins with a foundation model, which undergoes a pretraining phase to acquire foundational knowledge and emergent capabilities (see Figure 9-2). Enterprises require a secure method to access SaaS or open-source LLMs and an efficient approach to rigorously test these models for specific use cases through comprehensive prompt engineering. Subsequently, the model is aligned with human preferences, behavior, and values using a curated dataset of human-generated prompts and responses, enhancing its precision in the following instructions.

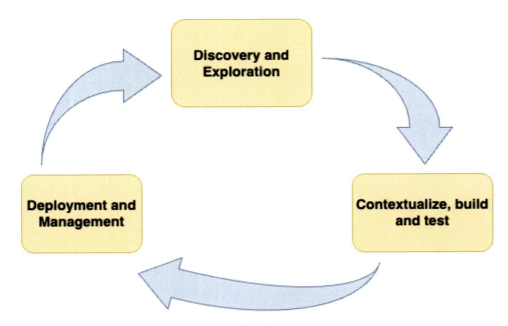

Figure 9-2. *Lifecycle of a generative AI application*

Organizations can opt to train their own foundation model or utilize a pre-trained one. During the customization phase, a foundation model is either augmented with task-specific prompts or fine-tuned on a curated enterprise dataset. However, the knowledge embedded within a foundation model is confined to its pretraining and fine-tuning data, necessitating continuous retraining to remain current—a process that can be costly. Post-customization, the model is primed for real-world deployment, either stand-alone or as part of a chain integrating multiple foundation models and APIs to deliver comprehensive application logic. At this stage, it is essential to rigorously test the entire AI system for accuracy, performance, and vulnerabilities, and to implement guardrails ensuring the model's outputs are precise, safe, and secure. The feedback loop is then closed, with users interacting through the user interface or automated data collection via system instrumentation. This feedback is used for continuous model updates and A/B testing, enhancing its value to customers.

Enterprises typically manage numerous generative AI applications tailored to various use cases, business functions, and workflows. This AI portfolio demands continuous monitoring and risk management to ensure seamless operation, ethical use, and prompt responses to incidents, biases, or regressions.

GenAIOps expedites this journey from research to production through automation, optimizing development and operational costs, enhancing model quality, adding robustness to the evaluation process, and ensuring sustained operations at scale.

Imagine AI as a series of nested layers (Figure 9-3). At the outermost layer, machine learning (ML) encompasses intelligent automation, where program logic is not explicitly coded but derived from data. Delving deeper, we encounter specialized AI types, such as those based on large language models (LLMs) or retrieval-augmented generation (RAG) frameworks. Similarly, there are layered concepts ensuring reproducibility, reuse, scalability, reliability, and efficiency.

- **MLOps** is the overarching concept covering the core tools, processes, and best practices for end-to-end machine learning system development and operations in production.

- **GenAIOps** extends MLOps to develop and operationalize generative AI solutions. The distinct characteristic of GenAIOps is the management of and interaction with a foundation model.

- **LLMOps** is a distinct type of GenAIOps focused specifically on developing and productionizing LLM-based solutions.

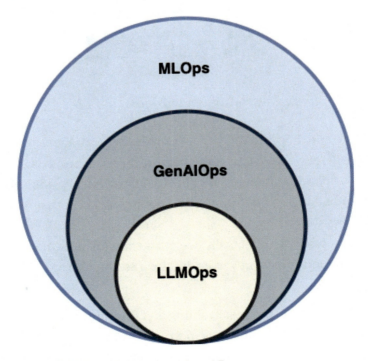

Figure 9-3. *Layers of MLOps for generative AI*

Let's start from the lowest layer to understand the comprehensive MLOps elements for Generative AI.

LLMOps

LLMs have gained significant traction in business and media, and their impact is poised to transform numerous industries (Figure 9-4).

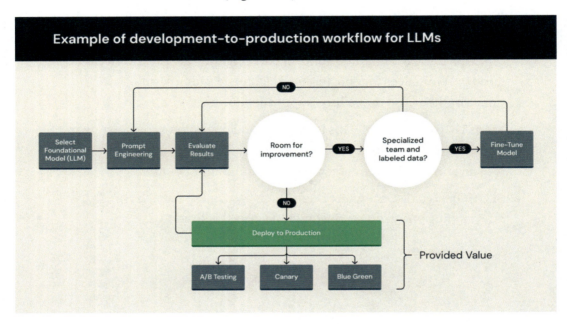

Figure 9-4. *Development-to-production workflow of LLMs*

Large language model ops (LLMOps) encompasses the practices, techniques and tools used for the operational management of large language models in production environments. The operational requirements of MLOps typically apply to LLMOps as well, but there are challenges with training and deploying LLMs that require a unique approach to LLMOps.

To adjust MLOps practices effectively, we must examine how machine learning (ML) workflows and requirements evolve with the introduction of LLMs. Critical considerations include:

- **Computational Resources**: Training and fine-tuning large language models necessitate significantly more computations on extensive datasets. To accelerate this process, specialized hardware such as

GPUs is utilized for vastly faster data-parallel operations. Access to these specialized compute resources is crucial for both training and deploying large language models. Additionally, the cost of inference highlights the importance of model compression and distillation techniques.

- **Transfer Learning**: Unlike traditional ML models often built or trained from scratch, many large language models begin with a foundation model and are subsequently fine-tuned with new data to enhance performance in a specific domain. This fine-tuning enables state-of-the-art results for particular applications while requiring less data and fewer computational resources.

- **Human Feedback**: A significant advancement in training large language models is achieved through reinforcement learning from human feedback (RLHF). Given the often open-ended nature of LLM tasks, feedback from end users is crucial for evaluating LLM performance. Incorporating this feedback loop into your LLMOps pipelines not only streamlines evaluation but also supplies valuable data for future fine-tuning of your LLM.

- **Hyperparameter Tuning**: In traditional ML, hyperparameter tuning primarily focuses on enhancing accuracy or other performance metrics. However, for LLMs, tuning is also crucial for minimizing the cost and computational power needed for training and inference. Adjustments to parameters such as batch sizes and learning rates can significantly impact the speed and expense of training. Therefore, while both classical ML models and LLMs benefit from a well-managed tuning process, the priorities differ, with LLMs placing a greater emphasis on cost and computational efficiency.

- **Performance Metrics**: Traditional ML models have well-defined performance metrics like accuracy, AUC, and F1 score, which are relatively simple to calculate. However, evaluating LLMs involves a different set of standard metrics, such as the Bilingual Evaluation Understudy (BLEU) and the Recall-Oriented Understudy for Gisting Evaluation (ROUGE). Implementing these metrics requires additional considerations.

345

- **Prompt Engineering**: Instruction-following models can process complex prompts or sets of instructions. Designing these prompt templates is crucial for obtaining accurate and reliable responses from LLMs. Effective prompt engineering can mitigate the risks of model hallucination and prompt hacking, such as prompt injection, sensitive data leakage, and jailbreaking.

- **Constructing LLM Chains or Pipelines**: LLM pipelines, created with tools like LangChain or LlamaIndex, integrate multiple LLM calls and interactions with external systems such as vector databases or web search. These pipelines enable LLMs to perform complex tasks, such as knowledge base Q&A or responding to user queries based on a set of documents. Consequently, LLM application development frequently emphasizes building these pipelines instead of developing new LLMs from scratch.

Benefits of LLMOps

While LLMs are particularly straightforward to use during prototyping, integrating an LLM into a commercial product presents significant challenges. The LLM development lifecycle comprises numerous complex components, including data ingestion, data preparation, prompt engineering, model fine-tuning, deployment, and monitoring. This process also demands collaboration and seamless handoffs across various teams, such as data engineering, data science, and ML engineering. Maintaining operational rigor is essential to ensure these processes remain synchronized and effective. LLMOps encompasses the experimentation, iteration, deployment, and continuous improvement throughout the LLM development lifecycle. The primary advantages of LLMOps are enhanced efficiency, scalability, and risk reduction.

- **Efficiency**: LLMOps enables data teams to accelerate the development of models and pipelines, produce higher-quality models, and expedite deployment to production.

- **Scalability**: LLMOps supports extensive scalability and management, allowing thousands of models to be overseen, controlled, managed, and monitored for continuous integration, delivery, and deployment.

It ensures reproducibility of LLM pipelines, fostering closer collaboration among data teams, minimizing conflicts with DevOps and IT, and speeding up release cycles.

- **Risk Reduction**: Given that LLMs often require regulatory oversight, LLMOps enhances transparency and allows for quicker responses to such requests, ensuring better compliance with organizational or industry policies.

LLMOps Best Practices

The scope of LLMOps in machine learning projects can vary widely based on the project's requirements. In some instances, LLMOps may cover the entire process from data preparation to pipeline production, while in other cases, it might only involve the model deployment process. The following best practices can be applied to different stages of the process:

- **Exploratory Data Analysis (EDA)**: Iteratively explore, share, and prepare data for the machine learning lifecycle by creating reproducible, editable, and shareable datasets, tables, and visualizations.

- **Data Preparation and Prompt Engineering**: Iteratively transform, aggregate, and de-duplicate data, making it accessible and shareable across data teams. Develop prompts iteratively to ensure structured and reliable queries to LLMs.

- **Model Fine-Tuning**: Utilize popular open-source libraries such as Hugging Face Transformers, DeepSpeed, PyTorch, TensorFlow, and JAX to fine-tune models and enhance their performance.

- **Model Review and Governance**: Track the lineage and versions of models and pipelines, managing these artifacts throughout their lifecycle. Discover, share, and collaborate on ML models using an open-source MLOps platform like MLflow.

- **Model Inference and Serving**: Manage model refresh frequency, inference request times, and other production-specific details in testing and QA. Employ CI/CD tools, including repositories and orchestrators (borrowing from DevOps principles), to automate the preproduction pipeline. Enable REST API model endpoints with GPU acceleration.

- **Model Monitoring with Human Feedback**: Establish model and data monitoring pipelines with alerts for both model drift and malicious user behavior.

GenAIOps

GenAIOps incorporates best practices to manage all generative AI workloads, encompassing language, image, and multimodal models. The processes of data curation, model training, customization, evaluation, optimization, deployment, and risk management need to be rethought for generative AI. Building a Gen AI application involves multiple components such as an LLM, data sources, vector store, prompt engineering, and RAG. GenAIOps defines operational best practices for the holistic management of DataOps, LLMOps, and DevOps for building, testing, and deploying generative AI applications.

Challenges in GenAIOps Automation

The following are some of the challenges that organizations have to overcome to achieve a successful GenAIOps pipeline:

1. **Access to Enterprise Data**: This involves creating connectors to various storage solutions and databases, considering different ingestion formats like files, tabular data, or API responses. Unlike traditional ETL, extraction, cleaning, masking, and chunking techniques require special attention, especially when dealing with complex structures like tables in PDFs or removing unwanted HTML tags from web crawls.

2. **Embedding Algorithms**: The constantly evolving nature of embedding algorithms means it's crucial to experiment with the top models to select the most effective one for your needs. Failure to do so can adversely impact the search process.

3. **Query Phase Management**: This phase can be vulnerable to adversarial actors who may try to "jailbreak" the prompts or overwhelm the system, impacting other users and potentially causing a cost spike.

4. **Chunk Retrieval Process**: For the chunk retrieval process, the similarity search may not retrieve adequate information or be unable to retrieve matching chunks, leading to insufficient context for comprehensive and relevant answers. Advanced retrieval chains are required to augment prompts with personalized context. (What are claims exclusions for "my" insurance plan?)

5. **Prompt Efficiency and Prompt Management**: Open-source LLMs are catching up fast with proprietary LLMs in language understanding, as evident in the open LLMs leaderboard on HuggingFace [1]. Hence, writing efficient prompts is important to get a relevant and comprehensive answer. Bad prompts can either confuse the LLMs or lead to inadequate responses.

6. **Understanding the Enterprise Domain**: While Generative AI effectively addresses numerous inquisitive challenges within enterprises, LLMs often struggle to grasp the specific nuances of individual enterprise domains. LLMs are trained on publicly available datasets by crawling the world wide web, but enterprise data is behind firewalls; hence, LLMs may not understand a specific internal term used within a business, leading to an "I don't know" response or a response related to a similar term in Wikipedia dictionary leading to hallucination.

7. **Content Safety**: LLMs may spout toxic or unsafe content without proper guardrails, leading to brand reputation issues. Imagine building these AI chatbots for children or other uninformed or vulnerable populations that may be led astray with misinformation.

8. **User Experience**: Most Gen AI systems do not focus on end-user experience. Chat GPT has set the standard for user experience, but OpenAI has control of the end-to-end pipeline, including the model. Lack of good experiences, such as streaming responses, A/B testing framework, lack of exhaustive user feedback mechanism, adequate seeding questions, or lack of follow-up questions, may diminish user engagement.

GenAIOps Best Practices for Enterprises

Effective GenAIOps operationalization requires skills such as AI engineers, safety and security experts, and domain experts. Here are some of the best practices:

1. **Data Management**: Utilize standard storage, database, and SaaS application interfaces to minimize bulk distributed data replication and incremental ingestion. To make it LLM-ready, utilize distributed runtimes for extraction, cleaning, masking, and chunking data. Maintain a copy of source metadata to the vector store to ensure downstream querying systems can use it for pre-filtering for more relevant answers.

2. **Model Selection**: Depending on your dataset, use the most appropriate embedding model for your use case. Try at least the top two embedding model techniques during the experimentation phase to understand search relevance based on human-generated standard questions and answer pairs. Utilize synthetic questions generated by LLMs if you don't have human-generated question-answer pairs.

3. **Query Phase Management**: To prevent intentional or unintentional adverse behavior, use a suitable classification model to block questions and provide canned responses. Monitor adverse prompts for trends and take appropriate action to improve classification methods iteratively. To safeguard against spam attacks, enable user- and token-based throttling to limit attack vectors.

4. **Retrieval Optimization**: Use user metadata for pre-filtering to produce a narrower set for semantic search for optimal retrieval. Many vector databases, such as OpenSearch, MongoDB, and Pinecone, provide hybrid search capabilities. Depending on your

source datasets, use additional retrieval chains to retrieve the entire or partial document to provide adequate context for your LLM query. For example, in an R&D chatbot, if the user asks to summarize a particular science paper, your retrieval chain must retrieve the entire science paper based on matching chunks.

5. **Building Efficient System Prompts**: Building system prompts is the most critical task to get the most optimal response. Because of the lack of a universal framework for prompts, ensure you follow the standards most appropriate based on LLM or your task (e.g., conversation, summarization, or classification). Maintain a library of best practice prompts for enterprise-specific use cases to benefit others. Including and enabling domain experts to design system prompts is essential as they are intimately familiar with datasets and expected outputs. Provide a prompt playground so domain experts can intuitively write system prompts, including examples, "Do not" rules, and expected response format. Provide a playground to quickly compare against authorized models for your enterprise. Maintain versions of the prompts so you can promote the best version to production.

6. **Model Experimentation**: Many enterprises start with SaaS model providers such as Azure OpenAI or Amazon Bedrock. Open-source models such as Llama2, Mistral, and MPT and their variants are catching up fast. Try out your application against at least two to three leading SOTA models to understand response time, domain understanding, and quality of response. Typical enterprise applications may not need the bells and whistles of multi-headed SaaS models, so using open-source models may be as effective as you scale out and offer a better price per performance. For the rapid testing, build an evaluation script to utilize the "LLM as a judge" approach to compare the responses' relevance, comprehensiveness, and accuracy. If the general purpose model does not provide relevant and comprehensive responses, resort to domain-specific fine-tuning or instruction fine-tuning techniques and employ the fine-tuned model in your RAG.

7. **Content Safety**: To prevent harmful, toxic responses, augment system prompts to instruct LLMs to redact harmful content from the response. Employ additional controls using other classifiers to block harmful responses entirely to ensure trust and safety. Use a standard set of questions for automated testing to ensure RAGs are regression tested to account for any changes in LLM, system prompts, or changes in data. Guardrails intercept adversarial or unsupported inputs before they reach a foundation model, ensuring that outputs are accurate, relevant, safe, and secure. They monitor and verify the state of conversations and active contexts, detect intents, and make decisions while enforcing content policies. These guardrails extend the rule-based pre/postprocessing of AI inputs and outputs covered under model management.

8. **Enhancing User Experience**: Ultimately, user experience is essential to increase engagement and attract new users. Add streaming if you are building a conversational system, provide appropriate feedback options so users can rate responses, and volunteer to provide correct responses to build the knowledge base. Provide custom instructions, seeding questions to start the conversation, and follow-up questions. Generative AI is rapidly evolving, so it is vital to continue to monitor user feedback and incorporate additional capabilities such as multimodal (image and text).

These best practices enable enterprises to execute rapid prototyping, production deployment, and continuous monitoring. The generative AI application's observability capabilities, evaluation, and central performance monitoring allow continuous quality and enterprise governance improvement.

MLOps

MLOps establishes a structured framework for the development, training, evaluation, optimization, deployment, inference, and monitoring of machine learning models in production environments. The principles and capabilities of MLOps are equally pertinent to generative AI, including the following aspects:

- **Infrastructure Management**: Programmatically request, provision, and configure compute, storage, and networking resources to access the underlying hardware.

- **Data Management**: Handle the collection, ingestion, storage, processing, and labeling of data for training and evaluation. Implement role-based access control; facilitate dataset search, browsing, and exploration; track data provenance; log data; version datasets; index metadata; validate data quality; and utilize dataset cards and dashboards for data visualization.

- **Workflow and Pipeline Management**: Integrate data preparation, model training, model evaluation, model optimization, and model deployment steps into an end-to-end automated and scalable workflow, utilizing either cloud resources or local workstations.

- **Model Management**: Train, evaluate, and optimize models for production, store and version models with model cards in a centralized model registry, assess model risks, and ensure compliance with standards.

- **Experiment Management and Observability**: Track and compare various machine learning model experiments, including changes in training data, models, and hyperparameters. Automatically explore the space of possible model architectures and hyperparameters, analyze model performance during inference, and monitor model inputs and outputs for concept drift.

- **Interactive Development**: Manage development environments, integrate with external version control systems, desktop IDEs, and other stand-alone developer tools, facilitating team collaboration, job launching, and project prototyping.

From the perspective of MLOps, LLMs bring new requirements, with implications for MLOps practices and platforms. Table 9-1 summarizes key properties of LLMs and the implications for MLOps.

Table 9-1. *Key Properties of LLMs and Their Implications on MLOps*

Key Properties of LLMs	Implications for MLOps
LLMs are available in many forms: • Very general proprietary models behind paid APIs • Open-source models that vary from general to specific applications • Custom models fine-tuned for specific applications	**Development process:** Projects often develop incrementally, starting from existing, third-party, or open-source models and ending with custom fine-tuned models.
Many LLMs take general natural language queries and instructions as input. Those queries can contain carefully engineered "prompts" to elicit the desired responses.	**Development process:** Designing text templates for querying LLMs is often an important part of developing new LLM pipelines. **Packaging ML artifacts:** Many LLM pipelines will use existing LLMs or LLM serving endpoints; the ML logic developed for those pipelines may focus on prompt templates, agents or "chains" instead of the model itself. The ML artifacts packaged and promoted to production may frequently be these pipelines, rather than models.
Many LLMs can be given prompts with examples and context, or additional information to help answer the query.	**Serving infrastructure:** When augmenting LLM queries with context, it is valuable to use previously uncommon tooling such as vector databases to search for relevant context
LLMs are very large deep learning models, often ranging from gigabytes to hundreds of gigabytes.	**Serving infrastructure:** Many LLMs may require GPUs for real-time model serving. **Cost/performance trade-offs:** Since larger models require more computation and are thus more expensive to serve, techniques for reducing model size and computation may be required.
LLMs are hard to evaluate via traditional ML metrics since there is often no single "right" answer.	**Human feedback:** Since human feedback is essential for evaluating and testing LLMs, it must be incorporated more directly into the MLOps process, both for testing and monitoring and for future fine-tuning.

Source: Databricks Big Book of MLOps, 2nd edition

MLOps for Generative AI on AWS

AWS provides an extensive ecosystem that supports every stage of the generative AI lifecycle, from data preparation and model training to development, deployment, and monitoring of Generative AI applications. The following are the key elements that contribute to the AWS generative AI landscape.

Building with Foundation Models

AWS provides a pathway to innovate faster with new capabilities, choice of industry leading foundation models (FMs), and the most cost-effective infrastructure.

Amazon Bedrock

Bedrock is a fully managed service that provides access to a selection of high-performance foundation models (FMs) from leading AI companies like AI21 Labs, Anthropic, Cohere, Meta, Mistral AI, Stability AI, and Amazon, all through a single API. It offers a comprehensive set of capabilities to develop generative AI applications with a focus on security, privacy, and responsible AI. With Amazon Bedrock, you can easily experiment with and evaluate top FMs for your specific use case, privately customize them using your data through techniques such as fine-tuning and retrieval augmented generation (RAG), and build agents that perform tasks using your enterprise systems and data sources. As Amazon Bedrock is serverless, there is no need to manage infrastructure, allowing you to securely integrate and deploy generative AI capabilities into your applications using familiar AWS services.

Flexibility of Model Choice

Amazon Bedrock helps you rapidly adapt and take advantage of the latest generative AI innovations with easy access to a choice of high-performing FMs from leading AI companies like AI21 Labs, Anthropic, Cohere, Meta, Mistral AI, Stability AI, and Amazon. The single-API access of Amazon Bedrock, regardless of the models you choose, gives you the flexibility to use different FMs and upgrade to the latest model versions with minimal code changes.

Secure Customization

To tailor models for specific tasks, you can privately fine-tune foundation models (FMs) using your labeled datasets in just a few simple steps. Amazon Bedrock supports fine-tuning for Cohere Command, Meta Llama 2, Amazon Titan Text Lite and Express, Amazon Titan Multimodal Embeddings, and Amazon Titan Image Generator. To adapt Amazon Titan Text models to your industry and domain, you can use continued pre-training with unlabeled data. With fine-tuning and continued pretraining, Amazon Bedrock creates a separate copy of the base FM that is accessible only by you, ensuring your data is not used to train the original base models. AWS allows you to customize a model privately by simply pointing to a few labeled examples in Amazon S3, enabling the service to fine-tune the model for a specific task with as few as 20 examples. For instance, a content marketing manager at a leading fashion retailer needing fresh, targeted ad and campaign copy for a new line of handbags can provide a few labeled examples of their best-performing taglines from past campaigns, along with associated product descriptions. Bedrock will then automatically generate effective social media, display ads, and web copy for the new handbags.

- **Security of gen AI applications**: With Bedrock, you maintain complete control over the data used to customize foundation models for your generative AI applications. Your data is encrypted both in transit and at rest. Moreover, you can create, manage, and control encryption keys through the AWS Key Management Service (AWS KMS). Identity-based policies offer additional control, allowing you to manage the actions users and roles can perform on specific resources and under certain conditions.

- **Data Protection and Privacy**: Bedrock ensures your data remains under your control. When you tune a foundation model, it is based on a private copy, meaning your data is not shared with model providers or used to improve the base models. You can use AWS PrivateLink to establish private connectivity from your Amazon Virtual Private Cloud (VPC) to Amazon Bedrock, avoiding exposure of your VPC to Internet traffic. Additionally, Bedrock complies with common standards, including ISO, SOC, and CSA STAR Level 2, is HIPAA eligible, and can be used in compliance with the GDPR.

- **Governance and Auditability**: Bedrock provides extensive monitoring and logging capabilities to meet your governance and audit needs. You can leverage Amazon CloudWatch to track usage metrics and create customized dashboards for audit purposes. Additionally, AWS CloudTrail can be used to monitor API activity and troubleshoot issues during the integration of other systems into your generative AI applications. You also have the option to store metadata, requests, and responses in your Amazon Simple Storage Service (Amazon S3) bucket and Amazon CloudWatch Logs. To prevent misuse, Amazon Bedrock incorporates automated abuse detection mechanisms.

Foundation Model Training and Hosting Infrastructure

Building foundation models (FMs) requires building, maintaining, and optimizing large clusters to train models with tens to hundreds of billions of parameters on vast amounts of data. AWS provides purpose-built accelerators for generative AI.

Amazon SageMaker HyperPod

Building foundation models (FMs) requires building, maintaining, and optimizing large clusters to train models with tens to hundreds of billions of parameters on vast amounts of data. Amazon SageMaker HyperPod simplifies the complex task of building and optimizing machine learning infrastructure for training foundation models, reducing training time by up to 40%. It comes preconfigured with SageMaker's distributed training libraries, allowing customers to automatically distribute training workloads across thousands of accelerators for enhanced model performance. Additionally, SageMaker HyperPod ensures uninterrupted FM training by periodically saving checkpoints. In the event of hardware failure during training, it automatically detects the issue, repairs or replaces the faulty instance, and resumes training from the last checkpoint, eliminating the need for manual intervention and enabling continuous training over weeks or months without disruption.

AWS Trainium and AWS Inferentia2

Training large-scale LLMs requires distributed training across more than 100 nodes, and getting elastic access to large clusters of high-performance compute is difficult. Even if you manage to get the required accelerated compute capacity, it's challenging to manage a cluster of more than 100 nodes, maintain hardware stability, and achieve model training stability and convergence.

For large-scale training of foundation models with billions of parameters, Trainium Trn1 and Trn1n instances are ideal due to their features. Trn1 instances are powered by advanced NeuronCore-v2 technology, offering ample accelerator compute and memory. Trn1n instances provide increased networking bandwidth (1,600 Gbps), making them well-suited for high-performance training with a focus on cost optimization.

AWS Inferentia, specifically designed for inference by AWS, is a high-performance and low-cost ML inference accelerator.

Each EC2 Inf2 instance is powered by up to 12 Inferentia2 devices, and allows you to choose between four instance sizes: Inf2.xlarge, Inf2.8xlarge, Inf2.24xlarge, and Inf2.48xlarge. See Figure 9-5.

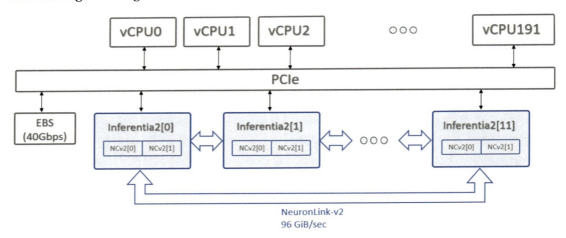

Figure 9-5. *AWS Inf2 architecture*

Amazon EC2 Inf2 supports NeuronLink v2, a low-latency and high-bandwidth chip-to-chip interconnect, which enables high-performance collective communication operations such as AllReduce and AllGather. This efficiently shards models across AWS Inferentia2 devices (such as via Tensor Parallelism) and therefore optimizes latency and throughput. This is particularly useful for large language models. Figure 9-6 shows the internal workings of the AWS Inferentia2 device architecture.

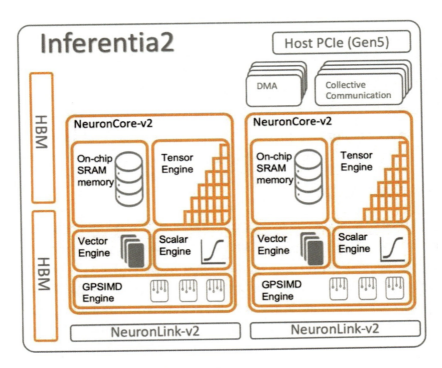

Figure 9-6. *AWS Inf2 device architecture*

DJLServing

DJLServing is a high-performance model server that supports AWS Inferentia2 in March 2023. AWS provides a container image suitable for LLM/AIGC use cases. DJL is integrated with Rubikon support for Neuron, which includes DJLServing and transformers-neuronx. These are core components of the container designed to serve LLMs supported by the transformers library. This container, along with the subsequent DLCs, enables models to be loaded on AWS Inferentia chips within an Amazon EC2 Inf2 host, utilizing installed AWS Inferentia drivers and toolkit.

SageMaker Deep Learning Containers (DLCs)

Large models often exceed the memory capacity of a single accelerator. For instance, the BLOOM-176B model may need more than 350 gigabytes of memory, surpassing the capabilities of current hardware accelerators. This requires model parallel techniques from libraries like DeepSpeed and Hugging Face Accelerate to distribute the model across multiple accelerators for inference. SageMaker's Large Model Inference Containers can be utilized with these libraries to enhance model performance.

SageMaker Jumpstart

SageMaker Jumpstart enables you to host your own machine learning models, allowing you to select infrastructure components such as instance sizes and deployment endpoints. One of the main challenges with training and deploying LLMs with billions of parameters is their size, which can make it difficult to fit them into single GPUs, the hardware typically used for deep learning. The scale of these models necessitates high-performance computing resources, like specialized GPUs with substantial memory. Additionally, the size of these models can make them computationally expensive, significantly increasing training and inference times. You can use Amazon SageMaker JumpStart to easily fine-tune a large language text generation model on a domain-specific dataset, similar to how you would train and deploy any model on Amazon SageMaker. JumpStart currently offers two types of fine-tuning: instruction fine-tuning and domain adaptation fine-tuning.

Operationalizing MLOps for Generative AI on AWS

As organizations increasingly adopt generative AI to drive innovation and enhance decision-making, the need for a robust operational framework becomes paramount. By leveraging AWS's comprehensive suite of tools and services, businesses can seamlessly operationalize their generative AI models, ensuring they deliver consistent, high-quality outputs in real-world applications.

LLMOps Using Amazon Bedrock

Amazon Bedrock is a fully managed service that simplifies access to high-performance foundation models (FMs) from leading AI companies via a single API. It enables developers to build and scale generative AI applications without managing the underlying infrastructure's complexity. It provides the following facilities:

- **Access to Foundation Models**: Bedrock offers a curated selection of high-quality models from Amazon and third-party providers like AI21 Labs, Anthropic, and Stability AI, allowing you to choose the best fit for your specific use case without being tied to a single provider.

- **API-First Approach**: Its API-centric design ensures seamless integration with existing workflows and tools, allowing you to incorporate Bedrock into your current development processes with minimal disruption.

- **Fine-Tuning Capabilities**: Bedrock enables you to customize models to meet specific needs, improving performance on domain-specific tasks. This is essential for organizations looking to leverage proprietary data for enhanced model performance.

- **Managed Infrastructure**: AWS takes care of the underlying infrastructure, letting you focus on model development and deployment instead of server management, significantly reducing the operational overhead of running large language models.

- **Built-in Security and Compliance**: Bedrock includes enterprise-grade security features to help you maintain compliance with various regulatory standards.

Referring to the lifecycle of generative AI application shown in Figure 9-2, the following section elaborates how Amazon Bedrock aids in achieving LLMOps.

Selecting the Right Foundation Model

Amazon Bedrock gives you access to a selection of high-performance foundation models from top AI companies such as AI21 Labs, Anthropic, Cohere, Meta, Mistral AI, Stability AI, and Amazon. With its single-API access, Bedrock allows you the flexibility to use various foundation models and upgrade to the latest versions with minimal code modifications. Amazon Bedrock offers a suite of foundation models that generate outputs in the following modalities:

Text: Generate various text types from text input. Examples include chat, question answering, brainstorming, summarization, code generation, table creation, data formatting, and rewriting.

Image: Generate or modify images from text or input images. Examples include image generation, editing, and variations.

Embeddings: Generate numeric vectors from text, images, or both. These vectors can be compared to other embeddings for semantic or visual similarity. Examples include text and image search, queries, categorization, recommendations, personalization, and knowledge base creation.

Customizing a Foundation Model

You can customize foundation models (FMs) privately and securely with your own data in Amazon Bedrock to develop applications tailored to your domain, organization, and use case. Custom models enable you to create distinctive user experiences that align with your company's style, voice, and services.

Fine-tuning allows you to improve model accuracy by providing task-specific labeled training datasets, further specializing your FMs. Continued pre-training lets you train models using your own unlabeled data in a secure, managed environment with customer-managed keys. This process enhances the models' domain specificity, building more robust knowledge and adaptability beyond their original training.

Amazon Bedrock currently offers the following customization methods:

- **Continued Pre-training**: Use unlabeled data to pre-train a foundation model, familiarizing it with specific input types. You can provide data on particular topics to enhance the model's domain knowledge. This process adjusts the model's parameters to better handle the input data. For instance, you can train a model with private data, like internal business documents, that aren't publicly available. You can further enhance the model by retraining it with additional unlabeled data as it becomes available.

- **Fine-tuning**: Use labeled data to train a model and improve its performance on specific tasks. By supplying a dataset of labeled examples, the model learns to produce the appropriate outputs for given inputs. This process adjusts the model's parameters, enhancing its performance for the tasks represented in the training dataset.

Prompt Engineering and Testing

Prompt engineering involves optimizing textual input to LLMs to achieve desired responses. It helps LLMs perform various tasks such as classification, question answering, code generation, creative writing, and more. The quality of prompts significantly influences the responses generated by LLMs. Amazon Bedrock offers a platform to create and test prompts using models it supports.

LLMs on Amazon Bedrock include various inference parameters like temperature, token lengths, Top-P, Top-K, and end token/end sequence. These parameters allow you to control the model's responses. LLMs on Amazon Bedrock perform best with clear and direct instructions, but you can also experiment with different prompting techniques such as few-shot prompting and chain-of-thought (CoT). Bedrock also provides prompt templates for the common tasks and use cases that can help you get started with prompt engineering.

Bedrock Guardrails

Bedrock guardrails allow you to establish safeguards for your generative AI applications based on your specific use cases and responsible AI policies. You can create multiple guardrails tailored to different scenarios and apply them across multiple foundation models, ensuring a consistent user experience and standardizing safety and privacy controls across generative AI applications.

Guardrails are also integrated with Bedrock Knowledge Bases and provide a comprehensive set of policies to protect users from undesirable interactions. You can customize denied topics to avoid in your application context, filter content based on prebuilt categories such as hate, insults, sexual content, violence, misconduct, and prompt attacks, and define offensive or inappropriate words to block. Additionally, you can filter user inputs containing sensitive information, such as personally identifiable information, or redact confidential information in model responses. Guardrails can be applied to both the input sent to the model and the content generated by the foundation model.

Contextualizing a Foundation Model

With Knowledge Bases for Amazon Bedrock, you can provide FMs and agents with contextual information from your company's private data sources for RAG, enhancing response relevance, accuracy, and customization. This feature automatically retrieves documents from various sources, segments them into text blocks, converts the text into embeddings, and stores them in your vector database. If you don't have an existing vector database, Amazon Bedrock can create an Amazon OpenSearch Serverless vector store for you. Alternatively, you can specify an existing vector store from supported databases, including Amazon OpenSearch Serverless, Pinecone, and Redis Enterprise Cloud, with support for Amazon Aurora and MongoDB.

Deploy Bedrock Agents

Generative AI agents are a versatile and powerful asset for large enterprises. They boost operational efficiency, improve customer service, and support decision-making, all while cutting costs and fostering innovation. These agents are particularly effective at automating a variety of routine and repetitive tasks, including data entry, customer support queries, and content creation. Additionally, they can manage complex, multistep workflows by decomposing tasks into smaller, manageable actions, and coordinating various steps to efficiently execute those actions.

Agents for Amazon Bedrock act as a conductor, orchestrating interactions between FMs, API integrations, user conversations, and knowledge sources loaded with your data.

Agents and Knowledge Bases for Amazon Bedrock collaborate to offer the following capabilities:

- **Task Orchestration**: Agents utilize foundation models to interpret natural language inquiries and break down complex tasks into smaller, actionable steps.

- **Interactive Data Collection**: Agents engage users in natural conversations to gather additional information.

- **Task Fulfillment**: Through a series of reasoning steps and actions based on ReAct prompting, agents fulfill customer requests.

- **System Integration**: Agents execute specific actions by making API calls to integrated company systems.

- **Data Querying**: Knowledge bases improve accuracy and performance with fully managed RAG from customer-specific data sources.

- **Source Attribution**: Agents perform source attribution, tracing the origin of information or actions through chain-of-thought reasoning.

You can test your agent in the Amazon Bedrock console or via API calls to the TSTALIASID. Adjust the configurations as needed. Use traces to analyze your agent's reasoning process at each orchestration step.

Once your agent is sufficiently modified and ready for deployment, create an alias pointing to a version of your agent. Configure your application to make API calls to your agent alias and continue refining your agent by creating additional versions and aliases as required. See Figure 9-7.

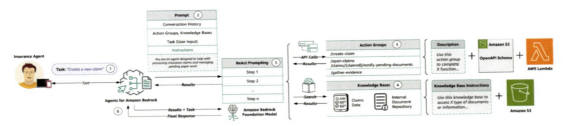

Figure 9-7. Example solution architecture using Bedrock agent and knowledge base

Inference with Amazon Bedrock

Amazon Bedrock allows you to perform inference with your chosen foundation model. When conducting inference, you provide the following inputs:

- **Prompt**: The input given to the model to generate a response

- **Inference Parameters**: Adjustable values that help guide or limit the model's response

You can perform model inference in the following ways:

- Use any of the playgrounds for inference in a user-friendly graphical interface.

- Use the Converse and ConverseStream API for conversational applications.

- Send an `InvokeModel` or `InvokeModelWithResponseStream` request.

- Prepare a dataset of prompts with your desired configurations and run batch inference with a `CreateModelInvocationJob` request.

You can run inference with base models, custom models, or provisioned models. To run inference on a custom model, you need to first purchase Provisioned Throughput. Use these methods to test foundation model responses with various prompts and inference parameters. Once you have explored these methods, you can configure your application to run model inference by calling these APIs.

Figure 9-8 shows a simple example of how you can invoke Bedrock APIs from your application.

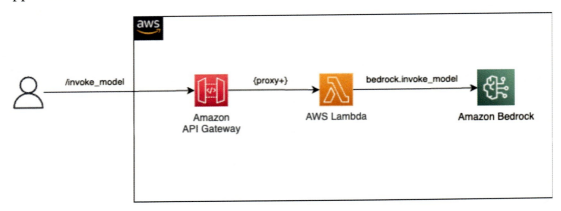

Figure 9-8. *Bedrock API invocation*

Monitoring and Governance

Amazon Bedrock provides extensive monitoring and logging features to meet your governance and audit needs. You can utilize Amazon CloudWatch to monitor usage metrics and create custom dashboards for auditing purposes. AWS CloudTrail allows you to track API activity and troubleshoot issues during the integration of other systems into your generative AI applications. Additionally, you have the option to store metadata, requests, and responses in your Amazon S3 bucket and Amazon CloudWatch Logs.

Evaluation and Continuous Improvement

The AI landscape is constantly evolving, and so should your models, prompts, agents and applications. Amazon Bedrock provides the following capabilities to support it:

- **Model Evaluation Jobs**: Model evaluations are critical at all stages of development. Amazon Bedrock provides options for automatic and human evaluation. Automatic evaluation uses predefined metrics like accuracy, robustness, and toxicity. For subjective or custom metrics, such as friendliness, style, and brand voice alignment, you can easily set up human evaluation workflows. You can use your datasets and define custom evaluation metrics, choosing either your internal teams or an AWS-managed team as reviewers. This simplifies the process of establishing and managing human evaluation workflows.

- **Prompt refinement**: Prompts and prompt engineering are model-specific. A prompt given to different models will typically yield varying results. Likewise, prompt engineering tips don't universally apply to all models. In some cases, many LLMs fine-tuned for specific NLP tasks may not require prompts. Conversely, very general LLMs benefit significantly from well-crafted prompts. Keep track of queries and responses to compare and iterate for prompt improvement. Consider developing prompt templates, especially for complex prompts. If your prompt includes user input, employ techniques to prevent prompt hacking by clearly distinguishing between your instructions and user input.

Managing Cost and Performance Trade-Offs

One major operational concern for LLMs is balancing cost and performance, particularly during inference and serving. With "small" LLMs containing hundreds of millions of parameters and large LLMs reaching hundreds of billions, computation can become significantly expensive. Fortunately, there are various methods to manage and reduce these costs when deploying and serving LLMs.

- **Start simple, scale later**: When creating a new LLM-powered application, rapid development is crucial, so using costlier options like paid APIs for existing models is acceptable. As you progress, collect data such as queries and responses. This data can be used to fine-tune a smaller, more cost-effective model that you can own.

- **Assess your costs**: Estimate how many queries per second you expect, whether requests will come in bursts, and the cost of each query. These calculations will help determine project feasibility and guide your decision on when to consider using in-house open-source models with fine-tuning.

- **Lower costs by adjusting LLMs and queries**: Utilize various techniques specific to LLMs to reduce computation and expenses. This includes shortening queries, modifying inference settings, and using smaller model versions.

- **Human feedback is critical**: Reducing costs is straightforward, but understanding how changes affect results can be challenging without feedback from end users.

Best Practices for LLMOps on AWS Bedrock

To optimize your use of LLMOps on AWS Bedrock, follow these best practices:

1. **Start with a Single Use Case**: Begin with one specific application and gradually expand. This approach helps your team master the complexities of Bedrock without becoming overwhelmed.

2. **Utilize Versioning**: Maintain records of model versions, prompts, and fine-tuning datasets. This is essential for reproducibility, auditing, and ensuring compliance.

3. **Automate Routine Tasks**: Employ AWS Step Functions or Lambda to automate repetitive tasks, minimizing human error and boosting efficiency.

4. **Prepare for Scalability**: Architect your system to accommodate growth as your LLM applications expand. This helps avoid performance bottlenecks and major architectural changes in the future.

5. **Establish Comprehensive Monitoring**: Implement thorough monitoring and alert systems to detect and resolve issues before they affect users.

6. **Emphasize Security and Compliance**: Incorporate strong security measures from the outset to safeguard your organization from data breaches and ensure regulatory compliance.

Conclusion

In an era characterized by data-driven decision-making and intelligent automation, the significance of MLOps is undeniable. MLOps provides the crucial framework for developing, deploying, and maintaining AI models at scale, ensuring they remain accurate and continue to provide business value. The rise of LLMOps underscores the rapid progress and specialized requirements of Generative AI. Yet, fundamentally, LLMOps is grounded in the core principles of MLOps.

Whether you are implementing traditional machine learning solutions or applications driven by LLMs, four core tenets remain constant:

1. **Business Goal**: Always align with your business objectives.

2. **Data-Centric**: Prioritize a data-centric approach.

3. **Modular**: Implement solutions in a modular fashion.

4. **Automated**: Strive to automate processes wherever possible.

By adopting a comprehensive LLMOps lifecycle, organizations can utilize AI responsibly and efficiently. This approach builds trust with users and stakeholders, ensures compliance with changing regulations, and positions the organization to leverage AI as a strategic asset while managing associated risks.

References

- https://www.databricks.com/glossary/llmops

- https://awsdocs-neuron.readthedocs-hosted.com/en/latest/general/arch/neuron-hardware/inf2-arch.html

- https://docs.aws.amazon.com/bedrock/latest/APIReference/API_runtime_Converse.html

- https://docs.aws.amazon.com/bedrock/latest/APIReference/API_runtime_ConverseStream.html

- https://docs.aws.amazon.com/bedrock/latest/APIReference/API_runtime_InvokeModel.html

- https://docs.aws.amazon.com/bedrock/latest/APIReference/ API_runtime_InvokeModelWithResponseStream.html

- https://aws.amazon.com/blogs/machine-learning/automate- the-insurance-claim-lifecycle-using-agents-and-knowledge- bases-for-amazon-bedrock/

- https://developer.nvidia.com/blog/mastering-llm- techniques-llmops/

- https://aws.amazon.com/blogs/machine-learning/deploy- large-language-models-on-aws-inferentia2-using-large- model-inference-containers/

- https://aws.amazon.com/blogs/machine-learning/fmops-llmops- operationalize-generative-ai-and-differences-with-mlops/

CHAPTER 10

Future Trends in MLOps

The AI era is not just approaching; it's already here, reshaping industries and societies at an unprecedented pace. As artificial intelligence continues to evolve, its impact on business operations, data management, and technological infrastructures will be profound and far-reaching. Among the transformativ(e technologies, generative AI stands out as a catalyst for the next wave of data-driven innovation. It will redefine how companies manage, analyze, and utilize data, driving the need for advanced machine learning operations (MLOps) practices to keep pace with these changes. See Figure 10-1.

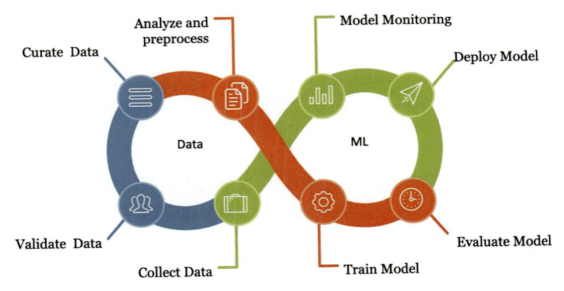

Figure 10-1. *MLOps pipeline*

© Neel Sendas and Deepali Rajale 2024
N. Sendas and D. Rajale, *The Definitive Guide to Machine Learning Operations in AWS*,
https://doi.org/10.1007/979-8-8688-1076-3_10

Generative AI is set to revolutionize the data strategies of tomorrow's leading enterprises. By centralizing data on managed service platforms, businesses can achieve the security, governance, and unified data repositories necessary to train and deploy large language models (LLMs) and other AI systems effectively. This centralization creates a single source of truth, streamlining operations and enhancing decision-making processes.

However, the rise of generative AI also signals the end of the era of on-premises data storage. The sheer scale and complexity of AI workloads are pushing businesses toward cloud-based solutions, which offer the scalability and flexibility that on-premises systems simply cannot match. Yet, this shift to the cloud introduces new challenges, particularly in terms of security and compliance. As organizations adopt multi-cloud strategies, they often find themselves managing distributed data and models across various platforms, each with different security and governance capabilities. This fragmentation makes it increasingly difficult to maintain a cohesive security posture and meet compliance requirements.

In this chapter, we will explore the future trends in MLOps as we move into 2025 and beyond. We will examine how businesses can navigate the evolving landscape of AI, the challenges and opportunities presented by generative AI, and the strategies needed to maintain performance, security, and compliance in an increasingly complex digital world. The chapter will provide insights into the critical role that MLOps will play in ensuring that organizations can harness the full potential of AI while mitigating the risks associated with this powerful technology.

Navigating the Next Wave of Gen AI Evolution

As we enter the Gen AI era, the landscape of machine learning operations is poised for transformative changes. The convergence of advanced technologies such as large language models, generative AI, and cloud computing is reshaping how organizations manage and deploy AI models in production environments. This shift requires not only a deep understanding of Gen AI technologies but also the adoption of innovative tools and practices to handle the complexities of modern data ecosystems.

MLOps has evolved from a niche practice to a critical component of AI deployment in enterprises. The integration of MLOps with LLMOps and GenAIOps introduces significant challenges to the existing MLOps paradigm. As organizations increasingly deploy large language models and generative AI models, the complexity of managing these models throughout their lifecycle grows.

MLOps is shaping it's path to automate and optimize the management of AI models at scale. Additionally, the need for real-time observability, robust data pipelines, and ethical considerations intensifies, pushing the boundaries of traditional MLOps frameworks. This convergence demands new tools and practices that can accommodate the unique demands of LLMOps and GenOps while ensuring scalability, reliability, and compliance across diverse environments.

This convergence is also enabling organizations to efficiently handle the networking requirements and hardware configurations of distributed, heterogeneous infrastructures. The ability to manage these complexities is becoming increasingly important as AI adoption accelerates across various industries, from space exploration to automotive manufacturing. See Figure 10-2.

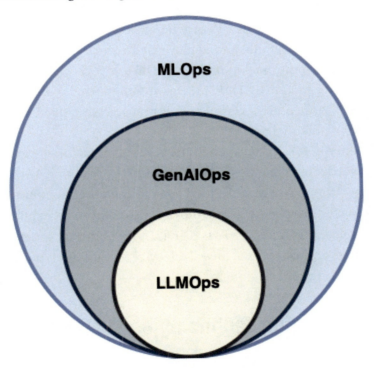

Figure 10-2. *Integration of MLOps with LLMOps and GenAIOps*

The Convergence of MLOps and Generative AI

The convergence of generative AI and MLOps represents a transformative shift in how AI models are developed, deployed, and maintained. This fusion allows for the automation of complex processes, enabling the creation and scaling of generative models at an unprecedented pace. By integrating MLOps practices, organizations can handle the vast datasets required for training generative AI models, ensuring efficient management and deployment across distributed systems. This integration not only accelerates the AI development lifecycle but also enhances the reliability and scalability of AI applications.

Furthermore, this convergence addresses the ethical challenges associated with generative AI by embedding rigorous reliability checks and ethical guidelines within the MLOps framework. This ensures that AI systems are not only effective but also aligned with ethical standards, reducing the risk of generating biased or misleading content. As a result, organizations can build and deploy generative AI models with greater confidence, knowing that they are upholding ethical integrity and fostering public trust. This synergy between generative AI and MLOps sets the stage for the next generation of AI technologies that are both powerful and responsible, driving innovation while safeguarding against potential risks.

This convergence of MLOps and generative AI is essential for efficient management of AI workloads, particularly in industries that are rapidly adopting AI-based solutions, such as space exploration, power and energy, media and entertainment, and healthcare life sciences. As AI continues to permeate these industries, the demand for more sophisticated orchestration frameworks is rising. These frameworks are specifically designed to address various stages of the ML lifecycle, including re-training, re-deployment, monitoring, and versioning.

The Role of Emerging Technologies in MLOps

As the technology is evolving, emerging technologies are poised to redefine MLOps, driving innovation, scalability, and efficiency in AI operations. Organizations that strategically integrate these advancements into their MLOps practices will lead the charge in the next phase of AI-driven transformation, setting new standards in performance and capability.

Advancements in High-Performance Computing (HPC)

As AI models become more complex, the need for HPC to support large-scale machine learning operations is more critical than ever. HPC systems, equipped with advanced GPUs, TPUs, and AI accelerators, provide the computational power necessary to train and optimize massive models efficiently. This evolution in HPC is driving a new era in MLOps, enabling faster model development, more accurate predictions, and the ability to handle ever-growing datasets with unprecedented speed and precision.

Revolutionizing MLOps with High-Speed Networks

The advent of 5G and the development of 6G networks are set to transform MLOps by delivering the high bandwidth and low latency required for real-time AI processing. These next-generation networks enable seamless access to AI models deployed across distributed environments, including cloud, edge, and on-premises systems. The increased speed and reliability of these networks are crucial for applications demanding instant decision-making, such as autonomous vehicles, smart cities, and IoT. MLOps frameworks must evolve to fully leverage these capabilities, ensuring models can operate effectively at the edge and in the cloud.

Harnessing the Power of LLMs and Big Data in MLOps

Large language models are revolutionizing the way we process and analyze unstructured data. The rise of LLMs necessitates robust MLOps frameworks capable of managing the complexities of training, deploying, and maintaining these models at scale. Handling vast amounts of data efficiently and effectively is key to maximizing the potential of LLMs, leading to new tools and methodologies within MLOps. Organizations that can seamlessly integrate LLMs into their operations will gain a competitive edge in processing and deriving insights from big data.

Edge Computing: The Frontier of MLOps Innovation

Edge computing is rapidly becoming a cornerstone of MLOps, enabling AI models to be deployed closer to data sources, which reduces latency and increases efficiency. With the proliferation of IoT devices and sensors generating vast amounts of data, the ability to process information at the edge is essential. MLOps frameworks are evolving to support the deployment and management of models in decentralized environments, ensuring robust performance even in resource-constrained settings. The integration of edge computing with MLOps is paving the way for advancements in federated learning and distributed AI.

Cloud Services Evolution and Its Impact on MLOps

The continuous evolution of cloud technologies is playing a pivotal role in the advancement of MLOps. Innovations such as serverless computing simplify infrastructure management, allowing developers to focus on deploying and refining AI models without the burden of managing hardware. Cloud providers are offering a growing array of specialized AI services, from managed model hosting to automated tuning, that streamline MLOps processes. As cloud services continue to evolve, they will become increasingly integral to scaling AI initiatives efficiently and effectively across industries.

Challenges and Opportunities in Data Management

Data management is the backbone of any successful AI project, and with the ever-increasing volume and complexity of data, the challenges associated with managing this data have become more pronounced. As organizations integrate big data ecosystems, manage unstructured data, and adapt to emerging technologies, they must navigate several key challenges. The following are some of the most critical challenges in data management within the MLOps framework:

- **Handling Big Data Ecosystems:** Big data ecosystems are characterized by their volume, velocity, and variety. Managing such vast amounts of data requires robust infrastructure and sophisticated data management strategies. The challenge lies in efficiently collecting, processing, and storing this data so that it can be used effectively in AI models. Organizations need to implement scalable data pipelines that can handle the influx of data from various sources while ensuring data integrity and accessibility.

- **Managing Unstructured Data with LLMs and Generative AI:** The shift toward using large language models and generative AI has introduced new complexities in data management. Unlike structured data, unstructured data such as text, images, and audio require different processing techniques to be made ready for AI models. Preprocessing this data to extract meaningful features and ensure compatibility with LLMs is a significant challenge. Moreover, the heterogeneity of unstructured data adds another layer of complexity, requiring innovative solutions for data integration and standardization.

- **Data Quality and Integrity:** Ensuring the quality and integrity of data is essential for training accurate and reliable AI models. Poor data quality can lead to biased or inaccurate models, which can have severe implications in real-world applications. Data management strategies must include rigorous data validation, cleaning, and normalization processes to ensure that the data used in training and inference is of the highest quality. Additionally, maintaining data integrity across distributed systems and during data transfers is critical to preventing data corruption and ensuring consistency.

- **Scalability of Data Pipelines:** As AI models grow in complexity and scale, so too must the data pipelines that feed them. Scalable data management solutions are needed to handle the increasing demands of larger datasets and more sophisticated models. This includes optimizing data storage, retrieval, and processing techniques to ensure that data pipelines can accommodate growth without becoming a bottleneck. Organizations must also consider the scalability of their infrastructure, ensuring that it can support the growing computational requirements of AI workloads.

- **Data Security and Compliance**: With the rise of data privacy regulations and the increasing importance of data security, managing sensitive data has become a critical challenge in MLOps. Organizations must implement robust security measures to protect data from unauthorized access and ensure compliance with regulatory standards. This includes encrypting data at rest and in transit, implementing access controls, and conducting regular security audits. Additionally, organizations must navigate the complexities of data governance, ensuring that data is used ethically and in accordance with legal requirements.

- **Real-time Data Processing:** The need for real-time data processing is becoming increasingly important in AI applications, particularly in use cases such as autonomous systems and predictive analytics. Managing real-time data streams requires advanced data management techniques that can handle high-throughput, low-latency data processing. This includes implementing distributed processing frameworks, optimizing data ingestion pipelines, and ensuring that data is processed and made available to AI models in real time.

In conclusion, effective data management is a critical component of successful MLOps implementations. As organizations continue to embrace big data, unstructured data, and emerging technologies, they must overcome significant challenges in data handling, processing, and security. By addressing these challenges, organizations can ensure that their AI models are trained on high-quality data and are capable of delivering accurate, reliable, and scalable solutions.

Future Directions in MLOps

Looking ahead, the future of MLOps will be shaped by the ongoing evolution of AI technologies, particularly in the areas of LLMs, AIOps, and next-generation networks. As these technologies continue to mature, they will enable new levels of automation, scalability, and efficiency in the management of AI workloads. However, this will also require organizations to adopt more sophisticated approaches to data management, model versioning, and monitoring to ensure that their AI systems remain performant and reliable in increasingly complex environments.

- **Enhanced Model Lifecycle Management:** Generative AI models, particularly large language models and generative adversarial networks (GANs), are far more complex than traditional machine learning models. Managing their lifecycle—encompassing stages such as training, deployment, monitoring, and retraining—requires more sophisticated tools and processes. The future of MLOps will see the development of advanced frameworks designed to handle the intricacies of generative AI, such as continuous model updates, real-time inference, and automated retraining triggered by performance metrics or data drift.

- **Scalability and Resource Optimization:** Generative AI models demand significant computational resources, both during training and inference. As these models become more prevalent, MLOps practices must adapt to optimize resource allocation and ensure scalability. This includes the implementation of HPC environments, distributed training frameworks, and efficient data management strategies that can handle the vast amounts of data required by generative models. Additionally, cloud and edge computing will play a critical role in providing the necessary infrastructure to support the deployment of generative AI at scale.

- **Integration with Automated Machine Learning (AutoML):** The complexity of generative AI models necessitates the use of automated tools to streamline the development process. AutoML, which automates tasks such as model selection, hyperparameter tuning, and feature engineering, will become increasingly integrated with MLOps practices. This integration will allow organizations to rapidly iterate on generative models, reducing the time and expertise required to bring new AI solutions to market. Moreover, AutoML can help manage the growing complexity of generative models by automating parts of the lifecycle, from data preprocessing to deployment.

- **Ethical AI and Governance:** As generative AI becomes more widely used, concerns around ethics, fairness, and transparency will intensify. MLOps will need to incorporate robust governance frameworks to ensure that generative models are developed and deployed in a manner that aligns with ethical standards. This includes implementing tools for bias detection, explainability, and accountability within the MLOps pipeline. Furthermore, regulatory compliance will become a key consideration, particularly as governments and industry bodies introduce new standards for the ethical use of AI.

- **Advanced Monitoring and Observability:** The dynamic nature of generative AI models requires continuous monitoring and observability to ensure they perform as expected in production environments. Future MLOps platforms will need to offer advanced capabilities for tracking model performance, identifying anomalies, and diagnosing issues in real time. This includes monitoring for data drift, model drift, and the impact of generative outputs on downstream applications. Enhanced observability tools will provide actionable insights that enable rapid response to potential issues, ensuring the reliability and robustness of generative AI deployments.

- **Collaboration and Cross-Disciplinary Integration:** The development and deployment of generative AI models often involve collaboration between data scientists, engineers, domain experts, and business stakeholders. MLOps will increasingly focus on fostering collaboration across these disciplines by providing platforms and tools that facilitate communication, knowledge sharing, and alignment of goals. This cross-disciplinary integration is essential for ensuring that generative AI models meet business objectives while adhering to technical and ethical standards.

- **Personalization and Customization of AI Models:** One of the most promising applications of generative AI is in creating personalized experiences for users. As generative models become more sophisticated, MLOps will play a crucial role in enabling the customization of these models to meet specific user needs. This includes developing pipelines that can handle the personalization of models based on user data, preferences, and interactions. Additionally, MLOps will need to ensure that personalized models maintain high performance and accuracy while safeguarding user privacy and data security.

- **Emergence of Specialized MLOps Tools for Generative AI:** As generative AI continues to evolve, there will be a growing demand for specialized MLOps tools tailored to the unique requirements of these models. These tools will focus on aspects such as model explainability, interactive debugging, and the orchestration of complex generative workflows. The future of MLOps will likely see the emergence of new platforms and solutions specifically designed to address the challenges posed by generative AI, enabling organizations to fully harness its potential.

In conclusion, the rise of generative AI is set to profoundly influence the future of MLOps. By adapting to the specific needs of these advanced models, MLOps practices will evolve to ensure the efficient, scalable, and ethical deployment of generative AI across a wide range of applications. As we move forward, the convergence of generative AI and MLOps will open new avenues for innovation, driving the development of cutting-edge AI solutions that can transform industries and enhance the way we interact with technology.

Open Issues and Challenges in MLOps

In the realm of machine learning and artificial intelligence, MLOps has emerged as a crucial discipline that combines machine learning with traditional software development and operations practices to streamline the deployment, monitoring, and governance of machine learning models. However, despite its growing importance, MLOps is still a relatively young field, and with that youth comes a host of open issues and challenges that organizations must navigate to successfully operationalize their AI-driven initiatives.

The Interdisciplinary Challenge

One of the primary challenges in MLOps stems from the interdisciplinary nature of the work required to successfully deploy and manage machine learning models in production environments. MLOps projects necessitate a combination of skills across data science, software engineering, and operations—a combination that is not easily found within most organizations. Data scientists often lack the necessary knowledge of software engineering practices, such as version control, modularization, and scalability, which are essential for maintaining and evolving AI solutions. On the other hand, software engineers may struggle with the intricacies of machine learning, including feature engineering, parameter tuning, and model selection. Operations engineers, meanwhile, must manage the complex infrastructure required to support these models, a task that demands a deep understanding of both the application and the platform on which it runs.

This fragmentation of expertise often results in silos within organizations, where data scientists, software engineers, and operations teams work in isolation, leading to misalignment in goals and priorities. The success of an MLOps project, therefore, hinges on fostering a collaborative culture that encourages cross-functional teams to work together, leveraging each other's strengths to overcome the challenges posed by the deployment of machine learning models in production.

Challenges in ML/AI Engineering

The convergence of emerging technologies with MLOps introduces significant challenges that require a rethinking of traditional approaches to ML engineering. To navigate this evolving landscape, MLOps must adopt more systematic, modular, and scalable strategies that can accommodate the growing complexity and demands of AI applications.

- **Systematic Lifecycle Management:** AI applications, particularly those leveraging advanced technologies, require a more structured and efficient approach to lifecycle management. Traditional software development practices often fall short in addressing the dynamic and iterative nature of AI model development, deployment, and monitoring. MLOps must adapt to support continuous integration and continuous deployment (CI/CD) pipelines that can handle frequent updates to models, manage versioning, and ensure robust monitoring of model performance in real-time. The emergence of sophisticated AI models, especially LLMs, further complicates this process, as these models require extensive computational resources and data management strategies throughout their lifecycle.

- **Complexity in AI Designs**: The design of AI systems has grown increasingly complex, particularly with the rise of multimodal models, deep learning architectures, and distributed systems. These designs are inherently more challenging to modularize and maintain, which complicates both the development and operational phases of the AI lifecycle. For instance, the integration of multiple AI models, each specialized in different tasks (e.g., text processing, image recognition), into a single coherent system requires careful orchestration and seamless communication between components. MLOps must provide frameworks and tools that support the modularization of AI systems, enabling easier maintenance, updates, and scalability.

- **Handling Emerging Technologies:** With the rise of HPC, edge computing, and high-speed networks, MLOps must also address the challenges of deploying and managing AI models across diverse and distributed environments. HPC enables the training of large models, but it also demands scalable and efficient resource management. Similarly, deploying AI models on edge devices introduces constraints such as limited computational power and the need for low-latency processing. MLOps frameworks must be equipped to handle these challenges by providing solutions for efficient resource allocation, model optimization, and seamless integration across cloud, edge, and on-premises systems.

- **Maintaining Consistency and Reliability**: The rapid pace of AI innovation, coupled with the increasing complexity of AI designs, makes it crucial for MLOps to maintain consistency and reliability in model performance. This includes ensuring that models continue to perform accurately as they are updated, scaled, and deployed in different environments. MLOps must implement robust monitoring and feedback mechanisms to detect and address issues such as data drift, model degradation, and performance bottlenecks. Moreover, as AI systems become more integral to critical business operations, MLOps must ensure that models adhere to ethical guidelines and regulatory requirements, adding another layer of responsibility to the already complex task of managing AI lifecycles.

Data Management Challenges

Data management is a cornerstone of both MLOps and LLMOps, and its importance cannot be overstated. Effective data management encompasses various aspects, including data quality, access, preparation, labeling, validation, and integration. These activities are often overlooked but can consume a significant portion of a project's time and budget. Moreover, the tight dependency between machine learning models and their associated data adds another layer of complexity to data management in ML-based scenarios.

The advent of Big Data has further complicated data management in MLOps. Issues such as task distribution, data movement, and batch processing become even more relevant in Big Data environments, necessitating a joint effort between industry and academia to develop solutions. The complexity of managing large volumes of data, combined with the need for accurate and efficient processing, makes data management one of the most significant challenges in MLOps.

- **Complexities in Handling Large Volumes, Varieties, and Velocities of Data:** The integration of big data within MLOps frameworks introduces significant challenges due to the sheer volume, variety, and velocity of data. Managing large datasets, especially those with diverse data types and formats, requires robust architectures capable of handling high throughput and ensuring data integrity. Moreover, the rapid influx of data necessitates real-time processing capabilities, making it crucial to implement scalable solutions that can efficiently process and analyze data without compromising performance.

  To address these challenges, one effective strategy is to decompose big data workloads into smaller, more manageable subsets. By characterizing and segmenting datasets, organizations can train models independently on these subsets, thus simplifying the complexity of big data workloads. This approach not only makes the training process more efficient but also allows for parallel processing, thereby accelerating the overall machine learning pipeline.

- **Strategies for Managing Datasets and Model Versions**: Another critical aspect of managing big data in MLOps is the effective handling of dataset and model versions. Dedicated tools and architectures are essential for tracking and managing different versions of datasets and models, ensuring consistency and reproducibility across the machine learning lifecycle. Version control systems tailored for machine learning, such as DVC (Data Version Control), help teams maintain a structured approach to dataset management, enabling them to revert to previous versions when needed and ensure that models are trained on the correct data.

- **Orchestration of ML Solutions in Big Data Environments:** The complexity of integrating big data with machine learning and AI solutions has heightened the need for advanced orchestration tools. These tools help manage the training and inference processes, ensuring that models are deployed efficiently in production environments. Orchestration frameworks like Kubernetes and Apache Airflow are increasingly being adopted to streamline these operations, allowing developers to focus on model development while the infrastructure handles the complexities of scaling and deployment.

- **Automating Data Labeling and Handling Labeled Datasets:** In addition to managing big data, MLOps must also address the challenge of labeled datasets, which are crucial for supervised learning models. The scarcity of labeled data often hinders the training process, leading to suboptimal model performance. To mitigate this, novel methods for automating data labeling are being developed, reducing the reliance on manual labor and expert intervention. For example, automating the labeling of log messages can significantly speed up the creation of labeled datasets, enabling faster iterations and improvements in model accuracy.

To summarize, managing big data within MLOps frameworks is a complex but essential task that requires specialized strategies and tools. By breaking down workloads, implementing robust version control, and utilizing advanced orchestration frameworks, organizations can overcome the challenges associated with big data and ensure the successful deployment of machine learning models in production environments. As the field of MLOps continues to evolve, these strategies will become increasingly important in harnessing the full potential of big data for AI-driven solutions.

Orchestrating the ML Lifecycle

The orchestration of the machine learning (ML) lifecycle has become challenging with the integration of emerging technologies such as generative AI, edge computing, and advancements in cloud computing. As organizations strive to efficiently manage data and computational resources across distributed environments, they face a host of new challenges that require innovative solutions. This section explores the key challenges in orchestrating the ML lifecycle and the strategies needed to address them.

Distributed and Parallelized Workflows

With the advent of cloud and edge computing, ML workflows are no longer confined to centralized data centers. Instead, they are distributed across multiple environments, each with its unique set of computational resources, storage capabilities, and latency constraints. The challenge lies in efficiently distributing and parallelizing tasks across these environments while minimizing traffic overhead, bandwidth limitations, and latency delays. Ensuring that data is consistently and securely transferred between cloud and edge devices is critical for maintaining the integrity and performance of ML models.

Resource Constraints in Edge Computing

Edge computing introduces additional challenges due to the constrained environments in which edge devices operate. These devices often have limited computational power, storage, and energy resources, making it difficult to deploy and manage ML models effectively. Furthermore, protecting the intellectual property and integrity of deployed models in edge environments is a significant concern, as these models may be vulnerable to tampering or theft. Ensuring reliable and secure communication between edge nodes and more resourceful infrastructural devices is essential for the success of ML projects in these settings.

Containerization and Dependency Management

Containerization has emerged as a popular solution for delivering ML solutions across diverse environments. However, it also brings challenges related to dependency and filesystem management. Containerized environments must be carefully managed to ensure that all dependencies are correctly configured and that the filesystem is optimized for the specific requirements of the ML model. Additionally, the deployment of containerized ML workflows across distributed environments requires robust orchestration tools that can handle the complexities of managing multiple containers, each with its dependencies and configurations.

Automation and AutoML

Automation is a key factor in achieving maturity and efficiency in ML models deployed in production environments. Techniques such as AutoML (Automated Machine Learning) automate many aspects of the ML process, including feature engineering, model selection, and hyperparameter tuning. However, automating these processes in distributed environments introduces new challenges, such as ensuring that the best-performing models are selected for deployment across diverse architectures. Balancing the trade-offs between high computational resources and more modest architectures is crucial to the success of MLOps projects.

Orchestrating AI Workloads Across Complex Environments

The orchestration of AI workloads across cloud and edge environments requires sophisticated tools and frameworks that can manage the entire ML lifecycle, from data preparation to model deployment and monitoring. These tools must be capable of handling the unique challenges of distributed ML workflows, such as ensuring consistency in data processing, optimizing computational resources, and maintaining model performance over time. As AI applications become more complex, the need for robust orchestration tools that can seamlessly integrate with existing MLOps practices will only grow.

Ensuring Security and Compliance

The distributed nature of modern ML workflows introduces additional security and compliance challenges. Protecting sensitive data, ensuring model integrity, and adhering to regulatory requirements are critical considerations for organizations deploying ML models across cloud and edge environments. MLOps teams must implement security measures that address these concerns while maintaining the flexibility and scalability needed to support emerging technologies.

In conclusion, the orchestration of the ML lifecycle in the context of emerging technologies presents several challenges that require innovative solutions. As organizations continue to adopt cloud computing, edge computing, and IoT technologies, they must invest in robust orchestration tools and frameworks that can manage the complexities of distributed ML workflows. By addressing these challenges, MLOps teams can ensure the successful deployment and management of AI models across diverse environments, ultimately driving the advancement of AI applications in the real world.

Hardware and Architectural Challenges

The integration of emerging technologies into machine learning operations brings a myriad of hardware and architectural challenges that require innovative solutions and careful consideration. As MLOps evolves to accommodate more sophisticated models, distributed environments, and varied use cases, the complexities associated with hardware platforms and architectural designs grow in tandem. The following are some key challenges and considerations.

Heterogeneity of Hardware Platforms

MLOps now involves a diverse array of hardware platforms, ranging from GPUs and TPUs to specialized AI accelerators and edge devices. Each of these platforms has its unique characteristics, capabilities, and limitations, making it challenging to ensure compatibility and optimal performance across different stages of the ML lifecycle. For instance, deep neural networks (DNNs) may perform exceptionally well on one type of hardware but may require extensive optimization to run efficiently on another. The need to manage and optimize ML workflows across such heterogeneous environments is a significant challenge for MLOps practitioners.

Incompatibility of Machine Learning Libraries

The diversity of hardware platforms is further complicated by the incompatibility between machine learning libraries and the underlying hardware. Many ML libraries and frameworks are designed with specific hardware architectures in mind, which can lead to difficulties when attempting to deploy a model across different environments. This challenge is particularly pronounced in scenarios where the deployment involves both cloud-based resources and edge devices, each requiring different configurations and optimizations. Ensuring seamless integration and performance across these platforms necessitates a deep understanding of both the software and hardware involved.

Architectural Design Complexities

As ML models become more complex, so too do the architectural designs required to support them. The deployment of advanced AI solutions often involves intricate architectures that integrate multiple components, such as data pipelines, model training environments, inference engines, and monitoring systems. These components must be carefully orchestrated to ensure that the overall system performs efficiently and reliably. However, differences in architectural designs across various ML frameworks add another layer of complexity, making it difficult to standardize processes and ensure consistency in performance.

Security and Isolation in ML Workflows

The distributed nature of modern ML workflows, particularly those that span across cloud and edge environments, introduces significant security challenges. Ensuring the isolation and protection of sensitive data and intellectual property is critical, especially in environments where different components of the ML pipeline are distributed across multiple hardware platforms. This requires robust security measures that can prevent unauthorized access and tampering while maintaining the integrity of the data and models being used. Additionally, the degree of isolation between different components of the ML pipeline must be carefully assessed to prevent potential security breaches and ensure reliable operation.

Optimizing Resource Allocation

Effective resource allocation is crucial for managing the computational demands of modern ML workflows. With the rise of edge computing and the increasing complexity of AI models, MLOps must adapt to allocate resources dynamically across distributed environments. This involves not only optimizing the use of GPUs and other accelerators but also ensuring that storage, memory, and network bandwidth are utilized efficiently. The challenge lies in balancing these resources across different stages of the ML lifecycle, from data ingestion and preprocessing to model training and inference, without compromising performance or scalability.

Scalability and Flexibility in Architectural Design

The architectural designs supporting ML workflows must be scalable and flexible enough to accommodate the growing demands of AI applications. As models become larger and more complex, the infrastructure must be capable of scaling up to handle increased workloads while maintaining performance and efficiency. This requires careful planning and the use of advanced technologies, such as containerization and serverless computing, to ensure that the infrastructure can adapt to changing requirements. Additionally, the architecture must be flexible enough to support the integration of new technologies and frameworks as they emerge, ensuring that the ML workflow remains up-to-date and capable of leveraging the latest advancements in the field.

High-Performance Computing (HPC) Integration

As machine learning (ML) workloads become increasingly complex, managing the underlying infrastructure presents significant challenges. High-Performance Computing (HPC) emerges as a powerful solution for addressing these challenges, offering the computational power necessary to handle large-scale ML tasks, particularly those involving deep learning and large language models (LLMs). However, leveraging HPC environments is not without its difficulties, particularly for data scientists who may not be familiar with the unique requirements and characteristics of HPC environments, such as specialized hardware configurations, parallel processing techniques, and the management of large datasets across distributed systems. Moreover, the scalability of computational resources in HPC systems must be carefully managed to avoid bottlenecks and ensure efficient utilization of available resources. See Figure 10-3.

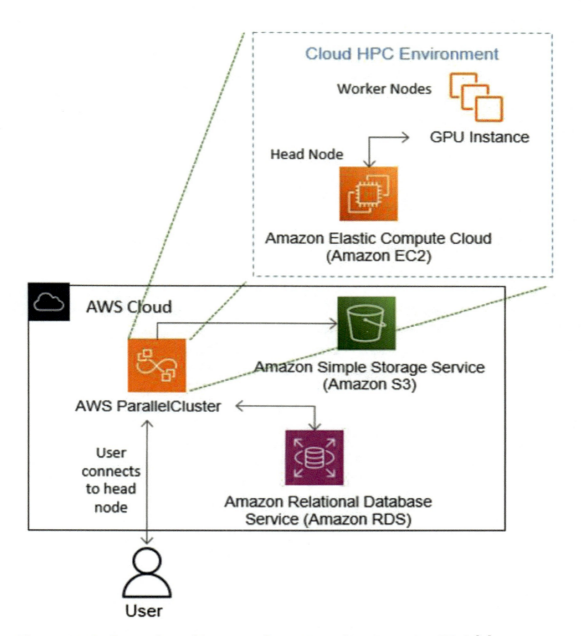

Figure 10-3. *Example architecture of an ML application using HPC [1]*

The following are the critical aspects of using HPC:

- **Scalability and Containerization:** One of the critical aspects of using HPC for ML workloads is the scalability of computational resources. As ML models grow in size and complexity, the ability to scale resources effectively becomes essential. Containerization has proven to be a promising solution in this regard, enabling the deployment of AI models on HPC systems more efficiently. By encapsulating applications and their dependencies into containers, this approach simplifies the process of scaling resources and managing the infrastructure.

- **Cloud Computing and Multitenancy Isolation:** While HPC offers immense power, cloud computing presents an alternative that combines scalability with flexibility. Cloud resources can be used to supplement HPC infrastructure, allowing organizations to manage ML workloads more dynamically. However, the use of cloud resources introduces challenges such as multitenancy isolation, where it is crucial to ensure that different workloads do not interfere with one another. Addressing these challenges requires careful consideration of cloud architecture and resource allocation strategies.

- **The Intersection of HPC and MLOps:** The integration of HPC with MLOps practices is key to managing complex ML workloads effectively. MLOps, which focuses on the continuous integration and deployment of ML models, benefits from the computational power and scalability offered by HPC. However, this integration requires a deep understanding of both ML workflows and HPC environments. By combining the strengths of HPC with the automation and efficiency of MLOps, organizations can build robust pipelines that can handle the most demanding ML tasks.

Edge Computing and Serverless Architectures

In addition to HPC and cloud computing, edge computing is becoming increasingly relevant for ML workloads. By deploying ML tasks on edge devices, organizations can reduce latency and improve real-time processing capabilities. This is particularly important for applications that require immediate responses, such as those in the Internet of Things (IoT) ecosystem. However, edge devices often have limited resources, making it necessary to optimize models for low power consumption and limited memory.

Serverless computing also plays a significant role in simplifying the management of infrastructure. By abstracting away the underlying hardware, serverless architectures allow developers to focus on writing code without worrying about scaling or resource management. This approach not only reduces operational overhead but also ensures that resources are used efficiently, further optimizing the cost and performance of ML workloads.

Frameworks and Tools for Effective Resource Management

To navigate the complexities of managing infrastructure for ML workloads, dedicated frameworks and tools are essential. These solutions help automate the deployment, scaling, and monitoring of ML models, ensuring that the infrastructure can adapt to the changing demands of the workload. For instance, frameworks like TensorFlow Lite and Core ML are designed specifically for running ML models on mobile and edge devices, enabling developers to harness the power of AI in resource-constrained environments.

Similarly, advanced algorithms, such as genetic algorithms, are being explored to optimize model configurations for edge deployments. These algorithms help find the balance between model size and accuracy, ensuring that ML models can run efficiently on low-power devices without sacrificing performance.

Managing infrastructure for complex ML workloads is a multifaceted challenge that requires a combination of HPC, cloud, edge computing, and serverless architectures. By leveraging these technologies and adopting the right frameworks and tools, organizations can overcome the challenges of scaling, resource management, and latency, ultimately enabling more efficient and effective ML operations. As the field of MLOps continues to evolve, the role of HPC and other advanced infrastructure solutions will become increasingly important in driving innovation and performance in AI.

Monitoring and Maintenance

Continuous monitoring is essential for detecting deviations in the performance of ML models during runtime. However, the static nature of trained models makes them susceptible to degradation in dynamically changing environments. This necessitates regular updates and maintenance to ensure that models remain responsive to changes in data, component wear, and biases.

Monitoring the production environment is crucial for detecting issues such as concept drift, where the statistical properties of the input data change over time, leading to a decline in model performance. However, defining appropriate performance metrics for monitoring is a challenge, as these metrics are often problem-specific and require careful consideration to ensure they accurately reflect the business's tolerance for error.

Continuous monitoring and feedback loops are crucial for maintaining model performance over time. Once a model is deployed, it needs to be monitored for performance degradation, concept drift, and other issues that could affect its accuracy and reliability. Implementing automated monitoring systems and establishing feedback loops allows for timely updates and retraining of models, ensuring that they continue to deliver value as conditions change.

The integration of large language models into AI workflows has dramatically reshaped the landscape of MLOps, bringing both new opportunities and challenges to model and performance monitoring. As LLMs grow in complexity and usage, traditional monitoring practices must evolve to ensure these models remain efficient, reliable, and aligned with ethical standards. In the next sections, we explore the key aspects of MLOps model and performance monitoring in the context of the rise of LLMs.

Increased Complexity in Model Monitoring

LLMs, with their billions of parameters, introduce a level of complexity that far exceeds that of traditional machine learning models. Monitoring these models requires advanced tools and techniques capable of tracking a wide array of performance metrics, including accuracy, latency, throughput, and resource utilization. The challenge lies in developing monitoring systems that can provide real-time insights while managing the sheer volume of data generated by LLMs. Future MLOps platforms will likely integrate more sophisticated AI-driven monitoring solutions that can automatically detect and diagnose performance issues, reducing the need for manual intervention.

Fairness, Transparency, and Explainability

As LLMs become integral to decision-making processes, concerns around fairness, transparency, and explainability have come to the forefront. MLOps must now incorporate mechanisms that ensure these models do not perpetuate biases or produce unfair outcomes. This involves not only monitoring the outputs of LLMs but also understanding the underlying decision-making processes. Explainable AI (XAI) techniques are critical in this context, providing insights into how LLMs arrive at their conclusions. MLOps teams will need to integrate XAI tools into their workflows to ensure models are both transparent and accountable.

Ethical and Responsible AI Deployment

The rise of LLMs has also highlighted the ethical implications of AI deployment, particularly in sensitive areas such as mental health. The use of LLMs in generative AI applications raises concerns about the potential harm that can result from AI-generated content. MLOps must incorporate robust ethical frameworks that guide the development, deployment, and monitoring of LLMs. This includes setting up automated checks to prevent harmful outputs, ensuring compliance with ethical guidelines, and creating feedback loops to continuously assess the impact of LLMs on users.

Real-Time Performance Monitoring

Given the dynamic nature of LLMs, real-time performance monitoring is crucial for maintaining model accuracy and reliability. As these models are deployed in production environments, they interact with continuously changing data streams, which can lead to performance degradation over time. MLOps platforms must provide real-time monitoring capabilities that track key performance indicators (KPIs) and alert teams to any anomalies. This is particularly important for LLMs deployed in critical applications where timely responses are essential.

Human-in-the-Loop Monitoring

While automation is a key aspect of modern MLOps, the rise of LLMs necessitates a more human-centric approach to monitoring. Human-in-the-loop (HITL) systems allow for the continuous involvement of human operators in the monitoring process, enabling them to intervene when necessary and ensure that LLMs operate within acceptable ethical and performance boundaries. This approach is especially important in applications where the consequences of AI decisions can have significant impacts, such as in healthcare or finance.

Scalability Challenges

As LLMs are scaled across organizations, ensuring consistent and reliable monitoring becomes increasingly challenging. MLOps must address issues related to the scalability of monitoring systems, particularly in distributed environments where LLMs may be deployed across multiple cloud and edge locations. Scalable monitoring solutions must be capable of aggregating data from diverse sources and providing a unified view of model performance. Additionally, these solutions must be resilient to network failures and capable of operating in resource-constrained environments.

Proactive Monitoring and Predictive Analytics

To stay ahead of potential issues, MLOps must move toward proactive monitoring strategies that leverage predictive analytics. By analyzing historical performance data, predictive models can forecast potential degradations or failures, allowing teams to take preemptive actions. This approach is particularly beneficial for LLMs, where early detection of issues can prevent significant downstream impacts. Predictive analytics will become a cornerstone of MLOps, enabling organizations to maintain high levels of performance and reliability in their AI deployments.

Challenges in LLM Observability

Model observability in LLMOps —the practice of monitoring and understanding the behavior of large language models (LLMs)—presents several challenges due to the inherent complexity, scale, and dynamic nature of these models. Here's an expanded look at these challenges:

- **Complexity and Scale:**
  - **Model Size:** LLMs, with their billions of parameters, are inherently complex, making it difficult to track how changes in the model or data affect its overall behavior. This complexity can obscure understanding and slow down debugging processes.
  - **Data Volume:** LLMs process and generate massive volumes of data. Monitoring these operations requires systems that can handle large-scale data ingestion and analysis, which often leads to significant challenges in data management and interpretation.

- **Interpretability:**

  - **Black Box Nature:** LLMs function as "black boxes," meaning their decision-making processes are not easily understandable. This opacity makes it difficult to trace the cause of specific outputs or behaviors, hindering efforts to explain or adjust the model's reasoning.

  - **Attribution:** Identifying the exact source of an issue or behavior within the model's output is challenging. This can complicate the process of refining the model, as it's hard to determine which part of the model or data is contributing to suboptimal results.

- **Dynamic Environments:**

  - **Data Drift:** Over time, the data that the model encounters may shift, leading to performance degradation if the model isn't updated to reflect these changes. This phenomenon, known as data drift, requires continuous monitoring and potential retraining of the model.

  - **Model Drift:** Similar to data drift, model drift occurs when the model's performance changes due to evolving input patterns. This can happen as the model encounters new types of data that were not present during its initial training, necessitating ongoing adjustments.

- **Monitoring Granularity:**

  - **Fine-Grained Monitoring:** Determining the appropriate level of granularity for monitoring is challenging. Too coarse, and you might miss critical issues; too fine, and you risk overwhelming operators with excessive data, making it hard to extract actionable insights.

- **Performance Metrics:**

  - **Choosing Metrics:** Selecting the right metrics to monitor is not straightforward. Different applications might prioritize different aspects, such as accuracy, latency, or resource utilization, and it's crucial to tailor metrics to each specific use case.

- **Metric Interpretation:** Even when the right metrics are chosen, interpreting them in the context of LLMs can be complex. Understanding how these metrics interact and what they indicate about the model's performance requires deep expertise.

- **Resource Constraints:**

  - **Computational Resources:** Monitoring LLMs at scale requires substantial computational resources, which can be costly and logistically challenging to manage. Ensuring that monitoring does not become a bottleneck is a significant concern.

  - **Storage Resources:** Storing the vast amounts of data generated by LLMs for effective observability can be expensive and complex, particularly as the need for long-term storage of logs and metrics grows.

- **Real-time Observability:**

  - **Latency:** Achieving real-time observability is challenging due to the processing delays inherent in handling large-scale data. Quick detection and response to issues are crucial, but latency can hinder these efforts.

  - **Streaming Data:** Continuously monitoring streaming data to assess model performance requires robust infrastructure that can manage the constant flow of information without delays or data loss.

- **Security and Privacy:**

  - **Sensitive Data:** Ensuring that observability practices do not compromise sensitive data is crucial. LLMs often process sensitive information, and observability tools must be designed to protect this data.

  - **Compliance:** Adhering to regulatory requirements while monitoring model behavior adds another layer of complexity, particularly in industries where data security and privacy are heavily regulated.

- **Tooling and Integration:**
  - **Lack of Standardization:** There is a lack of standardized tools specifically designed for LLMOps, making it challenging to integrate observability into existing workflows.
  - **Integration Complexity:** Integrating observability tools with other systems and workflows can be difficult, especially in environments where multiple tools and platforms are already in use.
- **Human Factors:**
  - **Expertise Required:** Understanding the outputs of observability tools often requires deep expertise in machine learning and domain knowledge, which can be a barrier for less experienced teams.
  - **Cognitive Overload:** The vast amount of data and metrics generated by observability tools can overwhelm operators, making it difficult to focus on the most critical issues.

Addressing these challenges requires a combination of advanced tools, comprehensive methodologies, and deep expertise. By overcoming these hurdles, organizations can ensure that their large language models are reliable, transparent, and maintain high performance throughout their lifecycle.

The Thriving Domains of MLOps: Current and Future

The integration of machine learning operations and large language models into various industries is transforming how businesses and research institutions leverage AI technologies. As these methodologies evolve, they are not only reshaping traditional industries but also enabling new forms of innovation and operational efficiency. This chapter explores the current thriving fields where MLOps and LLMOps are making a significant impact, as well as emerging areas where these practices are expected to grow.

Current Thriving Domains

MLOps is an emerging field that has seen significant growth across various domains. Here are some of the key areas within MLOps:

- **Automated Machine Learning (AutoML):** AutoML tools are streamlining the model development process by automating tasks such as feature engineering, model selection, and hyperparameter tuning. This allows data scientists to focus on higher-level tasks and accelerates the deployment of machine learning models. AutoML is increasingly adopted in industries like finance, healthcare, and retail, where rapid deployment of accurate models can provide a competitive edge.

- **Model Monitoring and Management:** As more machine learning models move into production, the need for robust monitoring and management solutions has increased. These tools track model performance, detect anomalies, and manage versioning, ensuring that models remain accurate and reliable over time.

  In the LLM era, continuous monitoring of LLMs in production to ensure they perform as expected is essential. This involves tracking performance metrics, identifying model drifts, and ensuring the model's outputs align with expected behavior. Advanced observability tools are being developed to provide insights into model behavior, helping teams maintain and improve model reliability over time.

- **Data Pipeline Automation:** Efficient data pipelines are critical for successful ML deployments. Tools that automate the extraction, transformation, and loading (ETL) processes are becoming essential, enabling continuous data flow from source to model training environments. The quality of data used in training LLMs is crucial for their performance. LLMOps involves sophisticated data engineering practices, including data preprocessing, augmentation, and the creation of robust data pipelines. The management of vast and diverse datasets, ensuring they are clean, relevant, and up-to-date, is a thriving area within LLMOps.

- **Scalable Infrastructure and Cloud Integration:** With the rise of cloud computing, MLOps platforms are integrating with cloud services to provide scalable, flexible infrastructure for training and deploying models. This includes the use of Kubernetes for container orchestration and tools like TensorFlow Extended (TFX) for end-to-end machine learning pipelines.

  Efficiently serving LLMs in production environments is a key area of focus. This includes developing methods to reduce latency, manage resource allocation, and ensure high availability of models. Innovations in model compression, quantization, and distillation are helping to make LLMs more accessible and practical for real-time applications.

- **Explainable AI and Fairness:** There is a growing demand for tools that can explain model decisions and ensure fairness in AI systems. This has led to the development of MLOps tools that provide insights into how models make decisions and help identify and mitigate bias.

- **LLMOps:** As LLMs grow in complexity, the need for efficient training and fine-tuning has become paramount. Organizations are focusing on optimizing training processes, reducing computational costs, and ensuring models can be scaled across diverse environments. Techniques such as distributed training, mixed precision training, and the use of advanced optimizers are critical in this space.

- **Security and Compliance:** As machine learning models handle increasingly sensitive data, the need for secure MLOps practices has become paramount. This includes encryption, access controls, and compliance with regulations like GDPR. For LLMOps, as LLMs are increasingly used in sensitive domains, ensuring their security and compliance with regulatory standards is a growing field. This includes protecting models from adversarial attacks, ensuring data privacy, and maintaining transparency in decision-making processes.

Following thriving fields in MLOps highlight the ongoing innovation and expansion of the discipline as organizations seek to scale their machine learning initiatives efficiently and securely.

Industry and Research

MLOps and AI have found substantial traction within traditional industries, where the demand for AI-driven solutions is on the rise. In sectors like manufacturing, predictive maintenance systems are being deployed to minimize unexpected equipment failures, thus reducing downtime and maintenance costs.

The building and construction industries are also embracing AI solutions, although their application in large-scale projects remains challenging. In innovative industries such as wind power, wireless sensor networks are crucial for monitoring power generation systems. Similarly, the automotive sector is leveraging MLOps to improve autonomous driving applications by deploying training tasks over cloud and edge resources while meeting stringent network and privacy requirements.

In the realm of space exploration, AI solutions are being utilized for enhanced monitoring, diagnostics, prediction, and image analysis. However, integrating AI on board spacecraft remains a challenge due to limited computational and network resources. In healthcare, recent advances in mobile technologies enable the development of ML-based patient monitoring systems on mobile devices, though this field requires further research to address associated challenges.

Academic fields such as physics are increasingly relying on MLOps to handle the vast amounts of data generated by experiments. For example, gravitational wave physics and high-energy physics are utilizing ML technologies and high-performance computing to meet the demands of data storage, transfer, and computation.

Information Technology

The information technology (IT) industry is at the forefront of leveraging Machine Learning Operations to streamline the deployment, management, and monitoring of AI models. MLOps practices have become integral to the development cycle in IT, allowing for the seamless integration of AI models into existing software and systems. These practices ensure that machine learning (ML) models are scalable, reliable, and maintainable in production environments, which is essential given the complex and dynamic nature of IT infrastructures.

Generative AI is rapidly transforming various aspects of the IT industry. From automating code generation and software testing to creating new digital content and personalized user experiences, generative AI is helping IT professionals improve productivity and creativity. By leveraging generative AI, organizations can reduce the time and resources required for software development, testing, and content creation, leading to more efficient and innovative IT solutions.

In software development, MLOps and generative AI are being used to automate and optimize various stages of the development lifecycle. For example, MLOps frameworks help in managing the deployment and continuous integration/continuous deployment (CI/CD) of AI-driven features in software applications. Meanwhile, generative AI can assist in automatically generating code snippets, user interfaces, or even entire applications based on high-level specifications, thereby speeding up the development process and reducing human error.

Future Thriving Domains

As MLOps continues to evolve, several emerging fields and trends are expected to shape the future of machine learning operations. Here's an overview of what to expect:

- **Federated Learning and Edge AI:** With the increasing need for data privacy and the proliferation of IoT devices, federated learning and edge AI are set to become central in MLOps. Federated learning allows models to be trained across decentralized devices without sharing data, ensuring privacy while enabling real-time processing at the edge. This will require robust MLOps frameworks to manage and monitor decentralized model training and deployment across heterogeneous environments.

- **MLOps for Hybrid and Multicloud Environments:** As organizations adopt multicloud and hybrid cloud strategies, MLOps solutions will need to evolve to manage model deployment, monitoring, and scaling across diverse cloud environments. Tools that provide seamless integration and interoperability between different cloud providers will become crucial, allowing organizations to optimize costs, performance, and compliance across their ML workloads.

- **AI Governance and Ethics:** The future of MLOps will heavily focus on governance and ethical AI. As machine learning models become more pervasive, the need for frameworks that ensure transparency, fairness, and accountability will grow. MLOps platforms will need to incorporate tools for bias detection, explainability, and compliance with regulations like GDPR and CCPA, helping organizations build and maintain trustworthy AI systems.

- **Automated MLOps Pipelines:** The automation of MLOps pipelines will continue to advance, enabling faster and more efficient deployment of models from development to production. This includes automated feature engineering, hyperparameter tuning, and continuous integration/continuous deployment (CI/CD) for ML models. These advancements will reduce the manual effort required and speed up the time to market for AI solutions.

- **AI for MLOps (AIOps):** The integration of AI into MLOps processes, known as AIOps, will become more prevalent. AIOps will leverage machine learning to optimize the operations of ML pipelines, including automated anomaly detection, predictive maintenance of infrastructure, and intelligent resource allocation. This will lead to more resilient and self-healing MLOps environments, reducing downtime and operational costs.

- **Quantum Machine Learning (QML):** As quantum computing matures, its integration with MLOps is expected to emerge as a new frontier. Quantum Machine Learning (QML) has the potential to solve complex problems that are currently intractable for classical computers. MLOps frameworks will need to adapt to manage quantum algorithms, hybrid quantum-classical models, and the unique infrastructure requirements of quantum computing.

- **Real-Time and Adaptive MLOps:** The demand for real-time analytics and decision-making will drive the development of adaptive MLOps frameworks. These systems will be capable of dynamically adjusting models based on streaming data, enabling real-time predictions and automated responses. This will be particularly important in industries like finance, healthcare, and autonomous systems, where timely and accurate decisions are critical.

- **Sustainability in MLOps:** As environmental concerns become more prominent, sustainability will play a significant role in the future of MLOps. Organizations will focus on optimizing the energy consumption of their ML workloads, using techniques like model compression, efficient data processing, and green computing practices. MLOps platforms will incorporate tools to monitor and reduce the carbon footprint of AI operations.

- **Collaboration and Open-Source MLOps:** The future of MLOps will see increased collaboration between organizations and the open-source community. Open-source MLOps tools and frameworks will continue to grow in popularity, providing organizations with cost-effective and customizable solutions. This trend will also encourage the sharing of best practices and innovations, accelerating the overall advancement of MLOps.

- **Observability of LLMs:** In the era of LLMs, continuous monitoring of models in production is essential. Advanced observability tools are being developed to track performance metrics, identify model drift, and ensure that outputs align with expected behaviors. LLM observability is particularly crucial in sectors like customer service, content generation, and education, where model outputs directly interact with end-users.

- **Human-in-the-Loop (HITL) MLOps:** Despite advances in automation, human oversight will remain essential in the MLOps process. Human-in-the-Loop (HITL) MLOps will focus on integrating human expertise into critical stages of the ML pipeline, such as data labeling, model validation, and ethical decision-making. This approach will ensure that AI systems are aligned with human values and expectations.

These future fields and trends highlight the dynamic nature of MLOps and its critical role in the successful operationalization of the ML pipeline . As the field continues to evolve, staying ahead of these trends will be essential for organizations looking to harness the full potential of ML and AI. Here are some of the industries that hold a lot of promise for the future of MLOps and AI.

Expansion of AI in Space Exploration

The future of AI in space exploration looks promising, with advancements expected in on-board AI capabilities. As computational and network resources become more robust, AI will play a critical role in autonomous space missions, real-time data analysis, and the development of intelligent systems for deep space exploration.

Growth of AI in Healthcare

The healthcare industry is poised for significant growth in AI applications, particularly in the areas of patient monitoring, diagnostics, and personalized medicine. The deployment of ML-based systems on mobile devices will become more prevalent, providing real-time health monitoring and improving patient outcomes. The integration of large language models into healthcare data management workflows will further enhance the efficiency and accuracy of medical records and patient care.

Generative AI in Creative Industries

Generative AI is starting to have a profound impact on creative fields such as art, music, and design. MLOps practices are crucial for managing the complex workflows involved in training and deploying generative models at scale. The rise of generative AI will likely lead to the development of specialized MLOps frameworks that cater to the unique needs of creative industries.

AI-Powered Autonomous Systems

MLOps is becoming increasingly important in the development and maintenance of AI-powered autonomous systems, such as self-driving cars and drones. These systems require real-time data processing and decision-making capabilities, which necessitate robust MLOps pipelines. As autonomous systems become more prevalent, there will be a growing demand for MLOps solutions that can handle the complexities of real-time, edge-based AI.

Integration with Edge Computing

The integration of MLOps with edge computing is another emerging trend. Edge computing allows for the deployment of AI models closer to the data source, reducing latency and improving real-time decision-making. Industries like manufacturing, logistics, and smart cities will increasingly rely on MLOps frameworks that support edge deployments, enabling faster and more efficient AI-driven processes.

Opportunities and Future Trends in MLOps

The integration of machine learning operations into modern data science practices is not just an emerging trend but an essential evolution in the field. As organizations continue to scale their AI initiatives, MLOps provides a structured approach to managing the complex lifecycle of machine learning models, from development and deployment to monitoring and iteration.

The following are some of the opportunities and future trends in MLOps that are set to shape the landscape of AI and data science in the coming years.

Industry Impact and Business Integration

MLOps is increasingly recognized for its ability to drive significant business value. However, for AI solutions to be truly impactful, they must be seamlessly integrated into the broader business strategy. This requires the active involvement of leadership, executives, and various stakeholders across the organization. The alignment of MLOps with business goals is critical to ensuring that AI initiatives are not only technically sound but also strategically relevant. As MLOps becomes more prevalent, there will be a growing need for education and training within organizations to bridge the gap between data science teams and business leaders. This will enable a more cohesive approach to AI adoption, where the impact of AI solutions is measured accurately and aligned with business objectives.

Advancements in the AI Lifecycle

The AI lifecycle, which encompasses everything from data collection and model development to deployment and monitoring, is central to the success of any machine learning project. One of the key trends in MLOps is the continuous refinement of this lifecycle to enhance efficiency and effectiveness. The adoption of continuous delivery practices in MLOps is crucial for automating and streamlining the various stages of the machine learning workflow. Additionally, the integration of large language models into the MLOps lifecycle presents new opportunities for innovation, particularly in the areas of data management and automation. As organizations strive to harness the full potential of AI, they will need to focus on improving data availability, standardization, and integration across the entire AI lifecycle.

The Cloud Continuum and Edge Computing

The cloud continuum, which includes everything from centralized cloud data centers to decentralized edge computing devices, is a major area of focus for MLOps. As data science projects become more complex, there is a growing need for advanced hardware capabilities that can provide the computational power and energy efficiency required for AI workloads. Edge computing, in particular, is gaining traction as a means of deploying machine learning models closer to the data source, thereby reducing latency and improving reliability. The use of Field-Programmable Gate Arrays (FPGAs) and other specialized hardware is also becoming more common, enabling more efficient processing of AI workloads at the edge. As these technologies evolve, they will play a critical role in the future of MLOps by enabling more scalable and efficient deployment of machine learning models across diverse environments.

Networking and Infrastructure

Networking is another area where MLOps is expected to see significant advancements. The complexity of modern networking technologies, driven by the increasing number of devices and services reliant on connectivity, presents significant opportunities for the application of AI-based solutions. The deployment of machine learning models across heterogeneous hardware and software architectures requires robust networking solutions that can support the continuous monitoring and redeployment of AI algorithms. Function-as-a-service (FaaS) technologies are emerging as key enablers of MLOps patterns, allowing for the deployment of event-driven AI solutions that can scale dynamically based on demand. Additionally, the need for more sophisticated version control systems tailored to the unique requirements of machine learning models and datasets is becoming increasingly apparent. As MLOps matures, there will be a growing emphasis on developing tools and frameworks that can support the complex networking and infrastructure needs of AI-driven projects. For example, AIOps or LLMOps can leverage graph theory for optimizing network lifetime, utilizing the capabilities of edge devices and software-defined network (SDN) controllers. By applying genetic algorithms, it can further minimize network delays, enhancing the overall performance and reliability of network infrastructures.

Opportunities in Data Management

Effective data management is the cornerstone of successful AI initiatives. As organizations continue to accumulate vast amounts of data, the ability to manage this data efficiently becomes increasingly important. MLOps offers several opportunities to improve data management practices, including data availability, standardization, and integration. By leveraging MLOps, organizations can ensure that their data is not only accessible but also of high quality, enabling more accurate and reliable machine learning models. Moreover, the use of MLOps can help organizations overcome the challenges associated with data collection, cleaning, and analysis, thereby enabling more effective decision-making and innovation.

The Role of Automation in MLOps

Automation is a key driver of efficiency in MLOps. By automating repetitive and time-consuming tasks, organizations can significantly reduce the time and resources required to develop, deploy, and maintain machine learning models. The continuous delivery of AI solutions, supported by automation, allows for faster iteration and deployment of models, enabling organizations to respond more quickly to changing business needs. Additionally, automation can help reduce the risk of errors and improve the overall quality of AI solutions. As MLOps continues to evolve, the role of automation in driving efficiency and innovation will only become more pronounced.

The Role of Emerging Frameworks in MLOps

Let's review how Upcoming Frameworks and Architectures Will Shape the Future of AI and ML Operations. The future of MLOps is set to be significantly influenced by the emergence of new frameworks and architectures that aim to streamline and optimize the machine learning lifecycle. These emerging frameworks will focus on addressing the growing complexity of AI models, the need for scalability, and the integration of advanced technologies like edge computing, serverless architectures, and hybrid cloud environments.

- **Scalability and Efficiency:** As machine learning models become more complex and datasets continue to grow, scalability becomes a critical concern. Upcoming frameworks will emphasize the efficient use of computational resources, enabling seamless scaling across distributed environments. This will involve leveraging containerization, microservices, and serverless computing to ensure that models can be deployed and managed effectively, regardless of the underlying infrastructure.

- **Automation and Integration:** Future MLOps frameworks will likely incorporate more automation, reducing the manual effort required to manage the end-to-end machine learning pipeline. This includes automated data preprocessing, model training, hyperparameter tuning, and deployment. Integration with AIOps (Artificial Intelligence for IT Operations) will become more prevalent, allowing for more intelligent monitoring, error detection, and automated remediation within ML systems.

- **Interoperability and Flexibility:** As organizations adopt multi-cloud and hybrid cloud strategies, the need for interoperability across different platforms will become more pronounced. Emerging MLOps frameworks will focus on providing the flexibility to deploy and manage models across various cloud environments, ensuring that organizations can choose the best tools and resources for their specific needs without being locked into a single vendor.

- **Security and Compliance:** With the increasing use of AI in sensitive and regulated industries, security and compliance will be key considerations in the design of new MLOps frameworks. These frameworks will need to incorporate robust security features, such as encryption, access control, and audit logging, while also ensuring compliance with industry standards and regulations.

- **Edge and IoT Integration:** The rise of edge computing and IoT (Internet of Things) will drive the development of frameworks that support the deployment of AI models on edge devices. These frameworks will need to address the unique challenges of edge environments, such as limited computational resources, latency requirements, and the need for real-time decision-making. This will open up new possibilities for AI applications in areas like autonomous vehicles, smart cities, and industrial automation.

The Path Forward: 2025 and Beyond

As machine learning (ML) continues to evolve, the operational frameworks surrounding it—collectively known as MLOps—are rapidly advancing. As organizations increasingly adopt ML and artificial intelligence (AI) as core components of their business strategies, the need for efficient, scalable, and automated MLOps practices becomes more crucial. Looking ahead to 2025 and beyond, several trends are poised to reshape the MLOps landscape, driving both technological innovation and operational efficiency.

Increased Automation and AI-Driven Operations

Automation will play a pivotal role in the future of MLOps. The manual tasks currently performed by data scientists and ML engineers—such as model retraining, hyperparameter tuning, and anomaly detection—are expected to be increasingly automated. AI-driven operations will enable self-healing systems that can identify and correct issues without human intervention. This will not only reduce the operational burden on teams but also ensure that ML models remain accurate and reliable over time.

In 2025 and beyond, we will likely see the rise of autonomous MLOps platforms that can manage the entire ML lifecycle, from data ingestion to model deployment and monitoring. These platforms will leverage AI to make real-time decisions, optimizing resource allocation and improving overall system performance.

Integration with Edge Computing

As edge computing becomes more prevalent, MLOps will need to adapt to manage ML models deployed on edge devices. The integration of MLOps with edge computing will facilitate real-time data processing and decision-making closer to the source of data generation. This is particularly important for industries such as autonomous vehicles, healthcare, and IoT, where low latency and immediate insights are critical.

The future will see MLOps platforms extending their capabilities to support distributed, edge-based ML models. This will include tools for managing model updates, monitoring performance, and ensuring compliance across a decentralized network of devices.

Emphasis on Model Interpretability and Ethics

With the growing reliance on AI in decision-making processes, there will be an increased emphasis on model interpretability and ethics. Organizations will need to ensure that their ML models are not only accurate but also transparent and fair. MLOps will evolve to incorporate frameworks and tools that can audit models for bias, explain their predictions, and ensure compliance with ethical standards.

It can be assumed that the future innovations in MLOps will include built-in capabilities for continuous ethical evaluation, ensuring that models align with regulatory requirements and societal values. This will be critical for maintaining trust in AI systems, especially in sectors like finance, healthcare, and law.

Scalability and Hyper-Automation

As the number of deployed ML models grows, the scalability of MLOps systems will be a significant concern. Hyper-automation, which combines AI, machine learning, and automation tools, will be key to managing this scale. Future MLOps platforms will need to support the seamless deployment, monitoring, and management of thousands of models across diverse environments.

Scalability will also extend to the infrastructure supporting MLOps. Cloud-native architectures, containerization, and serverless computing will play a vital role in enabling organizations to scale their ML operations efficiently and cost-effectively.

As organizations increasingly adopt AI-driven solutions, the need for scalable and automated processes becomes more pressing.

- **Scalability with LLMs**: The deployment of LLMs, which require immense computational power and resources, pushes the boundaries of scalability in MLOps. Organizations need to ensure that their infrastructure can handle the growing demands of these models, including large-scale data processing, distributed training, and real-time inference. This requires not only robust cloud-based solutions but also the ability to seamlessly scale resources up or down based on workload demands.

- **Hyper-Automation**: Hyper-automation refers to the extensive use of automation technologies, such as AI, machine learning, and robotic process automation (RPA), to streamline processes and eliminate manual intervention. In the context of MLOps, hyper-automation involves automating every aspect of the machine learning lifecycle—from data ingestion and preprocessing to model training, deployment, monitoring, and retraining. With LLMs, hyper-automation becomes even more critical as these models can be trained on vast datasets and continuously optimized without human oversight.

- **Automated Model Management**: As part of hyper-automation, the management of model versions, experiment tracking, and deployment pipelines can be fully automated, ensuring that the best-performing models are always in production. This reduces the time and effort required to manage models and allows data scientists and engineers to focus on more strategic tasks.

- **Real-Time Inference and Decision-Making**: Scalability and hyper-automation enable real-time inference and decision-making, a crucial requirement for many AI-driven applications. With LLMs, the ability to process and respond to data in real-time can significantly enhance the effectiveness of AI systems, particularly in scenarios where timely decisions are critical, such as in financial services, healthcare, and autonomous systems.

- **Resource Optimization**: As LLMs continue to grow in size and complexity, efficient resource utilization becomes paramount. Hyper-automation can help optimize the use of computational resources, ensuring that models are trained and deployed in the most cost-effective manner. This includes automating the allocation of resources based on the specific needs of the models, such as utilizing GPU clusters for training and scaling down during periods of low demand.

- **Continuous Learning and Adaptation**: Hyper-automation also supports the continuous learning and adaptation of LLMs. By automating the retraining process and integrating feedback loops, models can be constantly updated with new data, improving their performance over time. This is particularly important in dynamic environments where data patterns change frequently, and models need to adapt quickly to maintain accuracy.

- **Cross-Cloud and Multicloud Deployments**: Scalability in MLOps also involves the ability to deploy models across different cloud environments, leveraging the strengths of each platform. Hyper-automation can facilitate cross-cloud and multicloud deployments, ensuring that models are not only scalable but also highly available and resilient.

In summary, the future of MLOps is closely tied to the concepts of scalability and hyper-automation, particularly with the integration of LLMs. These trends will drive the development of more efficient, reliable, and adaptable AI systems, capable of meeting the demands of an increasingly AI-driven world. Organizations that embrace these trends will be better positioned to leverage the full potential of AI and maintain a competitive edge in the marketplace.

Adoption of Federated Learning and Privacy-Preserving Techniques

Data privacy concerns are pushing organizations toward federated learning and other privacy-preserving techniques. Federated learning allows models to be trained across decentralized data sources without sharing sensitive data. This approach not only protects privacy but also enables the use of larger and more diverse datasets.

MLOps platforms will need to evolve to support federated learning workflows, providing tools for coordinating distributed training, aggregating models, and ensuring data privacy. The integration of differential privacy techniques will further enhance the ability to train robust models without compromising individual data security.

With increasing regulations around AI and machine learning, ensuring that models comply with legal and industry standards will be a significant focus in LLMOps. Future observability tools will likely include features for maintaining detailed audit trails, generating explanations for model decisions, and ensuring that all aspects of model behavior are transparent and accountable. MLOps platforms will integrate these features, providing a comprehensive solution for managing compliance across the entire ML lifecycle.

Advanced Monitoring and Observability

As ML models become more complex and are deployed in critical applications, advanced monitoring and observability will become essential. Future MLOps tools will offer real-time insights into model performance, including detailed metrics on model drift, data quality, and resource utilization. These tools will enable proactive management of ML models, ensuring they continue to meet performance requirements as conditions change. See Figure 10-4.

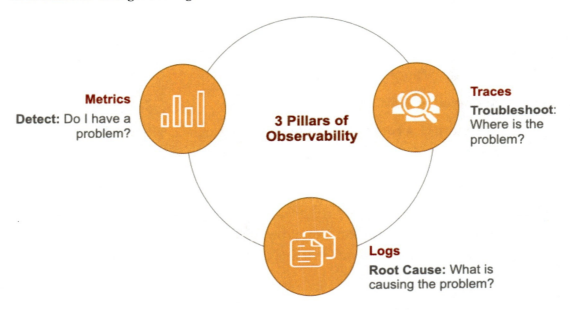

Figure 10-4.   *Three pillars of observability*

Model observability is becoming increasingly crucial in the field of LLMOps as it plays a vital role in ensuring the optimal performance, reliability, and trustworthiness of language models in production environments. As LLMs grow in complexity and are deployed in more critical applications, advanced observability mechanisms are necessary to monitor, analyze, and optimize their behavior continuously.

- **Ensuring Model Performance**

  Continuous monitoring and benchmarking of LLM performance metrics are essential to ensure that models perform as expected. Advanced observability allows for real-time tracking of key performance indicators (KPIs) and helps identify performance

degradation over time. This ensures that the models deliver
consistent, high-quality results, even as they are exposed to new data
or operational environments.

- **Identifying and Debugging Issues**

One of the primary benefits of advanced observability is the ability to
conduct detailed error analysis and root cause identification. When
an LLM produces incorrect or suboptimal outputs, observability tools
can pinpoint the specific instances where issues occur and facilitate
targeted debugging. This is crucial for maintaining the accuracy and
reliability of the models, especially in applications where errors can
have significant consequences.

- **Maintaining Trust and Reliability**

Advanced observability fosters transparency in the decision-making
processes of LLMs, which is critical for building trust with end-users.
By providing insights into how models arrive at their predictions,
observability ensures that stakeholders can understand and validate
the outputs. Additionally, in critical applications, observability
ensures that operators can be held accountable for the model's
decisions, which is essential for maintaining trust and reliability.

- **Adapting to Changes**

Observability is key to detecting data and concept drift, which
occur when the input data distribution changes or when the
model's predictions no longer align with real-world concepts.
Advanced observability allows for the timely identification of these
drifts, enabling model retraining or fine-tuning to adapt to the
new conditions. This adaptability is essential for maintaining the
relevance and accuracy of LLMs over time.

- **Regulatory Compliance**

In industries with stringent regulatory requirements, advanced
observability supports compliance by providing audit trails and
facilitating explainability. Detailed logs of model predictions and

behaviors are necessary for audits, while explainability features help generate the required explanations for model decisions, ensuring that LLMs operate within legal and ethical boundaries.

- **Optimizing Resources**

  Observability also plays a role in optimizing the use of computational resources. By highlighting performance bottlenecks and inefficiencies, organizations can make informed decisions on how to allocate resources more effectively. This not only improves the efficiency of LLM operations but also helps manage costs associated with model deployment and maintenance.

LLM observability is essential for maintaining the performance, reliability, and trustworthiness of language models in production. As LLMs continue to evolve and their applications expand, robust observability mechanisms will become increasingly important to ensure that these models meet the high standards required by modern AI-driven applications.

As the AI landscape evolves, observability will also extend to the entire ML pipeline, providing end-to-end visibility into the data flow, model training processes, and deployment pipelines. This holistic view will be crucial for identifying bottlenecks, optimizing performance, and maintaining system reliability.

Foreseeing the LLMOps Evolution

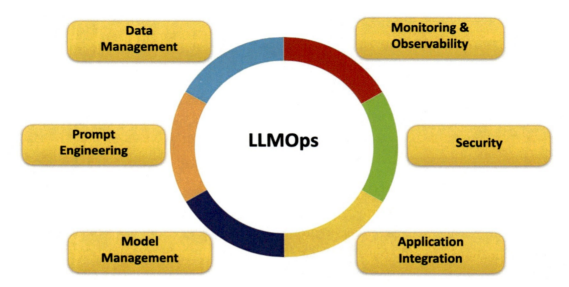

Figure 10-5. *Components of LLMOps*

The landscape of large language model operations (LLMOps) is poised to evolve rapidly as we approach 2025. As enterprises increasingly adopt generative AI and large language models, several key trends are expected to shape the future of LLMOps. These trends include the growing importance of data monetization, the shift toward consumption-based pricing models, and the integration of external data sources to enhance AI capabilities. This chapter delves into these emerging trends, exploring how they will impact the operationalization of LLMs in the coming years.

Data Monetization and LLMs

With the rise of LLMs, one of the most significant trends in LLMOps is the potential for LLMs and generative AI to drive new opportunities for data monetization. As organizations accumulate vast amounts of sensitive and proprietary data, there is a growing need to manage and leverage this data effectively. Enterprises are likely to develop in-house LLMs rather than relying on public tools like ChatGPT to protect their data's privacy and security. For instance, a shipping company might purchase a foundational model from a provider like OpenAI and then train it with their proprietary data to create a specialized AI solution. However, the need for data goes beyond internal datasets.

Business leaders increasingly recognize the importance of gaining a broader perspective that includes external data sources. To make informed decisions, organizations must understand regional trends, industry benchmarks, and other external factors that influence their market. This need for contextual information presents a significant opportunity for companies to not only consume data but also to become data providers. As demand for high-quality, industry-specific data grows, businesses can capitalize on this trend by selling their data products to a market hungry for insights. Companies like ADP, which offers data products that analyze pay growth across various demographics, exemplify this trend.

The Rise of Consumption-Based Pricing Models

Another emerging trend in LLMOps is the shift toward consumption-based pricing models. Traditional software pricing, which involved purchasing a package once and then upgrading every few years, has already evolved into subscription-based models. Now, with the rise of AI and LLMs, there is a growing push toward consumption-based pricing. In this model, users pay for the data they access or the compute power they consume, aligning costs more closely with actual usage.

This shift is particularly relevant for AI services and applications that rely on models trained with diverse data sources. As organizations integrate these models into their operations, data owners can be compensated based on how frequently their data is used. This approach not only ensures fairness but also encourages the adoption of usage-based models, which can be more efficient and cost-effective than traditional subscription models.

However, transitioning to consumption-based pricing presents challenges for organizations accustomed to fixed-cost models. To successfully implement this approach, businesses need visibility into their usage patterns, the ability to set budgets, and tools to monitor and control spending. This shift will also drive innovation, as companies can rapidly prototype AI solutions without the financial commitment of large, upfront contracts. While subscription models may still be relevant for high-usage scenarios, usage-based pricing offers a flexible entry point for experimentation and scaling.

In-House LLMs and the Integration of External Data

As enterprises increasingly develop their LLMs, there will be a growing emphasis on integrating external data sources to enhance AI capabilities. While in-house LLMs allow organizations to tailor AI models to their specific needs, external data provides the broader context necessary for informed decision-making. For example, a company might train its LLM with internal sales data but integrate external economic indicators to predict market trends more accurately.

This trend underscores the importance of data diversity in AI. By combining internal and external data, organizations can develop more robust AI models that deliver better insights and more accurate predictions. As a result, the demand for high-quality, industry-specific external data will continue to rise, creating opportunities for data providers to monetize their assets.

As the landscape of LLMOps evolves, organizations must adapt to new operational models and technologies. The shift toward data monetization, consumption-based pricing, and the integration of external data sources will require businesses to rethink their AI strategies. Companies that can effectively manage and leverage their data, adopt flexible pricing models, and integrate diverse data sources will be well-positioned to thrive in this new era of LLMOps.

Ethical Considerations of Deploying AI at Scale in MLOps

As AI continues to revolutionize industries, deploying AI at scale within machine learning operations environments presents significant ethical challenges. With AI becoming ubiquitous across sectors—ranging from healthcare to finance to e-commerce—addressing ethical concerns is increasingly critical. The rapid evolution of AI capabilities introduces complex questions regarding bias, privacy, and regulatory compliance. MLOps, with its ability to operationalize machine learning in a structured and automated way, plays a pivotal role in ensuring ethical AI deployment at scale.

Addressing Bias in AI Algorithms Through MLOps

One of the most pressing ethical concerns surrounding AI is algorithmic bias. AI models trained on biased data can perpetuate or even exacerbate societal inequalities. For instance, facial recognition technologies have been found to have higher error rates for certain demographics, and credit scoring models can unfairly disadvantage minority groups if historical biases are baked into the data.

MLOps can offer solutions to mitigate bias through continuous monitoring, automated retraining, and model transparency. By embedding bias detection mechanisms within the MLOps pipeline, organizations can ensure that models are regularly evaluated for fairness. For example, tools like Amazon SageMaker Clarify or IBM AI Fairness 360 can detect biases in datasets and models, providing insights into unfair outcomes. MLOps frameworks can also support automated retraining processes that incorporate diverse and representative data, helping to address evolving biases and ensuring that models reflect current realities.

Another important aspect is explainability. AI models, particularly complex ones like deep learning networks, often function as black boxes, making it difficult to understand how decisions are made. MLOps can help integrate explainability tools such as Local Interpretable Model-agnostic Explanations (LIME) or SHapley Additive exPlanations (SHAP), allowing stakeholders to understand and trust AI predictions. This is crucial for industries like healthcare, where transparency in decision-making directly affects outcomes.

Privacy Concerns in Large-Scale AI Deployments

Data privacy is another critical ethical consideration, especially as AI systems increasingly handle vast amounts of sensitive data. AI models trained on personal or sensitive data—such as healthcare records, financial information, or social media interactions—can raise privacy risks if the data is not handled securely or if models inadvertently expose personal information during inference.

MLOps frameworks offer several strategies to address privacy concerns. Federated Learning is an emerging technique that allows AI models to be trained across multiple decentralized devices or servers while keeping the data local. This ensures that sensitive data never leaves its original environment, thereby reducing privacy risks. Additionally, techniques like Differential Privacy add noise to the data, making it difficult to reverse-engineer individual data points while still maintaining model accuracy.

Data governance is another critical area where MLOps can play a vital role. MLOps pipelines can enforce strict data management protocols, ensuring that only anonymized, encrypted, or properly consented data is used for model training. By automating compliance checks, MLOps frameworks can also help organizations adhere to stringent privacy laws like General Data Protection Regulation (GDPR) and California Consumer Privacy Act (CCPA).

Regulatory Challenges in AI Deployment

As AI technology becomes more widespread, regulatory scrutiny is intensifying. Governments and regulatory bodies around the world are grappling with how to establish governance frameworks for AI that ensure accountability, fairness, and transparency. A significant challenge for organizations deploying AI at scale is ensuring that their models comply with evolving regulations, both regionally and globally.

MLOps can facilitate compliance by integrating regulatory checks throughout the model development lifecycle. Automated compliance validation, such as ensuring that models meet data protection requirements or that they do not engage in discriminatory practices, can be embedded into MLOps pipelines. Moreover, by maintaining version control of models and their training datasets, MLOps ensures full traceability—allowing organizations to audit the model's development history and demonstrate compliance when needed.

Additionally, many industries—such as finance and healthcare—operate under specific regulations that mandate fairness, transparency, and explainability in automated decision-making systems. MLOps can help operationalize these regulations by automating model validation against predefined ethical and regulatory standards before models are deployed into production environments.

Ethical Implications of AI at Scale: A Holistic Approach

Deploying AI at scale presents unique ethical challenges that require a comprehensive strategy for mitigation. It's not enough to address bias or privacy in isolation; organizations need a holistic approach that incorporates ethical considerations into every stage of the MLOps lifecycle—from data collection to model deployment and monitoring.

The future of MLOps lies in its ability to create systems that not only optimize model performance but also ensure that AI deployments align with societal values and regulatory standards. Continuous monitoring of deployed models, integrating human-in-the-loop processes for reviewing model outputs, and setting up proactive alerting mechanisms for ethical breaches are all ways that MLOps can contribute to this goal.

Moreover, as the field of AI ethics evolves, MLOps will need to integrate newer standards and best practices—such as Algorithmic Accountability, which mandates regular audits and evaluations of AI systems to ensure they are being used responsibly. Collaboration between technologists, ethicists, and regulators will be essential in shaping the future of AI deployment in a way that promotes both innovation and ethical responsibility.

Conclusion

The future of MLOps is characterized by the ongoing evolution of AI technologies and the increasing need for more sophisticated approaches to managing AI workloads. As organizations continue to scale their AI operations, they will need to invest in advanced tools and strategies to ensure that their AI systems remain performant, reliable, and secure in an increasingly complex environment. By embracing the trends and opportunities outlined in this chapter, organizations can position themselves to succeed in the AI-driven future, unlocking new levels of innovation, efficiency, and business value. By focusing on these ethical considerations, MLOps can ensure that AI technologies serve as tools for positive societal impact while safeguarding against unintended harm.

This chapter has explored the future trends in MLOps, highlighting the challenges and opportunities presented by the convergence of MLOps and AIOps, the rise of LLMs, and the ongoing evolution of cloud and edge computing. As we look toward 2025 and beyond, it is clear that MLOps will continue to play a critical role in enabling organizations to harness the full potential of AI, driving innovation and growth in an increasingly competitive landscape.

Sources

- https://aws.amazon.com/blogs/hpc/guided-multi-objective-generative-ai-for-drug-design/
- https://mlops.community/llmops-why-does-it-matter/
- https://dl.acm.org/doi/full/10.1145/3625289

Index

A

© Neel Sendas and Deepali Rajale 2024
N. Sendas and D. Rajale, *The Definitive Guide to Machine Learning Operations in AWS*,
https://doi.org/10.1007/979-8-8688-1076-3

S

Printed in the United States
by Baker & Taylor Publisher Services